Geographies of Media

Series Editors
Torsten Wissmann, Faculty of Architecture and Urban
Planning, University of Applied Sciences, Erfurt, Germany
Joseph Palis, Department of Geography, University
of the Philippines Diliman, Quezon, Philippines

Media is always spatial: spaces extend from all kinds of media, from newspaper columns to Facebook profiles, from global destination branding to individually experienced environments, and from classroom methods to GIS measurement techniques. Crucially, the way information is produced in an increasingly globalised world has resulted in the bridging of space between various scalar terrains. Being and engaging with media means being linked to people and places both within and beyond traditional political borders. As a result, media shapes and facilitates the formation of new geographies and other space-constituting and place-based configurations. The *Geographies of Media* series serves as a forum to engage with the shape-shifting dimensions of mediascapes from an array of methodological, critical and analytical perspectives. The series welcomes proposals for monographs and edited volumes exploring the cultural and social impact of multi-modal media on the creation of space, place, and everyday life.

More information about this series at
http://www.palgrave.com/gp/series/15003

Julia M. Hildebrand

Aerial Play

Drone Medium, Mobility,
Communication, and Culture

Julia M. Hildebrand
Eckerd College
St. Petersburg
FL, USA

Geographies of Media
ISBN 978-981-16-2194-9   ISBN 978-981-16-2195-6   (eBook)
https://doi.org/10.1007/978-981-16-2195-6

Cover image: © Edgardo Gonzalez

This Palgrave Macmillan imprint is published by the registered company Springer Nature Singapore
Pte Ltd.
The registered company address is: 152 Beach Road, #21-01/04 Gateway East, Singapore 189721,
Singapore

For my parents Magdalena and Albert Hildebrand

Series Editors' Preface

THE SKY AIN'T THE LIMIT

The exit of former Cheiron Studios at Fridhemsplan is getting smaller, as we slowly ascend into the Stockholm sky. Reaching an altitude of about 120 meters (i.e., about 400ft), we not only look back at the Swedish urban landscape, but at arguably the most significant hub of pop culture's global music industry. In *Songs from Sweden*, the fourth volume of our Geographies of Media series, Ola Johansson argues about cultural and economic interconnections that are largely enabled by digitalization. Without broadband internet, tracks of vocals, instruments, and audio loops would still be shipped physically to collaborating music producers. Without broadband internet, we would not be able to listen to the finished product via streaming services from radio stations (Peters 2018). Like music, audio from the remote control and video from our consumer drone, still hovering over Stockholm, can be streamed live to a range of media platforms. Thus, drone operators become content creators, may it be for a serious production or ludic fun.

Sarah Barns reminds us in *Platform Urbanism* (2020) that it is not only our content that is the message, but the platform itself. The platform does not only impact our ability to publicize our files but it changes the very places where we live, like Stockholm. In *Inhabiting Cyberspace and Emerging Cyberplaces* (2017), Tobias Boos provides a compelling link to *Aerial Play*: the merging of physical presence and media presence. Just like Siena's contrade which not only exists inside the city's borders but spreads into cyberspace, the drone imagery allows us to leave our body through external digital extensions of our senses while sitting still in our living room. The Cyberpunk culture of the 1980s might think of the Rigger, who is almost symbiotically bound to the vehicle he/she is operating.

In Julia M. Hildebrand's book, the drone is provided agency in a manner that both acknowledges and recognizes the machinic and emotional entanglements derived and generated from engaging with it. More than just for ludic enjoyment or for surveillance capabilities, the drone becomes a discursive concept that not only embodies and disembodies humans but also reorders and reassembles individual and collective encounter with the emotional, the corporeal, and the imaginative.

In Alex Rivera's neo-noirish sci-fi film *Sleep Dealer* (2008), the military drone that was responsible for the destruction of a subaltern community in Mexico became embodied as an exterminating angel that rebuilt the same community it destroyed. This liaison with a human-maneuvered machine, at once destructive and ultimately restorative, speaks to the hybrid space occupied by drones when viewed from its entanglement with humans, institutions, practices, and relationalities.

The affective aspect of drone engagement is given numerous exposure in several chapters. The excitement can be palpable like in Chapter 4:

"... I have learned to understand unfamiliar places and my own mobilities within them better once the drone extended my eyes into the sky...I remotely witnessed 4th of July fireworks a few hundred feet away from my doorsteps. As my neighbors watched the spectacle live on television, I felt a different sense of "liveness," visual control over, and active engagement with the event space from afar. My distant drone visuals were not nearly as compelling as the ones on television, but there was a sense of emancipation."

This "liveness" not only allows panoptical views of almost-otherworldly visual delights but the "super-power quality when accessing vertical space" (ibid.). These are likewise echoed by Hildebrand's informants who recount real experiences in imaginative and vividly captured language. Drones facilitate a visually-cued astuteness of one's environment. Like Boos' study of Siena's contrade, the borders may be real but the gateways that cyberplaces allow, and in the case of drones from Hildebrand's accounts, transcend the ether and nether worlds.

Drones are also about cohabitation. The drone might be perceived not only as technological equipment but as an emotional counterpart. Thus, operating the drone equals walking the dog or even conversing with another human. In this intimate companionship between operator and drone, borders of environmental experience and self-conception are blurred. Both humans and machine cohabit the same physical sphere that also changes spatial awareness.

One of the more interesting provocations in the book is about aerial gaze privileged from experiencing a vertical space point of view afforded by drones. The unfamiliar is familiarized and the familiar is made unfamiliar as map-reading and way-finding become enmeshed.

Ultimately, the drone is more than an optical toy that enables us to view the world from another angle. Otherwise, we could just climb the observation deck of any given skyscraper to reach a similar vantage point. Hovering in the air 120m/400ft above the ground, the medium becomes the message as we reach another conception of ourselves. Not only regarding human-machine interaction, but the very idea of what we might become once our senses are being separated from each other.

We cannot help but intuit that our perspective will get altered even more, once the flight controls are no longer bound to our thumbs and fingers. Given the progress in neural network research, we might look back at *Aerial Play* as the ending of what we call reality today.

Or, as William Gibson (1984: 3) puts it: "The sky above the port was the color of television, tuned to a dead channel."

Joseph Palis
Torsten Wissmann

Works Cited

Barns, S. (2020). *Platform urbanism. Negotiating platform ecosystems in connected cities.* London: Palgrave Macmillan.

Boos, T. (2017). *Inhabiting cyberspace and emerging cyberplaces. The case of siena, Italy.* London: Palgrave Macmillan.

Cravey, A., J. Palis., & G. Valdivia. (2015). "Imagining the future from the margins: cyborg labor in Alex Rivera's Sleep Dealer", *GeoJournal, 80*(6), 867–880.

Gibson, W. (1984). *Neuromancer.* London, Orion Publishing Group.

Johansson, O. (2020). Songs from Sweden. *Shaping pop culture in a globalized music industry.* London: Palgrave Macmillan.

Peters, K. (2018). Sound, space and society. *Rebel radio.* London: Palgrave Macmillan.

Rivera, A. (2008). *Sleep dealer.* Los Angeles: Maya Entertainment.

Acknowledgments

To begin, a heartfelt "danke" goes to my parents Magdalena and Albert Hildebrand for their wisdom, inspiration, and unwavering support, along with my siblings Susanne and Alexander for the positive energy and encouragement continuously sent and felt across the Atlantic.

At Drexel University, I owe immense gratitude to Mimi Sheller. As a dedicated mentor who always went above and beyond, she taught me the skills and sensitivity for developing and conducting this kind of research. I also sincerely thank the other members of my Doctoral Advisory Committee. Ernie Hakanen provided invaluable guidance particularly for situating my work on drones in communication and media studies. Brent Luvaas' creative scholarship and engaging classroom kept inspiring my own autoethnographic angle and voice. Thoughtful feedback by Pete Adey and Lisa Parks gave me the opportunity to strengthen my work's interdisciplinary ties between media studies and critical geography. Likewise, I am very grateful to all the study participants who generously shared their time, resources, and drone experiences with me during the interviews and fieldwork.

This research also benefitted from insightful comments received at the 2017 Doctoral Honors Consortium organized by the National Communication Association and the 2018 CAT MCIG Doctoral Consortium by the International Communication Association. In particular, I thank Mark Orbe, Jordan Frith, Klaus Bruhn Jensen, and Mike Yao for helping me further hone the research design. The project, moreover, received financial support and recognition with the 2018 Emerging Scholar Research Grant by the Mobile Communication Interest Group of the International Communication Association. Additional research funding came from Drexel University's Center for Mobilities Research and Policy and the Graduate Program in Communication, Culture, and Media.

My students and colleagues at Eckerd College have inspired the final version of this book. They continue to energize my ongoing research and teaching. Palgrave Macmillan's Senior Commissioning Editor Joshua Pitt was crucial in the making of this book. A special thank you also goes to drone photographer Edgardo Gonzalez for providing the book's beautiful cover image. Finally, for his love, support, and enthusiasm, I am immensely grateful to my husband Kyle Peer.

Praise for *Aerial Play*

"Julia M. Hildebrand's understanding of hobby drones as a 'mobile medium' offers novel insights into drone imaginaries and practices. With her rich theoretical background and innovative empirical research, her book will certainly be a reference in drone-related scholarship and interactions between humans and emerging technologies."

—Chantal Lavallée, *Assistant Professor at Royal Military College Saint-Jean, Canada*

"In a short amount of time, drones have become a ubiquitous technology. And while scholarly attention has been focused on commercial and military contexts, the recreational drone has been relatively overlooked. That is, until *Aerial Play: Drone Medium, Mobility, Communication and Culture*. *Aerial Play* addresses some of the complex debates around quotidian surveillance and mundane mobilities and how these practices recalibrate how we understand media ecology, mobile communication, mobilities research, and science and technology studies. Traversing themes such as drone geography, communication, mobility and new visualities, *Aerial Play* explores how drones can help us reinvent our digital

methods. Hildebrand's playful and yet robust approach encourages us to consider the drone as not just part of mobile methods for 'auto-technographic' self-reflection but also how they invite us to rethink the paradigm between media and mobility."
—Larissa Hjorth, *Distinguished Professor and Director of the Design &*
Creative Practice Research Platform, RMIT University, Australia

"In *Aerial Play*, Julia M. Hildebrand provides a serious, scholarly, and accessible study of a highly significant new medium that is altering the world that we live in, and the way that we view ourselves. Drones are not simply toys, they are our future, and this book offers us essential aid in understanding this important aspect of our evolving media environment. Drawing on the powerful tools made available via the media ecology intellectual tradition, combined with a multidisciplinary methodology, Hildebrand delivers an analysis that is both rigorous and readable, and above all insightful and provocative. Read it, and you will never look up at the sky in the same way again!"
—Lance Strate, *Professor of Communication and Media Studies, Fordham*
University, USA

"*Aerial Play* is a most welcome guide to an emerging phenomenon. Drones are increasingly showing their presence, and Dr. Hildebrand offers no-nonsense and straightforward insights into one of the growing niches of drone practices: flying for fun! Written at the crossroads of Mobilities and Media studies, *Aerial Play* is a must-read for students, researchers within media, Mobilities, geography, and technology studies. Recreational drone flyers may indeed also find it useful."
—Ole B. Jensen, *Professor of Urban Theory, Aalborg University, Denmark*

"With a focus on its recreational and hobby use, *Aerial Play* widens our understanding of drones as a socio-technical system with a growing presence in society. This is a welcomed contribution not only to studies on drones, but also to our knowledge on human-machine interactions."
—Bruno Oliveira Martins, *Senior Researcher at the Peace Research*
Institute Oslo (PRIO), Norway

Contents

1 Introduction: Powerful Play   1
   Consumer Drone Origins and Developments   5
   Discourses About Drones   12
   Approaches for the Aerial Medium   14
   (H)Overview of the Book   18
   References   22

2 Understanding (with) the Drone   27
   Introduction   27
   Theory: Hybrid Research/er   30
   Drone-Logs   34
   Auto-Affective Mobilities   38
   Conclusion   41
   References   42

3 Situating Hobby Drone Practices   45
   Introduction   45
   Theory: Media and Mobilities In Situ   50
   Drone Ecologies and Mobile Agencies   53

Drone Geomedia and Cybermobilities   65
Conclusion   68
References   69

4 **Communicating on the Fly**   73
Introduction   73
Theory: Mobile Media and Space   75
Drone Spatialities: Physical, Networked, Social   77
Conclusion   90
References   92

5 **Moving and Not Moving Up in the Air**   97
Introduction   97
Theory: Embodied Performances and Media Extensions   100
Drone (Im)mobilities: Body, Drone, Space   102
Conclusion   116
References   117

6 **Seeing like a Consumer Drone**   121
Introduction   121
Theory: The Aerial Gaze   124
Drone Visualities: Auratic Vertical Play   127
Conclusion   145
References   147

7 **Dancing with My Drone**   151
Introduction   151
Theory: Human-Medium Relationships   154
Drone Relationalities: Mobile Companionship   157
Conclusion   177
References   179

8 **Conclusion: Open Skies?**   183
Laws of Hobby Drone Media   187
Avenues for Future Research   190
Right to Fly Remotely   192
References   194

Index   197

About the Author

Dr. Julia M. Hildebrand is Assistant Professor of Communication at Eckerd College, Florida. Originally from Germany, she earned her Ph.D. in Communication, Culture, and Media at Drexel University. Her research lies at the intersections of critical media studies and mobilities research with a special interest in mobile technologies, visual communication, and human-machine interactions. Her work has been published in journals such as *Media, Culture, & Society, Digital Culture & Society, Mobile Media & Communication, Explorations in Media Ecology, Transfers,* and *Mobilities.*

Her research on consumer drones has won several awards: The 2020 Harold A. Innis Award for Outstanding Dissertation in the Field of Media Ecology, the 2019 Outstanding Dissertation Award by Drexel University, and the 2018 Emerging Scholar Research Award by the Mobile Communication Interest Group of the International Communication Association.

Her collaborative work in media ecology was honored with the 2019 Walter Benjamin Award for Outstanding Article and the 2019 John Culkin Award for Outstanding Praxis in the Field of Media Ecology.

In addition, she has won top paper awards for her consumer drone research by the American Association of Geographers and the National Communication Association.

At Eckerd College, she teaches such courses as "Media and Society," "Media Ethics," and "Critical Studies in New Media."

List of Figures

Fig. 1.1   The DJI Mavic Pro Platinum, named "Jay," with remote
            control   6
Fig. 2.1   The DJI Mavic Pro Platinum, "Jay," is actively tracking
            me   35
Fig. 3.1   Recreational drone use in situ (*Concept* Julia M.
            Hildebrand; *Graphic Design* Sofia Podesta)   47
Fig. 3.2   Physical (blue), visual (orange), virtual (green),
            atmospheric (yellow), and affective (pink) relations
            in hobby drone ecologies (*Concept* Julia M. Hildebrand;
            Graphic Design Sofia Podesta and Julia M. Hildebrand)   49
Fig. 4.1   Real-time map-reading of a Florida beach (Image taken
            with DJI Mavic Pro Platinum drone "Jay")   80
Fig. 4.2   DJI Mavic Pro app interface   84
Fig. 4.3   Animated DJI flight record   86
Fig. 6.1   Drone view of Philadelphia in the winter (taken
            with DJI Mavic Pro Platinum drone "Jay")   122
Fig. 6.2   Drone view of Bavarian village at sunset (taken with DJI
            Mavic Pro Platinum drone "Jay")   130
Fig. 6.3   Philadelphia skyline seen from the "mezzanine" level
            (taken with DJI Mavic Pro Platinum drone "Jay")   136

Fig. 6.4   Philadelphia skyline at dusk (taken with DJI Mavic Pro
            Platinum drone "Jay")   137
Fig. 6.5   Bridge crossing the Philadelphia Schuylkill (taken
            with DJI Mavic Pro Platinum drone "Jay")   137
Fig. 7.1   Florida beach sunrise (taken with DJI Mavic Pro
            Platinum drone "Jay")   161
Fig. 7.2   Jay follows the cyclist in a closed-off street in Active Track   172
Fig. 7.3   Drone tracks me while app is frozen (taken by DJI
            Mavic Pro Platinum drone "Jay")   176

List of Tables

Table 2.1   Types of mobilities based and expanding on Urry
            (2007: 47)   39
Table 5.1   Types of drone mobilities, expanding on Urry (2007)
            and Bolter and Grusin (1999), relevant for this chapter   99
Table 8.1   A tetrad of personal drone use inspired by McLuhan
            and McLuhan's "laws of media" (1988)   187

1

Introduction: Powerful Play

A new medium is entering everyday spaces, and it flies. You have seen it. You may have heard it. At minimum, you have heard *about* it: The unmanned aicraft system, the flying camera, the spying tool. This book is about expanding what we read, see, and think about the ambiguous consumer drone. Much scholarly and regulatory attention is rightfully on the variety of commercial, scientific, humanitarian, and military applications camera drones initiate and enhance. Yet, what about the recreational drone space? What about all those drones under holiday trees, the ones we hear buzzing in the local park, the kind we see over the river at sunset, the devices that bring us millions of aerial still and moving images from around the world on social media platforms? In the U.S. alone, an estimated 1.32 million consumer drones belonging to roughly 990,000 U.S. hobbyists log about 1.5 million hours of exclusively *recreational* flight time every month (FAA, 2020a). As industry professionals, lawmakers, and academics from a range of disciplines grapple with what our shared aerial spaces and traffic may look like in the near future, it is time for a deeper understanding of how everyday users are *already* adopting consumer drones for personal use. What does this new *aerial medium* afford in the context of *play*? What ways of seeing,

© The Author(s), under exclusive license to Springer Nature
Singapore Pte Ltd. 2021
J. M. Hildebrand, *Aerial Play*, Geographies of Media,
https://doi.org/10.1007/978-981-16-2195-6_1

moving, and being do hobby drones open up? And, what do those tell us about contemporary visual culture, mobilities, and human-machine relationships underway in our offline and online spaces?

The hobby drone is unquestionably polarizing. While the increasingly low-cost, ready-to-buy, and easy-to-handle swift aerial tool offers unprecedented access to the sky for leisure and creative expression, it also poses a threat to safety, privacy, and security. Consumer drones that injure people, damage property, collide with and potentially halt other aerial and ground traffic, disrupt wildlife, collect private and sensitive data, transport contraband, and that rogue actors and terrorist groups otherwise exploit or weaponize are just a few examples of the serious concerns surrounding their proliferation. Nevertheless, the safe integration of "unmanned aircraft systems," to use the terminology of the U.S. FederalAviation Administration (FAA), into national airspace holds enormous promise for a variety of domains. Examples includeinfrastructureinspection, construction, agriculture, package and medical supply deliveries, search and rescue missions, wildlife conservation, journalism, and so forth. Amidst such important applications, should we preserve *space* for *aerial drone play*?

My use of "play" is not meant to reduce consumer drones to toys. In fact, a key objective of this book is to more holistically delineate the technology as a *mobile medium* in response to the many different perceptions of drones as predominantly unmanned aircrafts, flying toys, surveillance tools, or weapons. Yet, before I dive into the drones as media argument, let me unpack what I mean with "play." Play describes the "conduct, course or action of a game" and as such signals the book's focus on drone use for leisure as well as the individual manners, maneuvers, practices, and performances that hobbyists adopt.[1] As I will discuss, the conversations about recreational drone use benefit from empirical depth and specificity about what the technology affords.

Over the past few years, I have closely followed, explored, and finally adopted this kind of play in ethnographic fieldwork, in-depth interviews with hobby users and drone experts, and personal drone flying

---

[1]See the definitions of "play" in Merriam Webster at https://www.merriam-webster.com/dictionary/play and in the Cambridge English Dictionary at https://dictionary.cambridge.org/us/dictionary/english/play.

and image-taking. In the process of becoming a camera drone user, I started to play with a DJI Mavic Pro Platinum, a foldable, football-sized quadcopter. In writing this book, I similarly play with the findings, weaving my own auto-ethnographic—in fact, auto-*technographic*—experiences through the interview excerpts, fieldnotes, online data, and policy documents. This empirical and analytical play is driven by a need to better understand what mobile, spatial, visual, and relational elements come *into play*. "Play" can imply a move, a series of moves, movements, and motions. The term thus speaks to the relevance of manifold forms of human and nonhuman mobility in personal drone use. Finally, I draw on "play" to denote the importance of staging and story in recreational drone use, the complex and indeed *dramatic* composition of people, things, space, and movement in consumer drone ecologies.

The story of the hobby drone warrants attention. I agree with drone ethnographer Adam Rothstein who claims that the technology "is in danger of becoming one of those simplified narratives" (2015: 51). He continues, writing "while it seems that the drone will definitely do something significant, we haven't done enough thinking about what that something should be, and how it will happen" (51–52). *Aerial Play* means to advance some of this thinking, to tell the story of personal drone use by complicating simplified narratives of consumer drones as tools for mostly spying, surveying, delivering, and disrupting. The public, academics, artists, activists, news media, businesses, lawmakers, and most of all hobby users are all disserved by reductionist assessments of everyday drone use.

A range of instructive scholarship on contemporary applications and competing public narratives helps advance the story of the drone. What this book adds is empirical research into the creative and playful, multi-spatial ways of seeing, moving, and being the aerial medium opens up. Without such grounded (and aerial) fieldwork that critically situates the flying camera in recreational spaces, we are short of the practical insights and theoretical nuance required to adequately respond to this technology's domestic uptake, its institutional embedding, and its creative and communicative potentials. Consumer drones in the hands of amateurs are powerful. As we consider the perils of hobby drones, let's also acknowledge and critically reflect on the promises that drive their popularity in the recreational space. We have much to gain from better understanding a device that can help you and I reach the sky, and much to lose from a lack thereof.

One objective of this book is to expand the FAA's official approach to consumer drones as first and foremost small unmanned aircraft systems. This framing of the consumer drone is one of the simplified narratives that benefits from conceptualizing the technology more broadly as a *mobile medium*. I identify consumer drones not only as aerial systems, but as mobile assemblages of human and nonhuman agencies in hybrid geographies, creative platforms for spatial exploration and visual discovery, and, last but not least, relational artifacts that shape spatial relations, social formations, and affective entanglements. Approaching consumer drones as media means centralizing the communicative character and relational quality of drones as flying cameras and social agents. Those affordances are more easily neglected in the dominant narrative of consumer drones as unmanned aircraft systems. At the same time, I argue for including consumer drones in media studies and mobile communication research as what media scholars Lisa Parks and Nicole Starosielski term an emerging media infrastructure that "challenges us to recognize a more extensive field of actants and relations in media and communication studies" (2015: 51).

Several intersecting fields and complementary methods shape this approach to consumer drones as mobile media. I draw on conceptual frameworks from media ecology, mobile communication studies, mobilities research, human geography, and science and technology studies (STS) when reflexively operating the consumer drone, engaging in hobbyist settings, and following the practices around producing and sharing drone imagery. Participant-observation during drone flight sessions in the rural and urban U.S. Northeast substantiate the auto-technographic findings. In addition, I make use of data from online recreational drone communities on Facebook in which users discuss drone-related issues and drone-generated content. In-depth interviews with twenty-five drone hobbyists and experts provide further insights into the motivations, processes, and outcomes of personal drone use.[2]

Regarding drone scholarship more generally, I agree with cultural anthropologist Adam Fish who emphasizes the importance of synthesizing "ethnographic, epistemological, and ontological to come to a more realistic notion of what the drone is, does, and why it matters" (2020: 253). The goal is to identify biases and effects of consumer drones as flying cameras, creative platforms, and socio-spatial agents in amateur contexts. Ultimately, this book also contributes to broader debates on emerging human-machine relations and mobile interactions in everyday spaces. In the following, I launch into an aerial drone perspective that briefly surveys consumer drone origins and developments, contemporary discourses about drones, and my interdisciplinary approach to the aerial medium. A (h)overview of the subsequent chapters lays out the book's flight plan, getting our drone minds ready for take-off.

Consumer Drone Origins and Developments

A multitude of circulating acronyms for the aerial technology commonly referred to as "drone" hints at its unstable conceptual footing. Consumer drones are referred to as unmanned aircraft systems (UAS), unmanned aerial vehicles (UAV), remotely piloted aerial vehicles, or remotely piloted aircraft systems to only name a few synonyms. "Drone" remains the most commonly-used term in not only the Anglophone world but also Switzerland, France, and Germany among other countries, which are generously using the term in both public and private discourses (Klauser & Pedrozo, 2015). Generally, "drone" refers to devices that are unmanned and controlled remotely by computer systems and/or pilots. Available in various shapes and forms, airborne drones can be as small as insects and as big as commercial airliners. According to Rothstein (2015: 27), the term originally stems from the "use of target drones in the 1930s, named for their unsophisticated, noisy, insect-like flight capacities."

---

[2]The names of all interviewees have been changed and identifying information omitted to maintain confidentiality.

Medea Benjamin (2013: 13), author of *Drone Warfare*, states that "The name is derived from the appearance of the small robotic planes used for target practice by World War II gun crews, which were colloquially named after 'drone' bees due to their black striped markings."

While sharing the common name, military background, and some technological principles with large armed military drones such as the Predator or Reaper, consumer drones differ significantly. Currently, civilian devices are present in the shape of fixed-wing or multi-rotor configurations, such as the DJI Phantom, Mavic, or Spark quadcopter series which are among the most popular off-the-shelf consumer drones in the U.S. This kind of technology dates back to 1907, when brothers Louis and Jacques Bréguet along with their professor Charles Richet built and flew the first quadcopter, called Gyroplace No. 1 (Kakaes, 2015). Back then, the aircraft weighed over 1,100 pounds and required a 40-horsepower engine. The miniaturization and stabilization of the quadcopter were not achieved until much later, which explains the more recent introduction and proliferation of consumer drones predominantly in the shape of multi-rotor platforms (Rothstein, 2015) (Fig. 1.1).

Fig. 1.1 The DJI Mavic Pro Platinum, named "Jay," with remote control

Contemporary uses of civilian drones encompass a multitude of domains: personal use, arts and entertainment, journalism, social advocacy and movements, environmental and wildlife conservation, agriculture, health and public safety, crime, surveillance, police, emergency services and disaster response, scientific research and education, commerce, and other uses, such as mapping or peacekeeping (Choi-Fitzpatrick et al., 2016). Unmanned aircrafts already far outnumber manned aircrafts (Kakaes, 2015) and non-military uses of drones have eclipsed those in the military context, causing drone scholar Austin Choi-Fitzpatrick and his colleagues (2016: 5–6) to speak of a shift from the military "Predator Era" (2003–present) to the commercial "Phantom Era" (2013–present). At the same time, current hobby drone registrations are almost three times higher than those by commercial drone users in the U.S. (FAA, 2020a, 2020c). With the continued advancement and proliferation of consumer drones that are both user-friendly and technologically sophisticated, recreational drone use is expected to remain popular (FAA, 2020a).

Sensors, optics, batteries, and processors continue to improve, and the current price point for some of the most popular ready-to-fly consumer models lies between 399 USD for the lightweight DJI Mavic Mini and 799 USD and up for devices like the DJI Mavic Air 2 capable of flying up to 34 minutes and producing high-end photos and cinematic videos. While some degree of knowledge and training is required to fly drones effectively and obtain high-quality aerial visuals, camera drones are self-empowering: Individuals interested in aviation and aerial image-taking face significantly fewer barriers with consumer drones than other motorized aerial modes. "While aerial photography has been practiced in various forms since the 19th century, its accessibility and popularity has exploded in recent years" (Gettinger et al., 2014: 15). This trend has resulted in an accumulation of stunning aerial imagery, frequently shared and stored on social media platforms such as YouTube, Vimeo, Instagram, and Facebook as well as drone-specific online platforms such as Skypixel, Travel by Drone, and Dronestagram. Drone film festivals and image competitions have blossomed around the world with both amateur and professional filmmakers showcasing their polished drone-generated views.

Meanwhile, the FAA has been implementing standards for unmanned aircraft systems and their safe operation. In 2015, the administration started to require hobby and commercial users to register any drones that weigh more than 0.55 pounds or 250 grams (including payload such as on-board cameras) for a $5-fee prior to accessing U.S. national airspace. Users would then receive a unique aircraft tail number, valid for three years, to attach on their small aircraft.[3] The purpose of the registration is to identify any drone, not currently airborne, to its owner. Aviation authorities in countries such as Mexico, France, Russia, Italy, Ireland, and the United Kingdom have introduced similar registration require-ments. Hundreds of thousands recreational and professional U.S.-based drone users have followed the FAA's guideline, helping the administra-tion build and maintain a large database of user locations and drone models (FAA, 2020d). In addition, the FAA established and continues to update a set rules for when, where, and how to conduct safe consumer drone use. Next to registering and marking their device with the registra-tion number, anyone flying strictly for recreational purposes is required to:

1. Fly your drone at or below 400 feet above the ground when in uncontrolled (Class G) airspace.
2. Obtain authorization before flying in controlled airspace (Class B, C, D, and E).[4]
3. Keep your drone within your visual line of sight, or within the visual line-of-sight of a visual observer who is co-located (physically next to) and in direct communication with you.
4. Do not fly at night unless your drone has lighting that allows you to know its location and orientation at all times.

---

[3]While commercial users are required to register each of their models separately, recreational users may use the same registration number on all of their devices. The registration requirement was temporarily halted in May 2017 following an order from the U.S. Court of Appeals and reinstated in December 2017 with the National Defense Authorization Act (FAA, 2020a).

[4]The FAA delineates different classes for the U.S. national airspace "to reflect whether aircraft receive air traffic control services and to note levels of complexity, traffic density, equipment, and operating requirements that exist for aircraft flying through different parts of controlled airspace. Generally, these classes of controlled airspace are found near airports" (FAA, 2019a: 84 FR 22554).

5. Give way to and do not interfere with manned aircraft.
6. Never fly over any person or moving vehicle.
7. Never interfere with emergency response activities such as disaster relief, any type of accident response, law enforcement activities, firefighting, or hurricane recovery efforts.
8. Never fly under the influence of drugs or alcohol.
9. Do not operate your drone in a careless or reckless manner. (FAA, 2020b)

Moreover, the FAA requires drone operators "to pass an online aeronautical knowledge and safety test and carry proof of test passage," which has yet to be implemented. Intentional violation of these safety requirements and otherwise reckless operations can make recreational drone users liable for criminal and/or civil penalties (FAA, 2020b).

To assist drone users with understanding airspace restrictions, the FAA developed the B4UFLY mobile safety app, "which provides real-time information about airspace restrictions and other flying requirements based on your GPS location" (FAA, 2018). The app informs users, for example, if they are within five miles of local, regional, or international airports or heliports, and near sensitive infrastructure such as stadiums, schools, hospitals, or national parks. In those cases, the service will warn users not to launch the drone or to fly with caution. The FAA emphasizes that hobbyists are "responsible for flying within FAA guidelines and regulations. That means it is up to you as a drone pilot to know the Rules of the Sky, and where it is and is not safe to fly" (FAA, 2018). To ensure safe drone operation, users need to take into account a number of additional factors that shape recreational drone spaces, discussed in Chapter 3.

As drone models and applications evolve, the FAA continues to reform their rules and regulations. Of interest to both recreational and particularly commercial users are revisions to the "line-of-sight"- and "over-people"-guidelines. For drone journalism to maximize camera drone use, for example, operators seek permission to fly over crowds of people. Similarly, for drone delivery to take off, the rule to fly within visual line-of-sight needs to be relaxed. Recognizing the immense potential of commercial drone use, the FAA has begun to conceptualize how drone-filled skies may be enabled and regulated. In December 2019, the agency published a Notice for Proposed Rule Making about implementing a drone identification system as a first step toward a large-scale "Unmanned Aircraft System Traffic Management System" (UTM) (FAA, 2019b). To locate both drone in the air and pilot on the ground, the proposed plan requires drone devices and users to broadcast a "Remote ID," a digital license plate, via radio frequency and the Internet. The goal is "to address public concerns and protect for public safety vulnerabilities associated with low altitude UAS operations, including privacy and security threats" (FAA & NextGen, 2020: 21). Drone and pilot locational information could then be available in real-time to law enforcement, the FAA, other officials, and the general public (FAA, 2019b).

Regulators, industry professionals, and also hobbyists generally agree on the necessity for a remote ID to increase operator accountability. However, the specifics of the proposal were met with much criticism from the commercial and particularly recreational sector (Broersma, 2020; I. Lee, 2020; T. B. Lee, 2020). The need for connecting to the Internet, for example, is a major issue for operations in remote areas. If an operator does not have an Internet connection, but the drone can still broadcast its remote ID, then the horizontal flight distance could be limited to 400 feet from the take-off location (FAA, 2019b). This distance would drastically limit what both recreational and commercial users can accomplish. If a drone does not include any remote ID capabilities, then operations would be restricted to "FAA-recognized identification areas" similar to the fields the Academy of Model Aeronautics maintains (FAA, 2019b). Such fields are likely to be unattractive for hobby aerial photographers and videographers seeking compelling landscapes, architectures, and scenes around the country as well as wanting to fly in their backyards, local parks, or nearby empty soccer fields. Furthermore, hobbyists criticized the proposed public availability of their location, which could be in a secluded area or their private home. This plan would make them and their valuable drone equipment vulnerable to potential harassment, assault, property damage, theft, or robbery (Broersma, 2020; Moss, 2019). What is meant to help reduce privacy and safety concerns of the public could flip into privacy and safety concerns of drone users. In addition, this implementation of a remote

ID would be accompanied by significant additional costs for users who may have to obtain unlimited data plans, pay monthly subscription fees to a remote ID service supplier who collects, records, and shares flight data, and replace their current drone fleet with models that include the required technical capabilities. The FAA (2019b) envisions all UAS operating in U.S. airspace to be compliant within three years of the rule's effective date.

The implementation of this version of the FAA proposal could result in considerable noncompliance or the end of the drone hobby as we know it. The plan impacts not only users of off-the-shelf consumer drones, but also the DIY community of first-person-view drone users who thrive on building their own models. Such users might be prohibited from flying their likely non-compliant home-made devices on their own property. There are similar concerns for schools with drone-building curriculum, possibly hurting education and innovation, and shutting down avenues for young people to get involved in aviation, drone racing, photography, and filmmaking. In light of these implications, the recreational drone community mobilized accordingly and left more than 53,000 comments on the proposal by March 2020 for the FAA to review (FAA, 2019b).[5]

As the subsequent chapters will illustrate, some of the proposed requirements would go against what makes personal drone use both exciting and dynamic but also safe and meaningful. As aviation agencies in the U.S. and around the world develop visions for widespread unmanned aerial traffic, there is a need to consider and understand not just commercial unmanned aviation, such as drone inspections and deliveries, but also the playful unmanned movements and creative mediations that have already found their way into our skies. "People do not and cannot know the exact modalities and aims of specific drone systems, and they therefore cannot be sensitive to all of the issues at stake," argue geographers Francisco Klauser and Silvana Pedrozo (2015: 289). They advocate that "Future academic work on drones should thus help to more fully inform citizens, public agencies and the private sector of the various dimensions and effects of drones" (Klauser & Pedrozo, 2015:

---

[5] A final rule is expected for the end of 2020 (French, 2020).

289). Approaching consumer drones as mobile media brings attention to both risks and benefits, the biases and effects of the aerial mode. The goal is to assess whether there should be space for such aerial play.

Discourses About Drones

Due to the still fairly recent rise of consumer drones, "sustained empirical research" on the full range of applications, including popular recreational ones, is limited (Klauser & Pedrozo, 2015: 291). Several studies focus on consumer drones more generally, such as by drone experts Ron Bartsch et al. (2016) who provide an overview of the history, present-day applications and regulations, and future possibilities of remotely piloted aircraft systems. Similarly, the edited volume by researchers of humanitarian studies Kristin Bergtora Sandvik and Maria Gabrielsen Jumbert (2016) insightfully covers debates about the "good drone" in the context of humanitarian, police, agriculture, and conservation uses.

Criminologist Amanda Graham and her colleagues (2021) as well as geographer Anna Jackman (2019) shift attention to the potentials for deviant and dangerous recreational drone use. Off-the-shelf drones can be repurposed, retrofitted, and exploited to harm, disrupt, or victimize. Highlighting both risks and counter-measures, Jackman delineates consumer drones as "inherently malleable objects – variously, multiply, and creatively deployed" (2019: 6). This book complements her assessment of potential terrorist, criminal, reckless, and subversive uses with the kinds of recreational, artistic, playful, and creative ways of seeing, moving, and being the "malleable object" also furnishes.

Approaching the drone as an aircraft, computer, and robot, Rothstein (2015) similarly addresses the technology's various characters and alludes to the merit of using media and mobilities research as theoretical lenses. According to him, "any drone built today will look and serve fundamentally as weapon" (Rothstein 2015: 143). Cultural studies scholars Caren Kaplan and Andrea Miller echo this approach in the context of U.S. border enforcement and civil policing and situate the drone "as a technology of atmospheric policing" (2019: 421) related to

other forms of "vertical mediation" (Parks, 2018: 14) and "security atmospheres" (Adey, 2014: 841). Keeping these relevant security, safety, and
privacy implications in mind, I shed light onto the malleable drone's
other vertical mediations and mobilities that still "shape where people
move and how they communicate" (Parks, 2016: 146–147), yet in the
context of aerial play. "UAVs and UAS at every scale and range change
and interact with the atmospheres through which they move and mediate
relations with the ground," note Kaplan and Miller (2019: 438) about
the unquestionable power of drones overall.

Relevant empirical work also comes from media scholar Maximilian
Jablonowski (2015, 2017), who analyzes amateur drone uses at the
crossroads of model flight cultures, DIY cultures, and military drone
applications. I follow in his footsteps by investigating the flying camera's
ambivalent position as "ego-technical device," which focuses on the self
(Sloterdijk, 2011), and "xeno-technical device," which shifts away from
the self (Jablonowski, 2017). According to Jablonowski, the drone is
more of a xeno-technical instrument as it "does not establish a particular self through media technologies, but destabilizes its individuality
and particularity" (2017: 100). Expanding on his approach, I understand camera drones as ambiguous ego-, xeno-, and geo-technical devices
that can make our particular spatial and (im)mobile selves visible to us
from a distance. As such, this book contributes to what Jablonowski
terms a "decentring of the drone" (2015: 13) and supports his idea
of a "'dronie citizenship' that does not fear drones, but explores their
ambiguous powers and pleasures" (2017: 97).

With respect to other social-scientific literature on drones, Klauser
and Pedrozo (2015) observe that "the existing academic work on [civil
and commercial applications of] drones suffers from a dramatic lack of
empirical research, which explains the generalist tone and research focus
that characterizes most of the literature in the field" (290). Similar to
my focus, the authors centralize the aerial visual affordances of drones,
but emphasize the relevance of space and power in connection to the
technology. While I recognize the aero-visual techniques of power and
draw on the rich literature on the aerial gaze to describe drone visualities, I also shift attention to the more playful, creative dimensions of the

personal drone gaze. Apart from these relevant discourses on unarmed drones, what frameworks shape my lens onto the flying camera?

Approaches for the Aerial Medium

This book approaches consumer drones as mobile media, embedded in medium-specific ecologies that encompass technical objects, spatial formations, social and visual arrangements, and affective entanglements, beyond mere flying machines. By analyzing the technology as a "medium," I refer to several definitions of the term as (1) means for producing, disseminating, and receiving communication, (2) content distributed through such means, and (3) the processes, sensations, and relationships "in-between" or in the "middle" based on the Latin origin of the term *medium*.

Several frameworks from multiple approaches and disciplinary fields inform this thinking. Those include the study of media as extensions and environments emphasized in media ecology; the study of physical and visual movements in the fields of critical mobilities studies, mobile communication research, and human geography; and the study of material and immaterial socio-spatial agencies in science and technology studies. Compelling intersections of these conceptual lenses come to light in personal drone ecologies, mobilities, and agencies. The following section lays out some of these relevant congruencies of particularly media ecology, mobilities research, and science and technology studies as foundations for this book.

Media ecology is the study of "media as environments" and explores "how media structure what we are seeing, why media make us feel and act as we do" (Postman, 1970: 161). Here, the term "media" refers broadly to any human-made technology. As such, media ecologists study traditional communication technologies such as the printed book, telephone, television, and the Internet, but also clothing, architecture, or vehicles and so on as "media." According to one of the field's key thinkers, Marshall McLuhan, media are extensions of human faculties, and "Any extension, whether of skin, hand, or foot, affects the whole psychic and social complex" (1964: 2). Rothstein draws from a similar conception of technologies and their relationship to humans when describing drones as "our own selves and culture, in technological form":

> The power of a drone to kill can be monstrous. The viewpoint from a drone's camera flying over us can be awe-inspiring. The way that swarm behavior allows a group of drones to seamlessly navigate through a small space can be amazing, intelligent, or even creepy. These feelings are part of narratives about ourselves, but through our technology. When we empathize with a cute-looking robot or fear the cold, expressionless head of a military drone's radome, we are really interacting with our own selves and culture, in technological form. (2015: xiii–xiv)

How do our interactions with camera drones "as our own selves and culture, in technological form" take effect and with what implications? According to media ecology, approaching media as extensions of human faculties and ultimately environments is essential for critically engaging with social and cultural shifts shaped by different technologies.

Media "are not passive wrappings but active processes" (McLuhan & Fiore, 1968: 26). This principle is at the core of McLuhan's (1964) famous aphorism, "The medium is the message." He clarifies that "When I say that 'the medium is the message' I don't question the 'content,' but point out that every medium is a hidden service environment" (McLuhan, 2003: 540). Following the media ecological approaches of Harold A. Innis (1999), Lewis Mumford (2010), McLuhan (1964), and Neil Postman (1970) and the closely related social and material orientations of medium theory (Meyrowitz, 1994), media scholar Lance Strate (2017) encourages critical media theorists to study the "biases" and "effects" of media. He explains that

> One way to study the biases of a medium is to ask what are its affordances and constraints? [...] How do different types of codes and symbolic form represent our environment and ourselves in different ways? How do differences in physical form provide affordances and constraints that open up certain possibilities and close others off? How do all of these differences influence the way that we construct our reality? (Strate, 2017: 217)

These are some of the key questions that drive my pursuit of understanding consumer drones as media. If the medium is the message, what kind of medium is the consumer drone and what are its "messages," meaning its biases and effects in personal flying and recording? Camera drones not only challenge industries, businesses, and organizations, but affect individuals and communities as the aerial device reconfigures the basic premises of seeing and moving by extending the human eye and foot. In exploring the what, how, and why of personal drone use, I shed light onto the biases and effects of the flying camera with attention to the ways of communicating, seeing, moving, and relating it affords and constrains.

Valuable concepts of mobilities research substantiate this media ecological approach and help conceptualize the drone medium and environment more carefully. As "fundamentally mobile" (Klauser & Pedrozo, 2015: 289), unruly, and motile (McCosker, 2015), I frame camera drones as an ambivalent mode of mobility and immobility within the "new mobilities paradigm" (Sheller & Urry, 2006). Urban theorist Ole B. Jensen (2016), in particular, advocates such a theoretical assessment of drones in how they relate to and manage everyday life mobilities. More concretely, sociologist Mimi Sheller explains that

> the new transdisciplinary field of mobilities research encompasses research on the spatial mobility of humans, nonhumans, and objects; the circulation of information, images and capital; as well as the study of the physical means for movements such as infrastructures, vehicles and software systems that enable travel and communication to take place. (2011: 1)

The focus of this wide field is thereby not only on the physical and corporeal ways of moving someone or something, but also on imaginative, virtual, and communicative forms of travel (Urry, 2007, Elliott & Urry, 2010), which are relevant in the context of the visual-communicative affordances of consumer drones as mobile media.

"Movement is rarely just movement; it carries with it the burden of meaning" states human geographer Tim Cresswell (2006: 7). Hence, similar to media ecology, mobilities research questions the neutrality of mobile forms (Hildebrand, 2018). Drones are not simply empty, *neutral* vessels enabling physical, virtual, and imaginative movements but implicitly and explicitly shape the relationships within and surrounding them. Mobilities theory complements media ecology in its attention to, what Sheller calls, the "socio-technical assemblages or human/material hybrids that perform mobile systems and support specific mobility regimes" (2011: 4). Hence, in both media ecology and mobilities research, the concepts of *media* and *mobilities* are viewed in a much broader sense that acknowledges the various material entities and immaterial agencies that influence relationships among subjects, objects, and environments.

In addition, I draw from science and technology studies to explore camera drones as "situated socio-technical systems," focusing on the specific materialities of media production, distribution, and consumption, including the "hardware, software, spectacular installations and imperceptible processes, synthetic objects, and human personnel" (Parks & Starosielski, 2015: 4–5). I follow such interdisciplinary scholarship in its approach to consumer drones as not isolated and static machines but a dynamic socio-technical formation, paying attention to the practical and affective ways users encounter, perceive, and use this relational medium. I am, thus, interested in both the "hard" media infrastructure that constitutes and enables recreational drone use and any "soft" relational infrastructure, such as social practices, dispositions, rhythms, and structures of feeling, that personal drone practices bring about (Harris, 2015; Parks & Starosielski, 2015). The flying camera invokes various kinds of relationships, which inform the respective socio-cultural environment and, hence, the behavior, feelings, and perceptions of users. Central is the understanding that people construct new "ways of relating" (Adey, 2010: xvii) in their use of different technologies.

Since this book focuses on not just drone flying but also image-production, I also follow STS scholarship in the analysis of "practices, methods, technology, actors and networks involved in the making of an image" (Burri & Dumit, 2008: 300). Similar to sociologist Janet Vertesi (2015) and her work on "seeing like a rover," I discuss "seeing like a consumer drone" through the socio-spatial processes of aerial image-production. Personal drone uses result from and contribute to a growing visual culture, i.e. "the shared practices of a group, community, or society through which meanings are made out of the visual, aural, and textual world of representations and the ways that looking practices are engaged in symbolic and communicative activities" (Sturken & Cartwright, 2009: 3). To understand the specific visual culture of personal drone use, I pay attention to the ways of remotely seeing the flying camera affords.

As mobile media for aerial play, camera drones connect the related fields of media ecology, mobilities research, and STS. The combined perspectives yield relevant insights into the technology, its material and immaterial agencies, and the embodied and disembodied "ways of relating" it opens up. In each of the subsequent chapters, I expand further on these approaches and their intellectual merit in relation to drone situating, communicating, moving, seeing, and dancing.

(H)Overview of the Book

The book's argument and my scholarly voice move from the more self-reflective, auto-technographic in Chapter 2 to a more "remote" assessment of hobby drone uses in Chapters 3–6. Chapter 7 comes full circle by placing greater emphasis again on my own situated entanglements with the drone.

More concretely, Chapter 2: Understanding (with) the Drone introduces the camera drone's unique ways of seeing, moving, and relating. I discuss how the drone gaze can serve as both a practical and metaphorical lens for research into physical, corporeal, virtual, communicative, and imaginative mobilities. In particular, I concentrate on the example of drone-logs, the juxtaposing of sky video with ground audio, as an innovative—technographic—method for video ethnography and elicitation. As a hybrid of multiple technologies and techniques, drone-logs sharpen the focus onto fleeting, slippery, sensory, and kinesthetic motions, notions, and emotions. Ultimately, I argue for the value of a larger "auto-drone" view for researchers to consider their own *affective mobilities* within research processes and acknowledge their respective relational emplacements from a distanced and detached top-down perspective. An earlier version of this chapter is published in the *Handbook of Methods and Applications for Mobilities Research* by Edward Elgar Publishing.[6]

Chapter 3: Situating Hobby Drone Practices outlines how recreational uses complicate our understanding of drones as mere "unmanned aircraft systems." Building on ethnographic fieldwork and interviews with drone hobbyists as well as online ethnographic research into Facebook drone communities, this chapter illustrates how aerial drone play is embedded in a complex assemblage of human and nonhuman factors across hybrid geographies. As hobbyists set out to fly their devices at a given time and place, a number of temporal, spatial, mobile, and social relations take effect. Those encompass weather conditions, daylight hours, GPS availability, volumetric obstacles, flight restrictions, aerial and ground traffic, physical and virtual bystanders and more. While drone hobbyists appear to be interested in keeping a "low profile" in their physical setting, many interviewees manage a comparatively "high profile" when editing, sharing, and live-streaming their drone imagery online. Ultimately, the assemblage-perspective brings together aviation-related *and* socio-cultural concerns relevant for understanding recreational drone ecologies and mobilities in situ. The chapter is based on arguments made in my article "Situating Hobby Drone Practices" published in *Digital Culture & Society*.[7]

In Chapter 4: Communicating on the Fly, I advance arguments for approaching camera drones as mobile media that help access, collect, and shape physical, digital, and social spaces. The medium affords what I call "communication on the fly" in the unique configuration of aerial navigation, visual production, and networked communication. The chapter first discusses what physical-material conditions the flying camera makes visible and the kinds of cartographic empowerment drone users attribute to their aerial play. An analysis of what digital-intangible formations the mobile interface illuminates in hybrid space follows. Finally, I turn to the social relations the noisy and potentially nosy medium can establish and

[6]Hildebrand, J. M. (2020). Drone mobilities and auto-technography. In M. Büscher, M. Freudendal-Pedersen, & S. Kesselring (Eds.), *Handbook of methods and applications for mobilities research* (pp. 348–364). Edward Elgar Publishing.

[7]Hildebrand, J. M. (2017). Situating hobby drone practices. *Digital Culture & Society*, 3(2), 207–218.

disrupt. These conditions of communication on the fly shape user practices of place-sensing and place-making and help expand our thinking of contemporary communication on the move. The chapter is an updated version of my article "Consumer Drones and Communication on the Fly" published in *Mobile Media & Communication.*[8]

Chapter 5: Moving and Not Moving Up in the Air turns to the unique mobilities of drone use. With attention to the premediated and remediated, the corporeal and imaginative, and the embodied and disembodied mobilities, I critically analyze the blurring boundaries between movement and stillness, subject and object, here and there in recreational drone flying and recording. Examples from immersive flying with first-person view (FPV) quadcopters and off-the-shelf consumer drones illustrate how pilot subject and drone object can collapse. Instead of finding themselves in their grounded bodies, users speak of *being* the drone up in the sky. Media ecological probes into media as extensions and amputations of human faculties find expression in this phenomenon. To describe the blurring boundaries of physical and imaginative movement, I introduce the concept of dis/embodied mobilities.

In Chapter 6: Seeing Like A Consumer Drone, I explore to what extent aerial views from consumer drones complicate theorizations of the aerial gaze as a top-down ordering form of surveillance. While this type of flying camera follows in the footsteps of balloons, airplanes, helicopters, and satellites, it nonetheless differs in what types of vertical and horizontal movements and speeds (and hence views) it affords. Consumer drones serve as powerful means for aerial exploration, creative expression, geographical literacy, and imaginative mobilities in ways that suggest expanding conceptualizations of the aerial gaze. Camera drones both establish "auratic views" and mobilize the aerial gaze in vertical play reminiscent of virtual gaming practices. As such, the flying camera shows clear alignments with other optical toys and can be understood as a playful technology of auratic visualization and vision. Ultimately, drone flying and image-taking curate "drone-mindedness," meaning an enhanced environmental awareness. I conclude with thoughts on the

---

[8]Hildebrand, J. M. (2019). Consumer drones and communication on the fly. *Mobile Media & Communication, 7*(3), 395–411.

ambiguous nature of the consumer drone gaze as both playful and powerful, externally extending and internally attuning.

Chapter 7: Dancing with my Drone brings attention to the subject-object-relationships in recreational drone use, in particular through the lenses of STS, feminist theory, and media psychology. Drawing from interviews with hobbyists and auto-technographic engagements with the DJI Mavic Pro camera drone, I illustrate some of the affective entanglements and agential negotiations inherent to this aerial play. Beyond visual production tools, camera drones serve as relational, evocative, and animated artifacts imbued with personal meaning. By illuminating how users address, describe, and interact with drones, I bring attention to human-drone figurations for a nonreductive analysis of what relations and affects come into play. Drawing on the metaphor of dancing, I argue that in such processes of affective association, agential negotiation, spatial intervention, and communicative disruption, subject and object are entangled as mobile companions.

Finally, Chapter 8 summarizes the overarching implications of consumer drones as mobile media and the merits of the interdisciplinary perspective. Based on the book's findings, I formulate an exploratory tetrad of what the technology enhances, retrieves, reverses into, and obsolesces (McLuhan & McLuhan, 1988). In this context, I point to avenues for future research into drone media, mobility, communication, and culture. With attention to plans and visions of unmanned traffic management, I make the case for a well-regulated but accessible "air commons." An individual "right to fly remotely" means accommodating an educational hobby that combines technology, aviation, and science with communication, creativity, and the environment. To complement our understanding of the risks and dangers of consumer drones, I conclude with a call for acknowledging the social, cultural, recreational, artistic, and educational potentials of such aerial play.

Overall, this book contributes to debates on recreational human-machine interactions, while responding to a larger trend toward an increasing mobile autonomy of media such as drones. The figure of the consumer drone can help us think about how such semi-autonomous robotic systems may shift our social, cultural, and technological relations in everyday horizontal and vertical spaces.

References

Adey, P. (2010). *Mobility*. Routledge.

Adey, P. (2014). Security atmospheres or the crystallization of worlds. *Environment and Planning D: Society and Space, 32*, 834–851.

Bartsch, R., Coyne, J., & Gray, K. (2016). *Drones in society: Exploring the strange new world of unmanned aircraft*. Routledge.

Benjamin, M. (2013). *Drone warfare: Killing by remote control*. Verso.

Broersma, M. (2020, March 2). Drone industry up in arms over "Remote ID" regulations. Retrieved June 4, 2020, from Silicon UK website: https://www.silicon.co.uk/workspace/drone-remote-id-333889.

Burri, R. V., & Dumit, J. (2008). Social studies of scientific imaging and visualization. In E. J. Hackett, O. Amsterdamska, M. Lynch, & J. Wajcman (Eds.), *The handbook of science and technology studies* (3rd ed., pp. 297–317). MIT Press.

Choi-Fitzpatrick, A., Chavarria, D., Cychosz, E., Dingens, J. P., Duffey, M., Koebel, K., Siriphanh, S., Yurika Tulen, M., Watanabe, H., Juskauskas, T., Holland, J., & Almquist, L. (2016). *Up in the air: A global estimate of nonviolent drone use 2009-2015*. http://digital.sandiego.edu/gdl2016report/1.

Cresswell, T. (2006). *On the move: Mobility in the modern western world*. Routledge.

Elliott, A., & Urry, J. (2010). *Mobile lives*. Routledge.

FAA. (2018, October 19). Where Can I Fly? Retrieved March 1, 2019, from Federal Aviation Administration website: https://www.faa.gov/uas/recreational_fliers/where_can_i_fly/.

FAA. (2019a, May 17). Exception for limited recreational operations of unmanned aircraft. Retrieved June 4, 2020, from Federal Register website: https://www.federalregister.gov/documents/2019/05/17/2019-10169/exception-for-limited-recreational-operations-of-unmanned-aircraft.

FAA. (2019b, December 31). Proposed rule: Remote identification of unmanned aircraft systems. Retrieved June 4, 2020, from Regulations.gov website: https://beta.regulations.gov/document/FAA-2019-1100-0001.

FAA. (2020a). *FAA aerospace forecast fiscal years 2020-2040*. Retrieved June 4, 2020, from Federal Aviation Administration website: https://www.faa.gov/data_research/aviation/aerospace_forecasts/media/FY2020-40_FAA_Aerospace_Forecast.pdf.

FAA. (2020b, February 18). Recreational Flyers & Modeler community-based organizations. Retrieved June 2, 2020, from Federal Aviation Administration website: https://www.faa.gov/uas/recreational_fliers/.

FAA. (2020c, March 10). UAS by the numbers. Retrieved June 4, 2020, from Federal Aviation Administration website: https://www.faa.gov/uas/resources/by_the_numbers/.

FAA. (2020d, April 9). FOIA library. Retrieved June 4, 2020, from Federal Aviation Administration website: https://www.faa.gov/foia/electronic_reading_room/#geo_list.

FAA, & NextGen. (2020, March 2). *Concept of operations v2.0: Unmanned Aircraft System (UAS) Traffic Management (UTM)*. Retrieved June 4, 2020, from Federal Aviation Administration website: https://www.faa.gov/uas/research_development/traffic_management/media/UTM_ConOps_v2.pdf.

Fish, A. (2020). Drones. In P. Vannini (Ed.), *The Routledge international handbook of ethnographic film and video* (pp. 247–255). Routledge.

French, S. (2020, September 18). Government hammers safety message, while hinting at remote ID future during FAA keynote. Retrieved October 22, 2020, from The Drone Girl website: http://www.thedronegirl.com/2020/09/18/faa-keynote-safety-remote-id/.

Gettinger, D., Holland Michel, A., Pasternack, A., Koebler, J., Musgrave, S., & Rankin, J. (2014). *The drone primer: A compendium of the key issues.* http://dronecenter.bard.edu/publication/the-drone-primer/.

Graham, A., Kutzli, H., Kulig, T. C., & Cullen, F. T. (2021). Invasion of the drones: A new frontier for victimization. *Deviant Behavior, 42*, 386–403.

Harris, S. (2015). Service providers as digital media infrastructure: Turkey's cybercafé operators. In L. Parks & N. Starosielski (Eds.), *Signal traffic: Critical studies of media infrastructures* (pp. 205–224). University of Illinois Press.

Hildebrand, J. M. (2018). Modal media: Connecting media ecology and mobilities research. *Media, Culture & Society, 40*, 348–364.

Innis, H. A. (1999). *The bias of communication.* University of Toronto Press.

Jablonowski, M. (2015). Drone it yourself! On the decentring of 'drone stories'. *Culture Machine, 16*. http://www.culturemachine.net/index.php/cm/article/view/589.

Jablonowski, M. (2017). Dronie citizenship? In A. Kuntsman (Ed.), *Selfie citizenship* (pp. 97–106). Palgrave Macmillan.

Jackman, A. (2019). Consumer drone evolutions: Trends, spaces, temporalities, threats. *Defense & Security Analysis, 35*, 362–383.

Jensen, O. B. (2016). New 'Foucauldian boomerangs': Drones and urban surveillance. *Surveillance & Society, 14*, 20–33.

Kakaes, K. (2015). What drones can do and how they can do it. In F. Greenwood & K. Kakaes (Eds.), *Drones and aerial observation: New technologies for property rights, human rights, and global development—A primer* (pp. 9–18). http://drones.newamerica.org/primer/Chapter%201.pdf.

Kaplan, C., & Miller, A. (2019). Drones as "atmospheric policing": From US border enforcement to the LAPD. *Public Culture, 31*, 419–445.

Klauser, F., & Pedrozo, S. (2015). Power and space in the drone age: A literature review and politico-geographical research agenda. *Geographica Helvetica, 70*, 285–293.

Lee, I. (2020, January 3). We're concerned about the FAA's proposed rule on remote ID. Retrieved June 4, 2020, from UAV Coach website: https://uavcoach.com/remote-id-nprm/.

Lee, T. B. (2020, February 29). New FAA drone rule is a giant middle finger to aviation hobbyists. Retrieved March 23, 2020, from Ars Technica website: https://arstechnica.com/tech-policy/2020/02/new-faa-drone-rule-is-a-giant-middle-finger-to-aviation-hobbyists/.

McCosker, A. (2015). Drone media: Unruly systems, radical empiricism and camera consciousness. *Culture Machine, 16*. https://www.culturemachine.net/index.php/cm/article/view/591.

McLuhan, M. (1964). *Understanding media: The extensions of man* (2nd ed.). Signet.

McLuhan, M. (2003). *The book of probes* (D. Carson, E. McLuhan, W. Kuhns, & M. Cohen, Eds.). Gingko Press.

McLuhan, M., & Fiore, Q. (1968). *War and peace in the global village*. Bantam.

McLuhan, M., & McLuhan, E. (1988). *Laws of media: The new science*. University of Toronto Press.

Meyrowitz, J. (1994). Medium theory. In D. Crowley & D. Mitchell (Eds.), *Communication theory today* (pp. 50–77). Polity Press.

Moss, V. (2019, December 27). FAA announces drone remote ID. Why we are disappointed. Retrieved May 28, 2020, from Drone U website: https://www.thedroneu.com/blog/faa-announces-drone-remote-id/.

Mumford, L. (2010). *Technics and civilization*. University of Chicago Press.

Parks, L. (2016). Drones, vertical mediation, and the targeted class. *Feminist Studies, 42*, 227–235.

Parks, L. (2018). *Rethinking media coverage*. Routledge.

Parks, L., & Starosielski, N. (Eds.). (2015). *Signal traffic: Critical studies of media infrastructures*. University of Illinois Press.

Postman, N. (1970). The reformed English curriculum. In A. C. Eurich (Ed.), *High school 1980: The shape of the future in American secondary education* (pp. 160–168). Pitman.

Rothstein, A. (2015). *Drone*. Bloomsbury Academic.

Sandvik, K. B., & Jumbert, M. G. (2016). *The good drone*. Routledge.

Sheller, M. (2011). Mobility. In *Sociopedia.isa*. Retrieved from http://www.sag epub.net/isa/resources/pdf/mobility.pdf.

Sheller, M., & Urry, J. (2006). The new mobilities paradigm. *Environment and Planning A, 38*, 207–226.

Sloterdijk, P. (2011). *Bubbles: Spheres volume I: Microspherology* (W. Hoban, Trans.). Semiotext.

Strate, L. (2017). *Media ecology: An approach to understanding the human condition*. Peter Lang.

Sturken, M., & Cartwright, L. (2009). *Practices of looking: An introduction to visual culture* (2nd ed.). Oxford University Press.

Urry, J. (2007). *Mobilities*. Polity.

Vertesi, J. (2015). *Seeing like a rover: How robots, teams, and images craft knowledge of Mars*. University of Chicago Press.

2

Understanding (with) the Drone

Introduction

The warm summer evening in Philadelphia was perfect for recording the sunset over the river with Jay, my drone.[1] As I try to locate a safe place to fly amidst the picnicking, strolling, jogging, and cycling activities next to the river, I have the FAA's rule to not fly over people or moving vehicles on my mind. Eventually, I detect a secluded spot next to a pathway with enough space for me to set up and launch the football-sized quadcopter. I have gotten used to the careful fumbling that setting up the foldable DJI Mavic Pro Platinum requires: Four propellers need to be correctly attached to the drone body, the camera lens protection comes off, my smartphone is wired to and clamped into the remote control, the app needs to be launched on the phone. Eventually, the remote control, drone app, and the small aircraft "detect" each other. Any software updates required? No. Good, that could have delayed me enough to miss this spectacular sunset. Finally, I am "good to fly" when Jay connects

---

[1] As I will detail later, I selected "Jay" as the official designation of my drone when registering the device on the FAA website. I spontaneously chose the name based on the initial of my first name.

© The Author(s), under exclusive license to Springer Nature Singapore Pte Ltd. 2021
J. M. Hildebrand, *Aerial Play*, Geographies of Media,
https://doi.org/10.1007/978-981-16-2195-6_2

to a sufficient number of satellites "nearby" for a stable connection in GPS flight mode and identification of his "home point." I carefully scan my surroundings horizontally and vertically using my eyes and ears. Will I be in the way of any pedestrians or cyclists? Do I detect the sound of aerial traffic nearby? Are there any birds that might get curious if I fly the drone above the river toward the sunset? All clear. I hold both controlling sticks down. "Take-off" the soft Siri-like voice inside the app for my Mavic drone tells me. After eight months and sixty-five flights, I have become comfortable with the remote control and the flight maneuvers it prompts.

Why am I beginning the chapter with this particular anecdote? Because what happened that evening not only taught me more about recreational drone use, but also prompted me to critically reconsider my auto-ethnographic positionality as a researcher. I reflectively stepped outside of myself, zoomed out, and looked back down onto myself from an aerial drone perspective. In this chapter, I want to make the case for such a self-aware, not only top-down but multidirectional, way of seeing and sensing as both a practical and metaphorical technique activated by the drone. As such, I discuss auto-*technography*—the self-reflective engagement *with technology through that technology* to tap into a "technological unconscious" (Clough, 2000; Thrift, 2004, 2011)—as a worthwhile supplement to the way we study technology, mobility, and our techno-mobile selves. Expanding ethnographers Philip Vannini and April Vannini's (2008) conception of "technography," the suggested approach has methodological merit in reconfiguring a range of mobile methods while asking auto-technographers to examine their own emplacements, relationalities, and mobilities.

So, what happened that summer evening? In short, a helicopter seemed to approach slightly beneath the 400-feet level in which drones are legally permitted to fly. Operating the drone at about 200 feet above the river, I noticed the familiar humming sound behind me, looked up away from the remote control, detected the helicopter, and tried to lower the drone above the river as fast and careful as I could. Alarmed yet focused, my gaze moved back and forth between the approaching helicopter and Jay who started to disappear behind trees. To keep the drone in my visual line of sight as required by the FAA, I stepped out of my protected spot, further up the pathway while hoping that the connection between my remote control and flying device wouldn't falter. In that case, the drone would automatically "return home" by rising up again to a pre-set height and traveling back to the launching coordinates. As I concentrated on getting the drone as far away as possible from the helicopter's potential path, I barely noticed how my body was getting in the way of passing cyclists. The ringing of bicycle bells joined the buzzing of the helicopter in my ears. Detached from my mind's and eye's fixation on the still invisible drone, my body managed to awkwardly move here and there, avoiding a crash on the ground. In the end, neither harm nor damage occurred on both vertical levels. The helicopter passed, and the drone returned "home."

Curious to learn more about the socio-cultural value of personal drone flying and eager to do justice to the practice by "being there" and "becoming" a hobby user, I briefly found myself in the position of potentially harming others and myself. Along with insights into human-machine interactions and aerial sensibilities that my engagement with the drone fosters, this experience left me questioning my investment into this research and the risks this aerial self-extension entails. Moreover, just as the drone perspective allows me to visually explore aerial geographies and quite literally opens up my horizon, the drone's visual and metaphorical gaze back at me on the ground cues me to critically reflect on my positionality in this research process beyond what might be mentioned in the limitations section of a journal article. In other words, the drone research medium prompts me to question, *where am I* and *where am I going with this*?

In the following, I briefly outline how this auto-technographic research design is informed by mobilities research and media ecological understandings of human-technology relationships. I then discuss the epistemological value of "drone-logs" as a mobile video ethnography and elicitation technique that evocatively reconfigures "sky video" with "ground audio." In this context, I argue for hybrid methods that juxtapose ways of knowing to sharpen the focus onto corporeal, physical, virtual, communicative, imaginative, and particularly (auto)-affective mobilities that imbue the flows of contemporary everyday life as well as the very research seeking to make sense of them. The chapter concludes with observations of how the distant and detached drone perspective can complement mobile methods practically and metaphorically. Adopting an aerial view onto themselves and the practice encourages researchers to more consciously take account of their own corporeal, intellectual, and affective mobilities within a larger research picture. The movements of the body and mind across space matter; the auto-drone view can make those visible.

Theory: Hybrid Research/er

For studying hobby drone practices, I combined multiple approaches: participant-observation in the Philadelphia region, in-depth interviews with hobby drone users, online ethnographies of drone community groups on Facebook, and visual analyses of drone-generated imagery. All of these methods gave me ideas about the ways of seeing, moving, and being that are relevant in personal drone adoption. While these methods provide rich data and insights, it is the auto-technographic component that allows me to connect the pieces, make sense of those relations, and, moreover, directly experience the fleeting, distributed, slippery, multiple, non-causal, sensory, emotional, and kinesthetic in drone flying and image-taking (Law & Urry, 2004). Learning to operate the quadcopter, studying the regulations, choosing times and places to fly, and creatively engaging with the collected imagery enabled me to discover some of the "non-representational ways" (Thrift, 2007) of relating toward the technology, the practice, the space, and myself.

Furthermore, the camera drone holds innovative means for reflecting, recording, and analyzing such multi-sensory mobilities beyond a drone-centric context. During each drone flight, the aerial views are live-streamed onto my smartphone's screen. I can thus see what the drone sees in real-time. In addition, my smartphone's microphone can be set to pick up sounds and noises around me. *Ground audio* thus connects with the corresponding *sky video*. While hobbyists may use this feature in combination with any live-streaming function of the drone's app, I juxtapose the audio and video into what I term *drone-logs*. Along with the natural sounds from the ground, I articulate my thoughts about the drone flying and image-taking in diagnostic voice-overs, which the drone app combines with the aerial recordings. I will return to the methodological merit of those drone-logs later.

Embracing the term "technography" as a "sensuous, engaged ethnography of technology" (Vannini & Vannini, 2008: 1299), I emphasize my attunement to such generative tools (what I am using), techniques (how I am using them), and corresponding tempers (what I think and feel while using them). I thus follow Vannini and Vannini (2008: 1275) and their understanding of technography "as a research strategy and art of representation" for their analysis of embodied media: "From our perspective technography is the study and writing of technical structures of communication processes, both their material and symbolic substance, and their potential for shaping social outcomes" (2008: 1299). I similarly study and write the socio-technical grammar of the remotely-controlled flying camera, engaging with both its material and immaterial affordances for hobbyists but also social scientists. Furthermore, I bring attention to what human geographer Nigel Thrift, (2004:176) describes as the "technological unconscious," mobilizing ways of knowing that

> do not belong to "us" or to the environment. Rather they have been coevolved, and so refuse a neat distinction between organic and inorganic life or between person and the environment.

In the auto-technographic, researchers orient themselves toward "the bending of bodies with environments to a specific set of addresses" (Thrift, 2004: 117) such as those of camera drones.

Just as Vannini and Vannini's creative project (2008) is inspired by some of McLuhan's "probes," so too is this exploration deeply informed by the lenses of media ecology. Central to this meta-disciplinary intellectual tradition are the biases and effects inherent to all human-made technologies. Such media are shaped by us as technological extensions of ourselves and may shape us back when we uncritically engage with them. Hence, media have an environmental quality; they surround us. After processes of media acclimatization, they and their biases tend to become invisible to us. For example, consider the alphabet as a medium. As a human-made technology of communication, its biases and effects have become somewhat invisible to us unless we make a deliberate effort to unpack them. Media ecologists make similar arguments about the inherent workings of other media like books, radio, film, television, and the Internet as well as cars, airplanes, satellites, and so forth independent of what specific content they transmit, contain, communicate. Since consumer drones remain fairly new and are not yet ubiquitous, their internal grammar is still legible. We have an opportunity to critically examine the socio-technical relationships this device affords and constrains. As technological extensions of human senses and faculties, as media that we shape and that shape us back, camera drones enclose knowledge about themselves, us, and any hybrid techno-social selves in-between.

The flying camera is consequently a compelling medium for understanding not only the technology itself, but our relationships to technology more generally in its convergence of multiple modalities: aerial navigation, visual production, and networked communication. McLuhan (1964: 57) writes, "The hybridization or compounding of these agents offers an especially favorable opportunity to notice their structural components and properties." The kind of hybrid interfacing innate to contemporary camera drones allows us to turn, what McLuhan (1964: 57) understands as, "make happen"-agents into "make aware"-agents. The drone-logs' configuration of ground audio and sky video, then, present a further level of revelatory hybridization. *Auto-drone-technography* is thus both a "make happen"- and "make aware"- process. According to McLuhan,

> The hybrid or the meeting of two media is a moment of truth and revelation from which new form is born. For the parallel between two media holds us on the frontier between forms that snap us out of the Narcissus-narcosis. The moment of the meeting of media is a moment of freedom and release from the ordinary trance and numbness imposed by them on our senses. (1964: 63)

In other words, the interfacing and juxtaposing of different media forms can serve as a mode of resistance to the sensorial numbness we may develop when engaging with our technological extensions. The same argument is valid for our ways of conducting research. Interfacing and juxtaposing multiple methods can similarly snap us out of an analytical Narcissus-narcosis. McLuhan expands on this idea, speaking to the alert media-user and critical researcher alike:

> Our very word "grasp" or "apprehension" points to the process of getting at one thing through another, of handling and sensing many facets at a time through more than one sense at a time. It begins to be evident that "touch" is not skin but the interplay of the senses, and "keeping in touch" or "getting in touch" is a matter of a fruitful meeting of the sense, of sight translated into sound and sound into movement, and taste and smell. (1964: 67)

Creatively experimenting with different media to "grasp" and "apprehend" our research subjects and objects can fruitfully stir routinized research and reflections. Auto-drone-technography is one of those ways that has mobilized me to not only protect my drone practice from unreflective drone use narcosis, but also pushed me to more deeply engage with my multiple selves as a researcher, amateur drone user, and visual subject from a bird's-eye view. By turning the drone into a "make aware"-medium in the effort to make myself more aware of the drone, I am increasingly being made *aware of myself, my temporal and spatial selves, and my evolving self-awareness*. When the FAA's registration website prompted me to enter a name for my brand-new Mavic Pro, I did not foresee how fitting the offhand initial of my first name would become. "J" keeps unmasking aspects of the consumer drone world along with parts of me, my role, and responsibilities as I self-extend into space.

Increasingly, researchers tap into the educational and epistemological potentials of consumer drones with social scientists Thomas Birtchnell and Christopher R. Gibson (2015) making a case for "aeromobile methods." The authors raise relevant questions about the politics and ethics of such personalized remote aeromobilities. Closer to my focus and conclusions, cultural geographers Adam Fish and Bradley L. Garrett acknowledge that

If in flying, the human operator is surrounded by the machine, is intimate with the machine, becomes the machine, is overcome by, or reins in the machine, then drone methodologies are already changing how we think and act. (2016: para. 1)

Going beyond the methodological purchase of consumer drones, Jablonowski (2017: 97) calls for a "'dronie citizenship' that does not fear drones but explores their ambiguous powers and pleasures." While endorsing his approach for a dronie citizenship, I shift away from his argument that the view from above "does not establish a particular self through media technologies, but destabilizes its individuality and particularity" (Jablonowski, 2017: 100). As I will show in the following, to my auto-drone lens, the aerial camera and its multidirectional gaze establish particular spatial selves and thus indeed represent philosopher Peter Sloterdijk's (2011) notion of an "ego-technical device." More than anticipated, the ego enters the auto reminding me of my ground while up in the air.

Drone-Logs

Combining sky video with ground audio, drone gaze with human voice, drone-logs sharpen the analytical attention to multi-scalar and multi-sensory mobilities. The hybrid format captures consciously and unconsciously communicated affects and "atmospheric attunements," as "the intimate, compositional process of dwelling in spaces that bears, gestures, gestates, worlds" (Stewart, 2011: 445) during the flying and recording process. An excerpt from a drone-log transcript illustrates this auto-technographic approach. In this February flight session, I experiment for the first time with one of the autonomous flight functions of the Mavic Pro: the Active Track. The ground audio picks up on the occasional wind gusts that interrupt my analytical voice-overs and the swishing sound of my winter jacket against the smartphone microphone when the drone animates me to run. The sky video is focused on me until I move out of the frame and the drone camera starts to visually search for me with subtle adjustments (Fig. 2.1). The drone-log transcript reads:

Fig. 2.1 The DJI Mavic Pro Platinum, "Jay," is actively tracking me

Ok, I am in Active Track right now, so that is what it is doing because I am not operating anything right now. [Video shows drone camera following me, but drone stays put; only one hand is on the remote controller]. It keeps tracing me, but not coming toward me. I thought it would be following me [skeptical tone]. Ah ok, I guess this is where I operate it. [Drone camera continues to trace my movement]. This is kind of cool. And, I have this green frame around me on the screen that says "GO" [chuckles]. It's like *the drone* is telling me to move, or *like the system* and *the screen* are telling me to move with this green square. It almost feels like as if I am in a video game. Like "go go go," "come on." Or like a first-person-shooter and I am the target. [Still walking] So, what happens if I go over there? Still focusing on me, I guess? Yep, still finding me. [I start running across the field]. It's still looking at me, but not coming. Has it lost me? [Drone zooms into where I stand]. No. Ok, now it's lost me. Oh, now it's found me again.

This serendipitous hide and seek play between the drone and I continues for a bit longer. The drone-log captures our experimental interactions as vocalized on the ground and depicted from the air. Both my and the drone's independent mobile agencies *come into play*.

A few weeks after this drone session, I am set to give a presentation at my university and debate whether or not to show this video despite its analytical richness for understanding the interactional mobilities between user and technology. Watching and listening to the drone-log shortly after the practice, I have second thoughts about the analogy to the first-person shooter game (and also find my running in the heavy winter jacket silly-looking and -sounding). For that research talk, I ended up selecting a different drone-log to substantiate my arguments. Today, the continued auto-technographic drone-logging and subsequent audio-visual exploring of my drone engagements have made me develop a more analytically distant and affectively detached lens onto my sky videos and ground audios. For example, as my drone-logging self struggles to describe what about the drone is telling her to move—"the drone," "the system," "the screen"—my elevated analytical self learns about the difficulty of locating and articulating agencies within drone ecologies. The same applies to the offhand first-person shooter analogy which I hesitated to endorse at first. Eventually, this angle became relevant to my thinking again as I will show in Chapter 6. Returning to those drone-logs from a stance of advanced comprehension if not emancipated elevation, I could (re)consider my immediate reactions and affective evaluative processes for additional conclusions.

The technographic format, consequently, aligns with and extends mobile video ethnography more generally. Embraced by mobilities researchers, mobile video ethnography taps into "a multitude of mobile, material, embodied practices of making distinctions, relations and places" (Elliot et al., 2017: 7) and enhances "recollection of sensory and affective encounters" (Spinney, 2015: 236). As human geographer Peter Adey states, "Video approaches to mobility therefore seem to collide different forms of sensing, witnessing and narrative" (2017: 275). The juxtaposition of affectively attached audio yet physically detached video along with an imaginative and imaged aerial gaze back at researchers themselves initiate new questions about this collision of different forms of sensing, witnessing, and narrative.

As such, auto-drone-technography combines features of mobile video ethnography with video elicitation techniques. Besides reflecting the visual maneuvers of the drone and the user's corresponding articulations, the drone-logs present what human geographer Justin Spinney calls

> sensual prompt[s] to recollection, helping to foreground the aspects of experience we are interested in knowing about and creating a framework through which to talk about felt experiences arising from relations with fleeting, mundane and easily forgotten phenomena. (2015: 236)

The immediate responses of drone-loggers and their bystanders in combination with the aerial imagery can thus be further contemplated from a (spatially and temporally) remote perspective. While my drone-logging self is often occupied with safely operating the drone, moving the gaze back and forth between drone and screen, surprised, amused, confused, and awed by the aerial play, my post-logging self can bring her critical attention to visual and auditory details as she reviews the mediated memories. Here, the experience continues to be a mobile one. However, to use sociologist Lesley Murray's words, the "range of emotional responses to space and mobility is reduced" (2009: 18). Recording from drone launch to landing, the unedited audio-visual diaries quite often *drone on.* Nonetheless, they include notions of the active and quiescent, the purposeful and accidental as central to the recollection of various mobilities.

There is more. While the drone-logs link ground audio with sky video, they assemble merely the *live-streamed version of the sky video* transmitted onto the smartphone. Occasionally, this image transmission is lagging or shaky. Sometimes the image will blur and go blank when the connection to the flying drone is poor. In the meantime, a high-quality version of the drone's recording is also saved onto a storage device inside the small aircraft. Those silent videos (there is no microphone on the drone itself) allow me to fill such visual disruptions in my drone-logs. With these data, I see what the drone saw in the short moments that my ground self was in the dark about the aerial gaze. On one occasion, the drone app suddenly froze, cutting off the live-feed of the aerial images onto my smartphone while the drone was locked in the tracking function. Pointing toward and moving with me, the drone camera continued to silently record my confusion, amusement, frustration, and pondering in this moment of shifted agencies (see Chapter 7). Later, I discovered this high-definition gem on the micro SD card inside the drone, enriching the dataset with a back-up record of this unusual event.

Auto-Affective Mobilities

Ethnographic studies stress the importance of "being there," "moving with," and researching "in situ" as crucial for data collection and analysis. With attention to the non-representational experienced in mobile methods, human geographer Peter Merriman (2014: 177) notes that "the practices of making a video, riding-along, and moving-with are perhaps more instructive or informative than the images, data or experiences gathered." The generated drone-logs and other mobile video ethnographic and elicitation methods are analytically valuable not only as collected data but as processes of uncovering the studied mobilities.

Auto-ethnographic approaches take the principle of being there and moving with a step further. As "systematic sociological introspection" (Ellis, 2004: xvii), auto-ethnography favors individualized and subjective accounts of the research topic, an abundance of which may never materialize as "data" or "fact" (Luvaas, 2016b: 90). In that sense, "Auto-ethnography does not just use the self to do research; it is explicitly about 'the self' as the medium through which research transpires" (Luvaas, 2016b: 90). In auto-drone-technography, it is the self in combination with technique and technology that poses the hybrid medium of research. By attending to the "auto," I take explicit account of my motions, notions, and emotions in the interplay with the drone during and after the practice. According to visual anthropologist Brent Luvaas, (2016a: 12), such data are "a meaningful form of knowledge in its own right." How I think and feel about my drone mobilities in the moment and after-the-fact may echo the ways of thinking and feeling not only other drone users and bystanders but also other researchers experience. A sense of a medium's inherent workings and users' engagement with them is key in assessing social, spatial, cultural, and political responses and effects.

Table 2.1 Types of mobilities based and expanding on Urry (2007: 47)

Corporeal	Bodies traveling, e.g., for migration, commute, leisure
Physical	Objects traveling, e.g., cargo, souvenirs
Virtual	Data traveling, e.g., through networks in realtime
Communicative	Communication traveling, e.g., via letters, audio, video calls
Imaginative	Minds traveling, e.g., when consuming visuals, reading a book
Affective	Senses and emotions traveling, e.g., when flying a drone, doing research

In this process of being/seeing/moving there (a mobilities principle that the drone as remote technology can complicate as I will discuss in Chapter 5), I experience the respective corporeal, physical, virtual, communicative, imaginative, and *affective mobilities* (Table 2.1). The last type of mobility is what I suggest adding to sociologist John Urry's (2007) typology.

Affective mobilities include the sensory challenges of and emotional responses to aerial drone play *as well as* research more generally. The opening anecdote about the helicopter is one prominent example that brings my vulnerabilities as remote pilot and researcher to the fore. The respective drone-log for that experience includes this segment:

Ok, I am flying toward the river. Uh oh, the birds. One of my interviewees said, when you encounter birds, you should go up with the drone because birds don't look up [chuckles]. Ok, so here is that uhm… [drone camera moves left and right overviewing the river]. That looks cool. [Camera clicking sound]. I am at 200 feet. I'm trying to always see it [the drone], but I am also sort of surrounded by trees. Oh wow. [Camera captures the sunset]. So, I've been looking up at the drone for the past couple of moments, and now I am looking at the screen and it is just so amazing. [Pause] Ok, I hear a helicopter [drone starts lowering]. It's behind me. [Bicycle swishes by. Helicopter buzzing gets louder and quieter again.] Ok, there was a … that was scary. I just kept coming down, down, down. My heart just dropped. That helicopter seemed lower than 400 feet. I just brought the drone straight down, so I'm not sure where it is hovering right now. Whew! [Sighs of relief]. Ok, there it is. Yeah, come back toward me.

Shifting between purposeful narration and *auto*matic reaction, this drone-log transcript gives a sense of the multiple emotions and motions active during this encounter. On other occasions, I enter the field wondering if something bad could happen today: What if the drone flies away, drops down, lands in the wrong spot, damages something, or worst of all hurts somebody? Are those risks worth it? Such and similar vulnerabilities and anxieties are not exclusive to my analytical practice and apply to other mobile methods. I see the auto-drone process foreground a "technological unconscious," understood as "the bending of bodies-with-environments to a specific set of addresses without the benefit of any cognitive inputs" (Thrift, 2007: 91). This process prompts me to metaphorically look up, out, and back down at myself as a researcher at a distance. It asks me to critically consider my role and responsibilities in the research process as well as the big picture of my work. A call for auto-drone perspectives encourages researchers to actively take account of such affective mobilities by shifting their analytical lens up, out, and back down onto themselves.

What does that mean and what is it good for? The idea is to consider the relational emplacements and mobile positionings of researchers in their work from a drone point of view. Camera drones capture views we are usually not in a position to see. They also capture us in ways that we do not usually see ourselves: *remotely*. In contrast to other valuable auto-ethnographic work which seeks visual immediacy as "a way of connecting with the field more intimately" (Luvaas, 2017: 164), the auto-drone lens can serve as a means for disconnecting from the field, for seeing oneself from an elevated angle. The aim is for a personal overview of the research processes and their multi-sensory mobilities. As such, the method speaks to the "sensuous turn" within ethnography that centralizes multi-sensuous, emplaced practices, and "attends to the question of experience by accounting for the relationships between bodies, minds and the materiality and sensoriality of the environment" (Pink, 2009: 25). Researchers' senses, emplacements, movements, and environments become central in the auto-drone angle.

Last but not least, as sociologist Chris Rojek (1993: ix) observes, "Up there in an airplane one is, as it were, suspended from earthly cares. Looking down from above the clouds one cannot avoid thinking." If the aerial is indeed a space for contemplation, then the drone perspective allows us to entertain celestial considerations while firmly on the ground. The auto-drone can serve mobile methodology as a lens for what Luvaas (2016a: 13) describes as moving "between embodied modes of practice and critical self-reflexivity." Hence, a worthwhile outcome of this approach is an increased attention to the researchers' corporeal, physical, communicative, imaginative, and affective mobilities in the conception, design, conduct, reflection, and presentation of their scientific work.

Conclusion

In this chapter, I addressed several dimensions of auto-drone-technography as a creative, self-reflective addition to mobile and ethnographic research. While the drone technique teaches me about drone technology, the medium has analytical purchase beyond that. In combining different modalities such as aerial navigation, image production, and virtual communication, the consumer drone presents a compelling hybrid medium that sharpens the perspective onto the individual mobile and mediating processes. Moreover, it provides a generative format for capturing and recalling multi-sensory mobilities in the combination of sky video and (research-reflective) ground audio. Auto-drone-technography merges the ground with the sky, the human with the nonhuman, the personal with the impersonal, the immobile with the mobile, the invisible with the visible, the immediate with the hypermediate, the up-close with the distant, the here with the (somewhere) over there, the anxious with the inanimate, the affective with the effective, the technically conscious with the technologically unconscious, the ego with the auto, *the topic and tool with the technographer*. Adey states that "artistic and creative practices may offer further insight into another range of methodologies attentive to mobility often through the making and juxtaposition of different kinds of visual and moving images" (2017: 294). Drone-logs have that potential.

More generally, the auto-drone view is meant to encourage researchers to zoom out, see the larger picture, and most notably see themselves inside of it along with the multiple material and immaterial mobilities the work demands, prompts, inspires. Supplemental to other mobile methods, data collection strategies, and elicitation techniques, this self-reflexive approach is one that takes note of the position, emplacement, role, and investment of the researcher in the research process. This aerial top-down angle can make us visible to ourselves within a larger context and aid us in making our research practices and processes—along with the multi-sensuous mobilities and auto-affective relationalities we encounter, animate, and enact—visible to our audiences.

References

Adey, P. (2017). *Mobility* (2nd ed.). Routledge.

Birtchnell, T., & Gibson, C. (2015). Less talk more drone: Social research with UAVs. *Journal of Geography in Higher Education, 39*, 182–189.

Clough, P. (2000). *Autoaffection: Unconscious thought in the age of teletechnology.* University of Minnesota Press.

Elliot, A., Norum, R., & Salazar, N. B. (2017). *Methodologies of mobility: Ethnography and experiment.* Berghahn Books.

Ellis, C. (2004). *The ethnographic I: A methodological novel about autoethnography.* Rowman Altamira.

Fish, A., & Garrett, B. L. (2016, December 18). Reframing drone methodologies. Retrieved September 1, 2018, from Centre for Mobilities Research website: https://www.lancaster.ac.uk/cemore/reframing-drone-methodologies/.

Jablonowski, M. (2017). Dronie citizenship? In A. Kuntsman (Ed.), *Selfie citizenship* (pp. 97–106). Palgrave Macmillan.

Law, J., & Urry, J. (2004). Enacting the social. *Economy and Society, 33*, 390–410.

Luvaas, B. (2016a). *Street style: An ethnography of fashion blogging.* Bloomsbury Academic.

Luvaas, B. (2016b). Urban fieldnotes: An auto-ethnography of street style blogging. In H. Jenss (Ed.), *Fashion studies: Research methods, sites and practices* (pp. 83–100). Bloomsbury Academic.

Luvaas, B. (2017). The affective lens. *Anthropology and Humanism, 42*, 163–179.

Luvaas, B. (2019). Unbecoming: The aftereffects of autoethnography. *Ethnography, 20,* 245–262.

McLuhan, M. (1964). *Understanding media: The extensions of man* (2nd ed.). Signet.

Merriman, P. (2014). Rethinking mobile methods. *Mobilities, 9,* 167–187.

Murray, L. (2009). Contextualising and mobilising research. In B. Fincham, M. McGuinness, & L. Murray (Eds.), *Mobile methodologies* (pp. 13–24). Palgrave Macmillan.

Pink, S. (2009). *Doing sensory ethnography.* Sage.

Rojek, C. (1993). *Ways of escape: Modern transformations in leisure and travel.* Palgrave Macmillan.

Sloterdijk, P. (2011). *Bubbles: Spheres volume I: Microspherology* (W. Hoban, Trans.). Semiotext.

Spinney, J. (2015). Close encounters? Mobile methods, (post)phenomenology and affect. *Cultural Geographies, 22,* 231–246.

Stewart, K. (2011). Atmospheric attunements. *Environment and Planning D: Society and Space, 29,* 445–453.

Thrift, N. (2004). Remembering the technological unconscious by foregrounding knowledges of position. *Environment and Planning D: Society and Space, 22,* 175–190.

Thrift, N. (2007). *Non-representational theory: Space, politics, affect.* Routledge.

Thrift, N. (2011). Lifeworld Inc—And what to do about it. *Environment and Planning D: Society and Space, 29,* 5–26.

Urry, J. (2007). *Mobilities.* Polity.

Vannini, P., & Vannini, A. (2008). Of walking shoes, boats, golf carts, bicycles, and a slow technoculture: A technography of movement and embodied media on protection island. *Qualitative Inquiry, 14,* 1272–1301.

3

Situating Hobby Drone Practices

Introduction

Consumer drones and their rapid rise in the domestic sphere over the past several years have been polarizing individuals, communities, regulators, and governments. The flying camera generates both excitement and concerns; the aerial sensor is both promising and perilous. For some, it provides unprecedented access to the skies, something akin to a visual and mobile liberation from our grounded bodies. Compared to helicopters, balloons, airplanes, and even model aviation, off-the-shelf consumer drones more readily provide access to horizontal and vertical spaces and breathtaking views. For others, however, the noisy and unruly aerial device raises significant concerns about the potential threats to privacy, safety, cybersecurity along with its impact on the natural environment. Drones crashing, hurting people, damaging property, shutting down aerial traffic, hindering emergency responses, or disrupting wildlife are just a few of the stories that tend to dominate public discourse about the problems with small unmanned aerial systems. In the recreational domain in particular, worries are justified about hobby users having only minimal, if any, aviation experience for safe drone flying (Bartsch et al.,

J. M. Hildebrand, *Aerial Play*, Geographies of Media, https://doi.org/10.1007/978-981-16-2195-6_3

2016). Other issues include the potential for purposefully "rogue" aerial activities such as spying, stalking, smuggling, and otherwise exploitative and harmful uses (Graham et al., 2021; Jackman 2019). Evident in this list of benefits and risks is that consumer drones are not just flying machines. Principles of aviation are constitutive elements in promising and perilous drone flying and image-taking. Yet, those are not the only factors in the interplay of people, things, and data on the ground and in the sky.

Amidst such tensions and frictions about what drones afford (and what drone users should and shouldn't do), I want to shed light onto how drones are used in everyday, specifically recreational spaces. The key argument in this chapter is that *consumer* drones are more than mere "unmanned aircraft systems" (FAA, 2019b: 72439). Yes, such drones consist of "an unmanned aircraft platform and its associated elements – including communication links, sensors, software and power supply – that are required for safe and efficient operation in the national airspace system" (FAA, 2020a: 41). However, in order to understand the technology's full range of affordances, the medium's biases and effects, we are in need of *zooming out* and acknowledging *what else* shapes consumer drone uses. Recognizing the roots of this technology in aviation, but then expanding our understanding of it as a complex assemblage of people, things, spaces, communication, and movement beyond the aerial mode, helps us more comprehensively understand, assess, and ultimately regulate ongoing and emerging practices. As an aerial device, the drone is part of the history of human aviation and subject to its regulations. As a military device, the drone is also part of the history of warfare and associated with surveillance and militarization. What I add to this list is how the drone is a mobile medium entangled in recreational ecologies and creative potentials.

Such a lens considers the drone's role as a visual production and digital communication tool, its spatially but also socially networked capacities, and its opportunities for interactive human-machine relations. The subsequent chapters will dive into the specifics of these different dimensions further. For now, I focus on how a shift in the way we think and talk about drones as hybrid mobile assemblages of human and nonhuman agents and socio-cultural dynamics sharpens our perspective onto everyday drone use. This chapter lays the groundwork, creates an inventory of key factors, and provides a map for the territories the subsequent chapters traverse more carefully.

The FAA officially refers to drones as "unmanned aircraft systems." More specifically, the term "system" encompasses both the unmanned aircraft and "its associated elements – including communication links, sensors, software and power supply – that are required for safe and efficient operation in the national airspace system" (FAA, 2020a: 41). This terminology is beneficial for recognizing the technology's networked character and for situating it in the larger aviation context. Nonetheless, this delineation is not ideal. It suggests a somewhat static and closed-off complex between ground control station, operator, drone, and other equipment. As such, the term obscures the medium's entanglement in larger spatial and socio-cultural ecologies as an assemblage of physical and virtual movement as well as human and nonhuman agencies.

Figure 3.1 illustrates, albeit much simplified, some of the constitu-

Fig. 3.1 Recreational drone use in situ (*Concept* Julia M. Hildebrand; *Graphic Design* Sofia Podesta)

tive factors that may shape aerial drone play on a given day. Beyond the user on the ground and unmanned aircraft in the air, the image situates the drone medium within a larger ecology of people, vehicles, structures, animals, things, and conditions. Starting with the sun and potential solar flares represented in the upper right corner, the user's practice can be impacted by the sun's geomagnetic effects and whether it is up or has set. Sunrises and sunsets also count as some of the most popular drone images. The depicted satellites hint at the relevance of GPS availability for a stable positioning of the drone during flight. Planes and similar aerial traffic factor into recreational drone ecologies in that hobbyists are required to stay away from or get prior approval for flights in such controlled airspace. Helicopters, birds, kites, and other model aircraft could pose potential hazards in "good to fly"-hobby spaces, too. Infrastructure and architecture on the mezzanine level, such as above-ground power lines, light poles and antennas, further shape user performances and similarly belong to hobby-drone ecologies. On the ground, other people and moving objects, such as cars and bicycles, demand hobbyists' attention. Finally, hybrid drone ecologies include real-time or delayed virtual audiences attending to and commenting on the practice from home when users share drone imagery online.

A number of those influential links between people, things, and data are highlighted in Fig. 3.2. The blue lines indicate potential physical relations of the flying drone to other hazards in the air and on the ground such as moving entities or volumetric obstacles. The orange lines represent the visual relations of drone users to their surroundings. Those people, things, and conditions are what remote pilots need to have their eyes on when flying and recording. They include bystanders and other hobbyists, moving vehicles on the ground and in the air, along with wind and weather. Next, the green lines signify data connections among the drone system, satellites, the operator, and the Internet. The reductionist sketch is only scratching the surface of the many virtual connections present and, for instance, excludes potential signals and data moving between one user's drone to another user's control system. The yellow line between sun and satellite hints at the atmospheric relations between the drone system—utilizing GPS—and satellites, which may be impacted by solar activity. The pink lines represent some of the affective relations

Fig. 3.2 Physical (blue), visual (orange), virtual (green), atmospheric (yellow), and affective (pink) relations in hobby drone ecologies (*Concept* Julia M. Hildebrand; *Graphic Design* Sofia Podesta and Julia M. Hildebrand)

among users, bystanders, and potential Internet audiences witnessing the practice.

As the two graphics suggest, looking beyond the specific dynamics between drone, ground control station, and pilot through an assemblage-perspective highlights many heterogeneous relations within recreational drone ecologies. Aerial drone play is shaped by not just aviation but also communication. Consumer drones are *socially-networked* aerial *cameras* and thus not just for flying, but also for capturing, creating, and communicating. Since the aerial device is merged with the communicative affordances of high-definition cameras and streaming capabilities—as manifested in the thousands of aerial still and moving images regularly uploaded onto the Internet—the recreational trend demands assessment from a social-scientific perspective that also considers contemporary digital practices and popular visual culture. In the following, I lay the theoretical groundwork for this analysis of situating personal drone uses, drawing from media ecology and mobilities research. I then trace drone mobilities in situ, inspired by Jensen's (2013) staging mobilities concept, by discussing drone temporal, spatial, mobile, and social dimensions. As such, this chapter is a foundation for the subsequent more in-depth explorations of drone communication, movements, visuals, and relationships.

Theory: Media and Mobilities In Situ

"What makes mobile situations happen?" asks Jensen (2013) when arguing for his staging mobilities framework. He turns to actor-network theory and philosopher Bruno Latour's definition of agency as anything that makes "a difference in the course of some other agent's action or not" (Latour, 2005: 71). Building on this comprehensive approach to agencies, mobilities research focuses on subject, objects, and spaces that make a difference in mobile situations "as they connect to embodiments, multisensorial engagements, affects, and materials" (O. B. Jensen, 2016b: 594). Similarly, media ecology uses the concept of "medium" as an agential, environmental force that shapes not only mobile situations, but us as thinking, feeling, and acting beings more generally. Media ecology's approach to media as extensions and environments (McLuhan, 1964; Postman, 1970; Strate, 2017) benefits from the material pragmatism much work in mobilities research advances (O. B. Jensen, 2016b). I adopt those frameworks along with the useful language of actor-network theory to illuminate what makes personal drone uses happen.

To understand the interplay of people, things, and environments in aerial drone play, the boundary-crossing foundations of media ecology help explore those often messy and invisible human-technology relationships. Media ecologists "study media environments as the sum total of all the technologies, codes and modes of communication available in any given time and place" (Strate, 2016: 1165). As such, media ecology understands media and environments as systemic, i.e., consisting of heterogeneous systems. Yet, Strate cautions from imagining "something like separate biological cells, each with their own membrane, maintain[ing] their own integrity and identity" (2017: 185). Instead, media, systems, networks, and environments are *ecological;* they overlap, link, shape, create. Media theorist Neil Postman (1998) suggests understanding the introduction of a new technology as equal to that of a drop of red dye into a glass of clear water. The red dye colors the water in the glass; it changes the environment it enters. This ecological effect occurs on micro- and macro-levels with attention to culture, society, economics, and politics, and media ecology directs critical attention to such changes. In the same vein, personal drone use asks to be unpacked as an ecology that draws from existing relations and shapes new ones. As such, media ecology provides a conceptual orientation beyond notions of "system" as a self-enclosed constellation. The official terminology of drones as small unmanned aircraft systems obscures the larger ecological factors that support and prevent the mobile drone practice. Instead,

> We can examine the ways in which an individual medium functions as an environment, mediating between ourselves and what would otherwise be our environment, and modifying or allowing us to modify our existing environment. Doing so allows us to study the effects of innovation, the ways in which a change introduced into a system affects the rest of the system. But a given medium rarely, if ever, functions as an isolated influence, but rather interacts with other media as part of a greater environment, one that includes the biophysical, technological, and symbolic. (Strate, 2017: 194)

The goal of this chapter consequently is to situate recreational drone use within a larger ecology of heterogeneous material and immaterial relationships.

Such intertwinement of technology and other atmospheric elements is also a point Fish (2020) makes, when describing drones as hybrids. He elaborates,

> The drone has a co-determining relationship with the objects—elements, other non-humans, and edges—alongside which it comes into being. Likewise, the mattering, programmatic, and ethical dimensions of the drone are interwoven with the messy practices of flying in elemental and social space. Drones become entangled with technologies, pilots, landscapes, and research subjects. (Fish, 2020: 253)

What then are these co-determining relationships, what are the objects, dimensions, messy practices, and entanglements in the spaces of aerial drone play?

Jensen's (2013) framework for understanding mobilities in situ, meaning the spaces in which movement occurs, aligns with such holistic perspectives. He encourages critical attention to how "mundane everyday life mobilities are dynamic and complex practices taking place in material sites and often complex infrastructures by and with people" (O. B. Jensen, 2016a: 69). Inspired by this agenda for studying such mobilities in situ, I adopt and reframe several of Jensen's (2013) questions for unpacking hobby drone ecologies:

1. What are the implications of the physical form and material design of sites and spaces that afford drone mobilities and socialities?
2. How does it feel to be a social agent remotely on the move by drone in public spaces and what normative and social ties are created among such social agents, places and objects?
3. How are personal drone mobilities being shaped and given meaning by semiotic systems of communication, circulation, and mobilities processing?
4. How are drone infrastructures creating new cultural practices and ways of using public spaces, and how are they creating mechanisms of social exclusion of power?

The staging mobilities approach opens up avenues for considering "the physical, social, technical and cultural conditions for the staging of contemporary mobilities" (O. B. Jensen, 2013: 4). This set of questions speaks to larger inquiries about how to situate personal drone mobilities across physical-material and digital-intangible environments, and what kinds of socio-spatial mobilities and techno-cultural relations camera drones open up, sustain, and complicate. Combining such approaches of media ecology and staging mobilities provides a comprehensive analytical framework for understanding hybrid drone ecologies, meaning drone-related agencies and mobilities in situ.

Drone Ecologies and Mobile Agencies

Participant observation and in-depth interviews with drone hobbyists highlight the complex relational dynamics between the aerial medium and its hybrid surroundings. In the following, I draw from fieldwork in different locations (such as the countryside, city park, over rivers and lakes, and close to urban infrastructure), weather conditions (sunny to drizzling), and during various times of the day (daytime and night-time flight sessions). Temporal, spatial, mobile, and social agencies all variously shape personal drone practices in situ.

Temporal Factors

Weather, sunlight hours, and satellite availability all fall under influential "temporal factors" in recreational drone ecologies. Weather plays a major role in making such aerial play happen as the standard off-the-shelf equipment is generally unsuitable for strong rain, wind, and extreme heat and cold. Strong winds in particular may overpower the smaller quad-copter models and thus present possibly dangerous flying conditions. When I meet several hobbyists in a local park in the spring of 2017, occasional wind gusts keep the hobbyists from initially launching their consumer drones. Two of the three users brought wind measuring tools and keep assessing whether their aerial devices would be stable enough for a safe flight. Eventually the wind calms down and a DJI Inspire 1, a Phantom 4, and a Mavic Pro drone take to the sky. All three aircrafts sound louder than usual; their propellers working against the wind gusts. Occasionally, the hobby pilots use the direction of the wind to speed up their drones and test how fast they can fly with the additional push from the windy conditions. Hence, wind and weather more generally can impact whether or not remote pilots can fly, how safe the flight will be, and how both users and drones may perform.

The important role of time and weather is also emphasized in the online local drone community I follow on Facebook. When users plan meet-ups, some of them share screenshots of their weather apps and discuss the viability of drone flying and recording. Flight sessions are usually not confirmed until several hours before to ensure favorable weather conditions. Consequently, the meteorological circumstances at a given place and time matter not only for manned and professional aviation, but also in the recreational spaces with stronger impact on the smaller devices.

In addition, an education campaign founded by the Association for Unmanned Vehicle Systems International (AUVSI) and the Academy of Model Aeronautics (AMA) in partnership with the FAA, called "Know Before You Fly," recommends recreational pilots not to fly during times of "reduced visibility," including nighttime hours (AUVSI et al., 2020). When I meet hobbyists Emanuel and Terrence for a flight session in the evening, they plan on collecting a few shots of the city lights and skyline at dusk. Emanuel registers the flight session in the FAA's B4UFLY app, which warns him about the reduced visibility and nearby heliports. The service advises him to "fly with caution" because of the nearby aerial infrastructures and the potential for helicopters. Emanuel and Terrence decide not to fly their respective quadcopters higher than 200 feet above the ground, half the height of what is legally permitted. The darkness presents an additional challenge as the DJI Mavic's grey shell is barely visible in the sky above us. For a moment, the white Phantom 4 and its strobe lights disappear behind one of the clouds and Emanuel relies completely on the image feed on his tablet to steer the drone back to his visual line of sight. Sunrises and sunsets are popular themes for hobbyists, yet, whether the flight begins before sunrise or continues after sunset has legal and practical implications for the drone session. During a sunset shoot near the river, another hobbyist decides to cut a session short because of nightfall. The time of day and respective lighting conditions again significantly shape recreational practices.

Another temporal dimension pertinent to personal drone uses is satellite availability for the GPS signal. The advancement and availability of Global Positioning Systems count as driving factors for the explosion of drone innovation next to improvements in battery technology, and lightweight cameras, along with the integration of multiple sophisticated sensors (Bartsch et al., 2016). Emanuel shows me his "drone" smartphone folder with the five apps that he regularly consults before launching his drone. Apart from four other drone-specific apps that display weather conditions, sunrise and sunset hours, or no-fly-zones, he uses the service Solar Sphere to check on the possibility of solar flares having caused geomagnetic storms on Earth's surface. Ground-based magnetic observatories around the world measure such disturbances with the so-called Kp-Index. The storms could affect satellites, which would then trigger GPS errors for consumer drones along with other disturbances. When the Space Weather Prediction Center warns about strong geomagnetic storms on a particular day, Emanuel shares the announcement with his Facebook drone community noting "Guys be careful flying today. Keep an eye on the Kp-index. The sun released a solar energy flare and we're getting it now." Aerial play with drones is thus entangled in complex and far-reaching temporal and social relations. I will return to the social relationships drone communities uphold online later.

Spatial Factors

Next to such temporal dimensions, a number of spatial relations make personal drone (im)mobilities happen. Volumetric obstacles, such as buildings, trees, power lines, fences, and antennas, could potentially interfere in the consumer drone flight path. The texture of the ground, too, may or may not be suitable for lift-off and landing. Furthermore, the "Know Before You Fly" education campaign asks operators to "not fly near or over sensitive infrastructure of property such as power stations, water treatment facilities, correctional facilities, heavily traveled roadways, government facilities, etc." (AUVSI et al., 2020). When I meet Ahmed, a drone hobbyist in his twenties, one Sunday afternoon, the task to find a safe place to fly becomes quite the challenge. An Ultimate Frisbee game is taking place on the open field that we had originally picked, so we continue to search for a suitable space. "Half the time is finding a place to fly," mentions Ahmed as he dismisses another location because of some power lines and a big antenna. While his drone's obstacle recognition and collision avoidance systems may prevent crashes into such volumetric formations, Ahmed prefers a wide-open space with less navigational challenges. Tara, a commercial and recreational drone user in her twenties, consults Google Maps prior to each flight session and goes over a number of questions to ensure a safe operation:

> I like to look at [Google Maps] at least to get some intel of the area, any other structures that are around, are there neighborhoods around? Are there schools around? Are there other potential hazards? Is it a bit busier? Is it downtown Center City in the middle of the day at lunch hour where everybody's out and about? That's not the best time to fly [laughs]. Things of that nature. Just know of any hazards.

Here, Tara considers various temporal and spatial agencies that shape the assemblage of her drone flying and image-taking.

Another afternoon, I join hobbyist Jim who is taking aerial images of rooftops on a street in Philadelphia. Behind a row of houses, he detects a small side street that sparks his "aerial curiosity." However, it is somewhat windy and the street is adjacent to railroad tracks behind a fence, so Jim decides against flying further in this direction. He expresses his worry about the drone being blown over the fence and crashing into the tracks. It would not only be difficult to retrieve the drone then, but the device could damage sensitive infrastructure and be a hazard for the rail traffic. The same applies to any flights conducted within five miles of an airport, for which the FAA requires drone pilots to obtain permission from the respective Air Traffic Control. When Emanuel finds himself in proximity of a regional airport, he calls the Tower and asks for permission to fly. According to the respective officer, Emanuel is clear to fly in the subsequent 25 minutes without posing a hazard to the airport operations. Hence, spatial particularities require special attention and occasionally standardized processes depending on the respective mobilities in situ.

Moreover, the material conditions that make up those human-made and natural geographies impact aerial play by drones. During a flight over a river close to two bridges, I learn about the magnetic disturbances the metal infrastructure can cause, triggering warnings in the drone system. In addition, the drone drifts softly when steered. Next to the near-by iron structure interfering with the GPS signal and drone stability, reflections from the water further destabilize the activity. Hence, not only the voluminosity of the geographic surrounding, its potential for opening up or obstructing a flight path, but also the materiality of the infrastructure and environment (such as metal and water) shape hybrid drone ecologies This example points to the relevance of what Jensen calls "other materialities": "as a shorthand for the different and sensual sensitivity to surfaces, structures, volumes, surfaces and spaces, as well as of the agencies and capacities of materials, things and artefacts" (O. B. Jensen, 2016b: 592). The affordances and agencies of materials, things, and artifacts the drone medium depends on, relates to, and makes legible come to light.

Mobile Factors

Next to temporal and spatial factors, the assemblage of the hobby drone practice is shaped by the mobilities and immobilities of people, animals, things, and spaces. First, consumer drone mobilities are closely regulated in terms of flight location, height, and distance. Besides the FAA's rule for unmanned aircraft systems to operate exclusively under 400 feet, remote pilots also need to respect controlled airspace and flight restrictions. The FAA adopted the classes A, B, C, D, E, and G for U.S. national airspace and requires drone pilots to either stay away from classes B to D or get flight permission from Air Traffic Control. While class A starts 18,000 feet above Mean Sea Level and is thus prohibited for recreational drone pilots, class G counts as the "good-to-go" uncontrolled airspace. Again several apps, such as Airmap and the FAA's own B4UFLY can help drone hobbyists responsibly situate their practice. Moreover, the apps also inform of any temporary flight restrictions, potentially put into effect due to "a temporary hazardous condition, such as a wildfire or chemical spill; a security-related event, [...]; or other special situations" (FAA, 2019a).

Beyond such regulatory frameworks, multiple other mobile relationships on the ground and in the air make or break aerial drone play. When tracing Ahmed's DJI Mavic Pro drone in the sky on a cloudy afternoon, I am surprised by the amount of aerial traffic occurring throughout the session. Apart from passenger planes visible in the far distance, a news helicopter passes well above us, several other quadcopters fly by, and a handful of model aircrafts are ready to take off once the battery of

Ahmed's Mavic runs out. Moreover, a ball and a frisbee occasionally enter the lower parts of the aerial space similarly posing as crash threats. All the while, Ahmed is cautious of the movements around him and the drone, his gaze moving back and forth between the screen on his controller and the device in the sky. The mobile ecologies of the drone flights at dusk with Emanuel and Terrence are similarly busy. A helicopter passes far above us and a police boat keeps patrolling the otherwise quiet river the drones hover above. Emanuel pays close attention to the sounds around him. When a motorcycle passes on the highway further away, the hobbyist wonders if there is another helicopter or boat nearby. "It's good to listen carefully," he tells me, referring to traffic on the ground and in the sky.

On another occasion, Terrence is flying his Mavic and a pair of birds starts to circle around the device. "The Mavic has sparked their interest" observes Ahmed standing next to him and recounts how frequently birds have gotten attracted by his own model. Not sure about what the birds will do, Terrence decides to land his drone. Other users experience the same and take measures to reduce the risk of attracting birds. On Facebook, a hobbyist shares a picture of his customized Mavic donning a bright orange instead of a grey coat. He writes "Ok, I change the color hopefully there's a keep the birds away [sic]. Every time I fly the birds are attracted to this drone. Also I can see it." The orange stickers on the device are meant to make the drone less attractive to animals in the sky and more visible to the pilot on the ground. In our interview, Tara tells me about a—in this case commercial—flight session in an abandoned warehouse that was "infested by giant hawks":

> Big birds, it wasn't like little pigeons, it was hawks. And, the crazy thing is, if I run into a hawk or a hawk runs into me, what am I going to do? And, really there is only so much you can do in that situation. If your drone gets hit while it flies, you'll try and save it, but the idea is to avoid that situation. So, when I see a hawk coming straight toward [the drone], am I going to go down or up? You have about 0.2 seconds to think about that. [...] I think they pose more of a hazard than manned airplanes just because where I fly, I don't fly near airports, so, to me birds and obstacles are my two biggest issues. Obstacles are easy because I can just fly around. Birds are not because you don't know what they are gonna do.

Tara is referring to both potential geographic and mobile hazards, emphasizing the additional challenges birds pose as unpredictable mobile agencies in the sky. Here, human (user) and nonhuman agents (drone, birds) can get entangled in complex mobile relationships. These examples allude to the variety of assembled human and nonhuman actors within consumer drone ecologies.

Finally, the impact of mobile traffic on the ground demands attention. The FAA (2020b) states, "Never fly over any person or moving vehicle." Following those guidelines, the remote pilots I observe make efforts to not fly too close or above busy streets, vehicles, and pedestrians. When Terrence flies his Mavic over a river to collect photos and videos of the sunset, a canoer comes out from under the bridge next to us. As Terrence's designated "co-pilot" for the evening, I notify him about an additional ten canoes coming our way. Surprised, Terrence navigates the drone further away. He admits, "This is why I prefer flying with others." A drone user needs to pay attention to so many factors that a second pair of eyes can help keep track of the many moving pieces in this aerial play.

Social Factors

The presence of a "co-pilot" can also help negotiate the multiple social relations in which drone users may get caught up. The photographers and videographers I accompany are careful not to disturb other people. While the majority of interviewees share positive encounters with bystanders, who are mainly curious about the hobby and technology, several users also mention being met with skepticism and distrust as to their intentions. More generally, "Peeping Tom"-privacy concerns are brought up in the discourse surrounding the flying camera. Another complaint relates to consumer drones' noise as a nuisance in public space. Such perceptions can shape hobbyists' practices regarding flight time, direction, height, distance, speed, and how the camera is used around bystanders. Ahmed tells me how "people can get really pissed" when they detect hobby drones nearby. He, consequently, tries to stay out of the way and "keep a low profile" with his flight maneuvers as much as he can. Georgine, a drone hobbyists in her sixties, tells me about the time she was approached by someone who thought she was spying on him:

> I had one guy in Hawai'i come up and – if I was a guy, he would have kicked my butt. He's like, "Do you have a license to fly?" He thought I was spying on him when the camera was clearly looking over the ocean at the sunset. I didn't fly over any people. I flew it over the sand to the ocean and was taking sunset shots. He thought I was filming his family, and he came running around the corner and sees me in my floppy hat. He still yelled at me, but, if I was a guy, he would have punched me. [...] He was that mad, yes. [...] That's the only incident I've had.

To prevent such potentially dangerous encounters and assure bystanders of her trustworthiness, Kristen, a FAA-certified drone pilot and hobbyists in her sixties, takes special precautions:

> What I do is I always wear a reflector jacket whether I'm flying, either way, I wear it, so it looks like I work for the town. One of the girls in Australia told me that she would write on the back "Certified FAA Pilot," so that people would just leave her alone, which is a really good idea. I think I may do that. I have a lanyard that I wear, and the lanyard has things in it that say – well, I have my FAA card. I have a copy of the photography field rights, and I have a copy of the law that pretty much wipes out any local regulations that are not officially regulated by the state.
>
> I'm always respectful, like that one time when the lifeguard came over. I said, "Hi." He goes like, "You can't fly here," and I said, "Well, with all due respect I can. The [regional] laws are not enforced. I have my flight laws here, which I'm happy to show you. I have permission from the flight tower, and they're aware of my location. They had given me permission to fly in their airspace. And, I'm not flying over people, I'm flying below 400 feet. So, I'm complying with all the regulations. Is there anything else that you need to ask me?" "No, we get a lot of bigwigs here [...]. I just wanted to make sure." I say, "Well, I can show you I'm not one of the idiots, thank you very much."

Bringing additional documentation, Kristen provides evidence of her internal and external credibility as an experienced drone user in case her activities are questioned and challenged by bystanders and local authorities. As such, Kristen, like the majority of my interviewees, also seeks to distance herself from "the idiots" that are unaware of consumer drone regulations and safe flying practices.

To avoid any encounters with bystanders in the first place, many remote pilots prefer secluded locations for launching, flying, and landing their drones. Terrence explains that he neither wants to bother, nor be approached and possibly distracted by others. When we look for a place to launch the drone for another sunset shoot, Terrence dismisses a spot because several children are playing nearby. "Kids tend to get curious and then ask questions when I need to focus on the drone," he tells me. This is another reason why he likes to go fly with others, he clarifies. Having a second pair of eyes on not just the drone but also the user and surroundings contributes to an overall safer practice. When one person is attending to the flying, for example, the other can respond to a bystander's questions and concerns.

The potential agency of social others, hence, influences the agency of the drone user. Laura, an interviewee in her sixties, mentions that she adjusts her flight times based on the presence of others:

> I am a real early-in-the-morning flyer because I don't like to bother people, and I like the light in the morning. I am sensitive to people wanting quiet etc., so you have to be a good neighbor. I always talk about the Golden Rule of droning: *Drone unto others as you would want others to drone unto you.*

The social agency of others is thus another influential component in aerial drone play, leading some hobbyists to develop a specific code of conduct, or in Laura's case a "Golden Rule" of droning.

The social factors that shape consumer drone ecologies are not only of interpersonal, unmediated nature, but extend into online environments. Such virtual social relations come into play when drone-generated imagery is shared or even live-streamed on online. The drastic increase in hobby drone use has resulted in the growth of multiple online archives thematically or geographically organizing millions of drone-generated photos and videos. Besides Instagram storing a multitude of still and moving images under hashtags such as #dronephotography, #dronevideo, or #dronefly and YouTube hosting a multitude of drone-specific channels, such as DronedOut, Epic Drone Videos, and Drone Compilations, several platforms exist exclusively for sharing amateur and professional drone imagery, such as Dronestagram, Travel By Drone, Skypixel, and Dronetrotter.

Next to this "delayed" sharing of aerial views, some drone users have the opportunity to live-stream their footage to social media platforms. The Chinese drone manufacturer and market leader DJI integrated the function to live-stream onto Facebook, YouTube, WeiBo, and QZone, for example, via its mobile app. Users of newer consumer drone models can thus broadcast aerial videos online while flying. With aerial drone play thus extending into virtual spaces in real time, I learn that my ethnographic inquiry needs to occur both offline and online.

One afternoon, Ahmed and I are unable to meet up. By coincidence, I later see that he is live with his drone video on Facebook and I am able to virtually observe his drone practice. The aerial visuals of suburban rooftops in the soft afternoon sunlight are combined with the sound of breathing and quiet mumbling: The video feed of the drone camera is linked to the audio of the smartphone attached to the remote control. The audio transmission is "on" by default and allows users to communicate directly with their live audience (provided users are aware of this default setting). At least one of my interviewees is making active use of this functionality, creating live drone diaries about what he is recording and why. Moreover, audience members can comment on the feed, which show on the user's screen and allow for reciprocity. This virtual interactive component happens simultaneously to the flying and recording and can thus influence recreational drone mobilities and mediation.

When Diego, a commercial and recreational drone user in his twenties, goes live with his drone on Facebook for the first time, several spectators comment in real time below the video ("It's cloudy tonight," "That's where I live"). During the footage, Diego can be heard saying to his companion, "I just went live on Facebook and everyone is lovin' it, bro." He is attentive to the responses of his Facebook audience while operating the drone. In our interview, Diego admits that initially he was not aware of the voice-over function in the Facebook live-stream and felt somewhat embarrassed about the random chat with his friend that accompanied his first aerial broadcast.

> When I got home, I was like "Oh my God, yeah that is live." The app gives you the option to turn it off. But to be honest with you, once I found out, I never turned it off. I just use it. I use it for my benefit. And whenever I go live, I just talk with the microphone and I explain what I am doing. And the return is unbelievable. People love it. And it is something that is so new that people are like "Oh my God." But you know I also have friends that are pilots, then it's all constructive comments. You're also gonna get the one that hates and is like "Oh no! You should not be doing this," etc.

After learning about the unintentional voice-over, Diego starts using the function "almost like a blog." In another live-stream, he directly addresses his virtual spectators by explaining, "And this is my little town where I live" along with highlighting certain landmarks his drone passes. More generally, Diego is impressed by the response he gets to his videos from his online community. The comments include admiration, advice, but also criticism from "the one that hates." Virtual bystanders and their real-time feedback may shape the hobbyist's aerial performance. Opportunities for influential interplay of virtual and physical components surface in the consideration of the (audio)-visual and communicative relations in the drone assemblage and its reaching into the digital sphere, a point I will return to in Chapter 4.

These findings belong to the more general category of virtual social relations which make hobby drone ecologies different to those of, for example, helicopter flying or model aviation. When pilots share their aerial images on personal websites, social media profiles, and drone-specific groups, their creations (real-time and delayed) generate feedback from their social networks. Consumer drones have made the sky accessible to hobbyists in new ways. The visuals obtained are insightful and often breathtaking, opening up everyday visual horizons. Sharing those images with the respective online communities is another way of making those vistas available to a wider audience. In the drone-specific groups I follow, members convey respect and admiration and give advice on how to improve flight maneuvers, camera settings, and image editing.

Similarly, problematic drone practices are identified and discussed, such as drones flying too close to architecture, sensitive infrastructure, and over people or traffic. In at least one case, a drone user was arrested after Internet users reported serious misconduct in the drone video of a plane landing in close proximity (McKirdy & Wang, 2017). When I run into a hobbyist in a park, he tells me that he prefers this location over another for drone image-taking because it is further away from a hospital. If the hospital, as sensitive infrastructure with a heliport, was visible in his videos, that "would trigger comments from the [online drone] community," he says. Here, the online drone community presents itself as a disciplinary force. Drone play means individualization of (aerial and visual) power. To maintain this power, drone communities have developed dynamics for holding individual members accountable. Elliott, a professional and recreational drone user in his thirties, explains this social dynamic thus:

> As drone pilots, we all consider ourselves to be part of this really great community. We all like to help one another. We all support one another, and we all try to police one another as well. So like if, for example, someone is flying a drone and they post that video, we know, somebody knows that was in illegal airspace or it was at night and the person did not have permission to be flying in that place at night. You'll be sure to see in the comments section below that video like "Hey man, I know this is illegal. I fly drones too. And, I know you don't have permission to be flying in there. No one can get permission to be flying here. So, you really should be more careful and please be more aware of your surroundings and your airspace." Like we do. You always see that under videos, like "This is illegal. You are ruining this for all of us. This is why we are getting regulation that we really don't need."

Users who share their drone images online not only accumulate social capital with the virtual appreciation of the extraordinary views from above but also attract scrutiny and criticism by their peers. The images shared online are subject to disciplinary comments that aim to keep drone usage within current legal parameters to avoid further restrictions of the hobby. Hence, the drone medium's reaching into online environments means taking into account another powerful dimension with influential dynamics; one that may be overlooked in the approach to consumer drones as closed-off network between aircraft, ground control station, and remote pilot.

Drone Geomedia and Cybermobilities

Two concepts from critical media studies and mobilities research help further describe the complex interplay of temporal, spatial, mobile, and social agencies in hybrid drone ecologies: media scholar Scott McQuire's (2016) "geomedia" and human geographers Peter Adey & Paul Bevan's (2006) "cybermobilities."

Based on their medial character and spatial relations, camera drones are what McQuire (2016) defines as "geomedia:" "Geomedia is a concept that crystallizes at the intersection of four related trajectories: convergence, ubiquity, location-awareness and real-time feedback" (McQuire 2016: 2). The exploration of the links between people, infrastructures, and data illuminates how consumer drones lie at the intersection of those four trajectories. First, convergence applies as different media merge in the drone assemblage (e.g. sky video and ground audio in the live-stream). Location-awareness is relevant regarding the close attention users need to pay to temporal, spatial, mobile, and social relations for safe practices in the physical space. The relevance of real-time feedback surfaces in the multiple signals and connections between drone system and the respective (physical and virtual) environments. McQuire (2016: 4–5) also speaks of "novel experiences of social simultaneity" and "new forms of recursive communication and coordination between the diverse actors even as events unfold." These kinds of feedback suitably describe both the interactive drone live-stream in online environments and the practice-specific precautions users take for offline encounters with bystanders. The concept of ubiquity, lastly, may become increasingly relevant with the proliferation of drones and the respective analog and digital infrastructures; some of which, such as satellites, are already ubiquitous. McQuire clarifies further,

It is this paradoxical conjunction of connection and disconnection — of placement and displacement, of the articulation or jointing of the local and global, of media and immediacy — that I am wanting to grasp with the concept of geomedia. (2016: 6)

As consumer drones span physical and virtual spaces, engender low-profile behaviors offline and high-profile activities online, they exemplify such paradoxical conjunctions, which the subsequent chapters further unpack.

The drone affordances of convergence, location-awareness, and real-time feedback may increase in relevance when multi-device cross-functionalities at the intersection of socially-networked communication and aerial navigation develop further. For instance, smartphone manufacturers are already thinking about how users may transmit real-time drone footage via direct video calls (Udin, 2019). Recognizing consumer drones as geomedia acknowledges the larger assemblage of spatial, temporal, technological, social, and cultural elements left underrecognized in simplified frameworks of a triangular relationship between remote pilot, controller, and small aircraft. The "unmanned aircraft system" is the technical basis for a variety of socio-spatial practices and techno-cultural potentials which the drone as geomedium ultimately brings about.

Equally relevant for situating aerial drone play is the concept of "cyber-mobilities," which helps describe the "connected movement that inhabits and inscribes both virtual and physical space simultaneously" (Adey & Bevan, 2006: 57). As I elaborate further in the subsequent chapters, the hobby drone practice is defined by multiple mobilities and immobilities ranging from the agile flight of the drone and comparative stillness of the pilot, to movements of information in physical and virtual spheres. The term "cybermobilities" helps illuminate the multiplicity of physical-material and digital-intangible movements with different temporal, spatial, mobile, and social relations. Physical "low profiles" and virtual "high profiles" of users suggest that the connected movement that "inhabits and inscribes both virtual and physical space simultaneously" can be influenced by competing forces since remote pilots, physical bystanders, and virtual audiences may have distinct interests regarding such kinds of aerial play. Moreover, understanding consumer drones as geomedia enabling cybermobilities illuminates the "hybrid space" (de Souza e Silva & Sheller, 2014) they occupy and create. Consumer drones are like other locative media which operate in a "hybridity of digital information and physical spatiality" (de Souza e Silva & Sheller, 2014: 6). Hence, the exploration and regulation of consumer drones benefit from an equally "hybrid crossing of various disciplinary boundaries" (de Souza e Silva & Sheller, 2014: 6), such as this book's assemblage of media ecology, mobile communication, mobilities research, and science and technology studies.

Ultimately, aerial drone play is more comprehensively understood as an assemblage of human and nonhuman agencies, a medium-specific ecology affected by situated mobilities. Similar to the telephone functioning as the placeholder for a much larger ecology of devices and connections, drone media go beyond mere aerial instruments. Following the media ecological lens, no medium stands alone, but is connected to and creates cultural, economic, political, and educational structures. The drone mobile medium functions within existing and creates new environments. The discussed examples highlight such ecological relationships and, moreover, allude to drone-specific "media life-forms." According to media scholar William Merrin (2014: 47),

> Each system will include particular media life-forms, with the dominant media creating specific epistemological environments: extending our senses in particular ways that bring the world to us in different forms, impacting upon and directing our experience and knowledge. But media forms can also be analyzed as their own separate systems; as systems constituted by the physical elements they comprise and their internal layers.

While the FAA's aviation-centric approach addresses the physical elements of the unmanned drone system, the assemblage and ecology approaches point to such "epistemological environments" impacting the way drone users perceive the respective place and time by extending their senses—and thus expanding their horizons—in specific ways. While this chapter pointed to some of those epistemological environments and potential agents within them, the book's subsequent chapters expand on such notions of "media-life forms" shaping experience and knowledge at the intersection of aviation and communication.

Conclusion

The aviation-centric approach of the FAA toward consumer drones as unmanned aircraft systems rightly points to the important links among pilot, control station on the ground, and flying object in the air. We benefit from expanding this framework with attention to the wider net of relations in which the drone system is emplaced. This general overview of different temporal, spatial, mobile, and social dimensions brings attention to some of the manifold agencies within consumer drone ecologies, while only scratching the surface of the dynamics between them and their impact on drone users' performances. Users' visibility and positionality in offline and online contexts are particularly noteworthy: Next to the suggested "low profile" that users seek in the physical space of the recreational drone practice, many hobbyists appear to manage a "high profile" in the virtual sphere with respect to the real-time or delayed sharing of their images. A user's desire for the hobby's visibility can thus significantly differ in offline and online environments. This move could also be viewed as a risk-and-return-process toward higher social capital with likes, shares, comments, and follows in the larger context of contemporary digital culture. Nevertheless, both the interpersonal and mediated social relations can function as a modifying, disciplinary force for recreational drone use due to simultaneous or subsequent (positive and negative) feedback.

In sum, a more holistic understanding of the "unmanned aircraft system" within such aerial play includes the critical consideration of the heterogeneous relations that configure aviation with visual and digital culture. To the ethnographic eye, the hobby drone practice presents itself as a mobile assemblage of physical and virtual movements as well as human and nonhuman agencies. Consumer drones can thus be approached as "geomedia" that converge with other media formats, are location-aware, and include real-time feedback functionalities. Moreover, consumer drone ecologies furnish "cybermobilities" with different performative qualities in offline and online environments. These two theoretical frameworks help illuminate the processes of mediation and movement that aerial drone play opens up in hybrid space.

This overview of the temporal, spatial, and mobile, and social factors in consumer drone flying and image-taking shed light onto the multiple human and nonhuman agencies that help or hinder drone mobilities in situ. Temporal conditions along with the physical form and material design of sites and spaces matter as much to personal drone ecologies as the normative and social relations that take effect physically and virtually. The subsequent chapters on communicating, moving, seeing, and dancing with drones delve more deeply into the questions of how personal drone uses are shaped and given meaning. They build on this broad survey of "the physical, social, technical and cultural conditions for the staging of contemporary mobilities" (O. B. Jensen, 2013: 16) such as aerial drone play. Consumer drone uses emerge out of and engender complex ecologies of human and nonhuman agencies in situ and beyond.

References

Adey, P., & Bevan, P. (2006). Between the physical and the virtual: Connected mobilities? In J. Urry & M. Sheller (Eds.), *Mobile technologies of the city* (pp. 44–60). Routledge.

AUVSI, AMA, & FAA. (2020). Recreational users. Retrieved June 11, 2020, from Know Before You Fly website: http://knowbeforeyoufly.org/recreatio nal/.

Bartsch, R., Coyne, J., & Gray, K. (2016). *Drones in society: Exploring the strange new world of unmanned aircraft*. Routledge.

de Souza e Silva, A., & Sheller, M. (Eds.). (2014). *Mobility and locative media: Mobile communication in hybrid spaces*. Routledge.

FAA. (2019a, February 7). Restricted or special use airspace. Retrieved July 2, 2020, from Federal Aviation Administration website: https://www.faa.gov/ uas/recreational_fliers/where_can_i_fly/airspace_restrictions/tfr/.

FAA. (2019b, May 17). Exception for limited recreational operations of unmanned aircraft. Retrieved June 4, 2020, from Federal Register website: https://www.federalregister.gov/documents/2019/05/17/2019-10169/except ion-for-limited-recreational-operations-of-unmanned-aircraft.

FAA. (2020a). *FAA aerospace forecast fiscal years 2020-2040*. Retrieved June 4, 2020, from Federal Aviation Administration website: https://www.faa.gov/data_research/aviation/aerospace_forecasts/media/FY2020-40_FAA_Aerospace_Forecast.pdf.

FAA. (2020b, February 18). Recreational flyers & modeler community-based organizations. Retrieved June 2, 2020, from Federal Aviation Administration website: https://www.faa.gov/uas/recreational_fliers/.

Fish, A. (2020). Drones. In P. Vannini (Ed.), *The Routledge international handbook of ethnographic film and video* (pp. 247–255). Routledge.

Graham, A., Kutzli, H., Kulig, T. C., & Cullen, F. T. (2021). Invasion of the drones: A new frontier for victimization. *Deviant Behavior, 42*, 386–403.

Jackman, A. (2019). Consumer drone evolutions: Trends, spaces, temporalities, threats. *Defense & Security Analysis, 35,* 362–383.

Jensen, O. B. (2013). *Staging mobilities*. Routledge.

Jensen, O. B. (2016a). Drone city: Power, design and aerial mobility in the age of "smart cities". *Geographica Helvetica, 71,* 67–75.

Jensen, O. B. (2016b). Of 'other' materialities: Why (mobilities) design is central to the future of mobilities research. *Mobilities, 11,* 587–597.

Latour, B. (2005). *Reassembling the social: An introduction to actor-network-theory*. Oxford University Press.

McKirdy, E., & Wang, S. (2017, January 17). Drone operator detained for flying near plane in China. Retrieved May 14, 2017, from CNN website: http://www.cnn.com/2017/01/17/asia/china-drone-passenger-plane-near-miss/index.html.

McLuhan, M. (1964). *Understanding media: The extensions of man* (2nd ed.). Signet.

McQuire, S. (2016). *Geomedia: Networked cities and the future of public space*. Polity.

Merrin, W. (2014). *Media studies 2.0*. Routledge.

Postman, N. (1970). The reformed English curriculum. In A. C. Eurich (Ed.), *High school 1980: The shape of the future in American secondary education* (pp. 160–168). Pitman.

Postman, N. (1998, March). *Five things we need to know about technological change*. Talk delivered in Denver, Colorado. Retrieved from http://web.cs.ucdavis.edu/~rogaway/classes/188/materials/postman.pdf.

Strate, L. (2016). Media ecology. In K. B. Jensen & R. T. Craig (Eds.), *The international encyclopaedia of communication theory and philosophy: Vol. I* (pp. 1159–1167). Wiley-Blackwell.

Strate, L. (2017). *Media ecology: An approach to understanding the human condition.* Peter Lang.

Udin, E. (2019, August 21). Huawei EMUI 10 comes with drone video call feature. Retrieved June 9, 2020, from Gizchina website: https://www.giz china.com/2019/08/21/huawei-emui-10-comes-with-drone-video-call-fea ture/.

4

Communicating on the Fly

Introduction

I am super fascinated by the technology that I felt had this much potential impact on my life and society similar to when the first iPhone came out. It was like "Oh, this changes everything." I feel the same way about drones. This has the potential to change a lot of the things that we do every day. (Mike, drone user in his thirties)

While the smartphone continues to reign supreme as a "personal, interactive, Internet-enabled and user-controlled portable platform" (Wei, 2013: 52), consumer drones as an increasingly popular and similarly personal, interactive, Internet-enabled, and user-controlled portable platform raise new questions about how we think of and with the concept of communication on the move. In this chapter, I discuss how consumer drones not only take visualization practices to the skies in novel ways, but also offer *communication on the fly*. This term alludes to both the literal sense of communication during flight and, more generally, to

© The Author(s), under exclusive license to Springer Nature Singapore Pte Ltd. 2021
J. M. Hildebrand, *Aerial Play*, Geographies of Media, https://doi.org/10.1007/978-981-16-2195-6_4

the communicative processes that are *in motion* among people, technology, and space. Moreover, my use of this expression includes the informal meaning of "on the fly" as doing multiple tasks simultaneously, potentially in a hurry, when users engage with aerial navigation, visual production, and virtual communication at the same time across multiple layers of space.

Drawing on literature from mobile communication, media ecology, and mobilities research, this chapter illuminates how the aerial technology conceptually aligns with but also goes beyond more traditional mobile media such as smartphones. Instead of showing how mobile media such as smartphones are drone-like in contemporary contexts of always-on monitoring, sensor-based data capture, and mediated locational tracking (Andrejevic, 2015), I discuss the extent to which consumer drones are mobile media-like in creative hobby practices.

This approach has multiple benefits: First, as argued in Chapter 3, understanding consumer drones as mobile media helps us broaden the official conceptualization of drones as "unmanned aircraft systems" (FAA, 2019). This means recognizing the impact of the communicative affordances of consumer drones as aerial visualization tool, social media interface, and augmented reality platform, which are key factors in the popularity of aerial drone play. A better understanding of how hobbyists use the flying device for technical mastery, creative expression, and spatial exploration can positively shape regulatory decision-making and ambiguous public perceptions of the practice. Second, situating the aerial camera and its adoption by hobby users in mobile communication research also expands the scholarly literature discussing personal drone uses in everyday spaces (Bender, 2018; Jablonowski, 2015, 2017; Klauser & Pedrozo, 2015; Rothstein 2015).

Finally—and most relevant for this chapter—categorizing drones as mobile media allows us to advance theoretical and practical frameworks in mobile communication research to account for such and other emerging mobile interfaces. This widening of the field beyond mobile phones is imperative in light of the growing mobile autonomy or "motility" of communication platforms such as drones. Equipped with sophisticated capacities for remote operation, independent flight maneuvers and automatically sensing and avoiding obstacles among other functions, consumer drones epitomize early stages of mobile autonomy for communication technologies. Consumer drones complicate our ongoing conceptual work around what mobile, motile, and portable mean for communication on the move. So, what can mobile communication studies learn from the drone?

In the following, I discuss interview data and ethnographic findings to highlight how personal drones align with mobile and "locative media" (Frith, 2015), and how hobby drone practices parallel communication on the move. Foundational to this discussion is the understanding that mobile media provide spatial knowledge and experience (Özkul, 2014), carve out "social spaces out of physical spaces" (Jensen, 2013: 26), manage public space as mobile interfaces (Katz, 2007; Sheller, 2014; de Souza e Silva & Frith, 2012), disrupt shared spaces (Campbell, 2013), as well as produce place via "performative cartography" (Verhoeff, 2012) and "emplaced visuality" (Hjorth & Pink, 2014). Drones embody such logics as mobile geomedia (McQuire 2016) and complicate them in their spatial extension into the air. As I will show, aerial drone play opens up physical, networked, and social spaces in processes I term communication on the fly. Ultimately, Sheller's (2014) "mobile mediality" framework helps explore how consumer drone ecologies enhance our perception of hybrid geographies and our entanglement within them. As avenues for future research specifically into communication on the fly, I conclude with key questions about the powers and potentials of camera drones as and beyond mobile media.

Theory: Mobile Media and Space

Before demonstrating how and why personal drones both align with but also expand contemporary notions of mobile media, I briefly return to the theoretical lenses that shape my explorations of everyday drone adoptions. Combining critical frameworks from mobile communication, mobilities, and media ecology is worthwhile in the example of camera drones, which configure communication, movement, and space in unique ways. In its attention to the ecological nature of technology, media ecology shares relevant common ground with mobilities research, which recognizes the close relations between communication and mobility and points to the increasing hybridization of physical and informational mobility systems across space.

This development is again of crucial interest in mobile communication studies, which "focus on changes in social and spatial practices of everyday life" (Goggin & Hjorth, 2009; Ling & Campbell, 2009) and "uses of the technology that alter how people relate to space in ways that connect to both people and places while on the go" (Campbell, 2013: 11). Smartphones, in particular, serve as a paradigmatic example of the shifts in our management of and relation to communication, mobility, and space. However, "they exist alongside an array of other mobile technologies, from wearables to smart watches, from tablets to RDIF cards" (Farman, 2016: xi) that inform such developments in mobile communication. Bridging media ecology, mobilities research, and mobile communication, my use of the term "mobile media" broadly includes any human-made artifacts, whether analog or digital, that shape the way we relate to our physical spaces and socio-cultural environments on the move. This angle also includes digital media scholar Jason Farman's definition of mobile media as "interfaces" which help us "connect with each other, with objects, and with data across material and digital landscapes" and thus transform "the ways we conceive of embodied space" (2011: 15). Drones are such mobile interfaces to public spaces and each other across hybrid space. Consequently, they also shape the ways we perceive those different kinds of environments.

What about the host of aerial media such as camera-equipped balloons, helicopters, airplanes, and RC model aircraft that precede consumer drones? While a case can be made for all of those to serve as mobile media, consumer drones differ in the extent that they afford non-specialist users recreational and artistic flying, image-taking, online live-streaming, and socially-networked communication. The genealogy of the aerial media eco-system can hence itself be understood as "on the move" toward increased physical and virtual access into vertical spaces by a growing number of user groups (from established institutions and corporations to communities and individuals) on the ground.

Those socio-spatial potentials and uses of camera drones are starting to receive increasing scholarly attention regarding their methodological purchase (Birtchnell & Gibson, 2015; Fish, 2020; Fish & Garrett, 2016), their socio-political implications (Birtchnell & Gibson, 2015; Hildebrand, 2020; Kaplan & Miller, 2019; Klauser & Pedrozo, 2015), their visual affordances (Jablonowski, 2017), their unruly motility (McCosker, 2015), their threat potential (Graham et al., 2021; Jackman, 2019), and evolving cooperative practices (Bender, 2018). Similar to other mobile communication technologies and applications, drones generate novel social and spatial practices in public and private spaces, blurring those boundaries further. For example, the way that the Pokémon Go app introduced new socio-spatial practices in private and public augmented spaces, so do camera drones afford new ways of engaging with the backyard, neighborhood, and region, raising concerns about privacy and safety. In my theorization of communication on the fly, I discuss how drones show characteristics of locative mobile media, albeit pushing—into three-dimensional space—the conceptual boundaries regarding drone users' collection and production of locational information in everyday life.

Drone Spatialities: Physical, Networked, Social

If camera drones are mobile media, then what exactly do they mediate, communicate, and mobilize in recreational contexts? In their unique combination of visual and mobile affordances, consumer drones provide distinct ways of relating to space. The aerial camera enhances ways of accessing, collecting, and carving out physical-material spaces. Moreover, as a networked interface, consumer drones allow for accessing, collecting, and creating digital-intangible spaces. In the sharing of visual space online and offline (sometimes simultaneously), the cyber-mobile geomedium also opens up social spaces. Nevertheless, similar to other mobile media, consumer drones can equally disrupt those physical, digital, and social spaces as I will discuss.

The flying camera serves as a mobile locative medium but also stretches the definition of the concept. Parallels exist in how drones rely "on spatial dispersion in order to pin sensor data to time-space location" (Andrejevic, 2015: 196). Visual and telemetric place-specific information guides remote pilots as they navigate through horizontal and vertical space. Similar to how users of locative media "are able to log and share their locations with others as they move about from place to place" (Campbell, 2013: 11), drone users can live-stream their aerial explorations to social media platforms and provide real-time commentary on the ground. While it is not the physical location and movements of the user on the ground that are visually shared with a social network, it is the drone's perspective from the air and its remote mobilities that are available to online audiences.

In uniquely distributing user and technology across space, the drone presents a different kind of *location-aware* geomedium. In drone practices, users become aware of geographical spaces beyond their typical visual and physical reach. The flying camera, moreover, makes users aware of their own locational positioning in the top-down aerial gaze directed back at them. When linked to social media, the drone's communicative potentials can also make aware any audiences that may witness the distributed and differential positions of the highly mobile drone and comparatively immobile pilot on the ground. Here, the drone complicates notions of "mobile" as a remotely controlled device that is portable, mobile, and motile, meaning capable of moving independently from a user's corporeal motions (McCosker, 2015). Beyond the users' manual remote-control operations, their and the drone's physical mobility are separate. Nonetheless, drone ecologies can visually and virtually mobilize the user by extending into physical-material and digital-intangible spaces. As a special kind of mobile and locative medium then, drones provide dynamic locational information and a medium-specific sense of place.

Similarly, personal drones are aerial interfaces to public spaces. Communication scholars Adriana de Souza e Silva & Jordan Frith describe mobile interfaces to public spaces as technologies that "enable people to filter, control, and manage their relationships with the spaces and people around them" (2012: 6). As I will show in the following, drones allow users to inscribe space with meaning creating personalized aerial spaces and senses of place. As a mobile and locative medium, the technology not only helps filter, control, and manage relationships with spaces and people, but also allows users to enhance and remake existing relationships while accessing, creating, and sharing novel spatial ways of relating *on the fly*.

Mediating Physical Space

Contemporary consumer drone models excel in the configuration of aerial navigation and image-taking. The flying camera enables users to access, collect, and carve out spaces in ways that exceed those of other visual mobile media by extending into the sky. Drone users tap into those potentials using the visual reach into the air for various purposes. Mike, a drone users in his thirties, for example, employed his device to increase his familiarity with a holiday location and drew from the visual, aerial, and mobile resources when planning his morning running route:

> I would fly up and then BOOM. I could see exactly how big the island is, I could see where we were on the island in relationship to all this other stuff. And then the next morning, I want to go on a hike, and I'm sitting there with the drone in the sky, and I'm like "ok, there's the hiking path, it goes over to this archipelago, and here I can go down this spot here and hook up with this trail over here. Ok, let me bring this around a little bit to see the other side of the mountain. Ok good, yeah, that trail connects along the backside, I can go down over here and loop back around." So, I mapped out my whole running path the next morning just because I sent my drone up and I was kind of like circling around the island a little bit.

The aerial vantage point gave Mike an overview of the location. Here, the camera drone joins other mobile and locative media "as a means of exercising control over one's local environment" (Katz, 2007: 392). Since Mike used the drone to gather information for the conquest of space, the practice alludes to a growing culture of surveillance in terms of data collection and processing. However, instead of a hawkish intelligence-gathering exercise contributing to the increasing militarization of society, Mike's drone use is closer to a visual and mobile extension and enhancement that centers on the self and its engagement with space as opposed to exercising control over others. Figure 4.1 exemplifies this real-time map-reading approach in a drone image taken on the east coast of Florida.

In addition, Mike's narrative illustrates the kind of multidirectional "performative cartography" that the temporal collapse of image production and image reception affords (Verhoeff, 2012; see also Bender, 2018). The smartphone often serves as the drone system's remote control and app interface, making evident the similarities to navigational practices with smartphones more generally. When Mike elaborates on his mapping approach, he compares this visual and spatial navigation by drone as reminiscent of using Google Maps with his smartphone.

> You can see from 500 feet up. It's like the first time you used Google Maps on your phone, and you're like "oh I know how to navigate Google Maps." I remember the first time I used Google Maps. You don't need

Fig. 4.1 Real-time map-reading of a Florida beach (Image taken with DJI Mavic Pro Platinum drone "Jay")

to tell me to turn left on this street and turn right here. I just have this phone that is guiding me along the way. It was that revelatory type of totally transformative experience where I... the closest thing I can say is that I kind of have a superpower. It was like when I first had my smartphone and everyone else had their flip phones and yeah, I'm like "I have smartphone superpowers. So, I got this." You really do feel like "I'm a little more capable than the average person because I have this thing." Same thing with the drone. I can learn things, I can see things, I can do more recon. I can get to places.

As a technological superpower, the aerial self-extension enhances Mike's sense of place and potential for inscribing personal meaning into the location. Despite the militaristic lingo ("recon"), Mike's sense of empowerment is akin to "the self-referential feeling of power" that Jablonowski's hobby drone research discusses; a sensation not to be confused with the "unearthly powers" of military drones (Jablonowski, 2015: 12). Comparing his drone superpowers with "smartphone superpowers," Mike points to the ways the aerial medium allows him to connect with spaces, people, and information, making him feel "a little more capable." This virtual extension of his capabilities lies closer to a sense of emancipation from bodily constraints than militaristic fetish. In the same spirit, Diego, a drone user in his twenties, tells me about an experience of spatial self-empowerment when he heard fireworks from his backyard:

So, I was sitting in my backyard, talking to my roommate, and all of the sudden I hear fireworks. And I'm like "Oh, that's cool, there is fireworks. I'd love to see them, but by the time I get there..." and then I went "wait a second." I took out the drone and put it maybe three, four floors above my house. And there you go. That was the right spot to see the fireworks. And I was like "wow this is pretty cool, I am in my backyard, I have the drone up, and I am seeing the fireworks from my backyard with my screen.".

The drone view allowed Diego to remotely yet quickly witness the fireworks from his backyard. Similar to Mike who can remotely "learn things" and virtually "see things" with his drone, Diego was able to get virtual access to the fireworks via the drone's combination of aerial mobility and image streaming.

By providing real-time visual impressions and affording users the sensation to "get to places" on the spot, consumer drone affordances exceed those of Google Maps and other location-based tools and services in these specific cases. Annie, a hobbyist in her sixties, explains: "When you're looking on the [drone] app, you can actually see where it's flying and it's like you're actually traveling to that place and I can take pictures." Instead of the drone bringing the location to her, she understands the aerial practice as *taking her to that place*. Furthermore, Annie concludes that the spatial drone practice "makes me more observant of my world." Just like other modes of mobile communication "have distinctive implications for how users relate to space" (Campbell, 2013: 10), the visual and mobile biases of camera drones affect how users observe, understand, and manage their "world." Mike even speaks of seeing the world differently now that he flies drones:

> This is like a whole other different type of experience that opens itself up to me. I go to different places; I look at things differently. I'm into different things because I have a tool that allows me to capture images in this way.

This quote exemplifies the impact of drone ecologies as media environments that affect human perception, understanding, feelings, and values. For Annie, Mike, many others, and myself, the physical world becomes visible and accessible in novel ways, thus shaping views and practices. This kind of "performative cartography" then does not initially centralize media scholar Nanna Verhoeff's "three principles of locative media practices," which encompass "tagging, plotting and stitching" (2012: 133). With Mike, Diego, and Annie reaching out into three-dimensional space in real time, aerial drone play begins with *spanning, traversing*, and *observing*. The drone allows users to visually span, aerially traverse, and remotely observe familiar and unfamiliar territory. To what extent the renewed attention—whether accurate or imaginative—to everyday spaces, as suggested by Annie and Mike, is an enrichment to ways of thinking, observing, and being in the world is a question I will return to.

From my own critical aerial play with a DJI Mavic Pro Platinum consumer drone, I can confirm this superpower quality when accessing vertical space. I also felt my aerial sensibilities and subsequent location-awareness enhanced. Like Mike, I have learned to understand unfamiliar places and my own mobilities within them better once the drone extended my eyes into the sky. Like Diego, I remotely witnessed 4th of July fireworks a few hundred feet away from my doorsteps. As my neighbors watched the spectacle live on television, I felt a different sense of "liveness," visual control over, and active engagement with the event space from afar. My distant drone visuals were not nearly as compelling as the ones on television, but there was again a sense of visual emancipation. Finally, like Annie, my aerial play has led me to adopt a drone perspective onto the locations I pass through on a daily basis. Attuned to my geographic environment, I more readily notice places that would make for interesting aerial shots and maneuvers and speculate what other perspectives would open up to me by drone. In addition, I have become attentive to local airspace restrictions, weather and wind conditions, and aerial traffic when visiting unfamiliar or revisiting familiar places (even without the drone). My new mental orientation is induced by both the drone's mediation of physical-material but also digital-intangible spaces, as I will explain now.

Mediating Networked Space

Along with providing almost instantaneous visual access to aerial spaces, consumer drones open up hybrid spaces. In the crossover of vertical mobility, image-production, and sensor capacities, consumer drones supply both visual and digital information about the surrounding geographies and infrastructures relevant for safe and reliable drone use. These data are often displayed on a smartphone screen as the interface between drone, remote control, and drone app. Depending on the hardware and software, the aerial imagery on the screen is overlaid with a range of telemetry: height and distance of the aircraft, the number of connected satellites, the status of the aircraft battery, a two-dimensional map of the area along with an indication of where the drone is facing and the launching coordinates as "home" location, the settings of the drone camera, the settings of any automated flight features, along with the occasional warnings about wind speeds, signal interference, local airspace restrictions, and so on (Fig. 4.2). This wealth of drone-related micro- and macro-data may be accompanied by smartphone-specific information about new text messages, incoming phone calls, or online push notifications if the smartphone is not fittingly set to "airplane" mode.

The interface's combination of aerial-visual and informational-digital space speaks to a range of concepts related to mobile communication: "hybrid space" (de Lange, 2009), "networked place" (Varnelis & Friedberg, 2006), "augmented space" (de Lange, 2009: 59), and "remediated space" (Bolter & Grusin, 1999). Drone-mediated space is hybrid space, a framework that refers to the diminishing "distinction between the physical and the digital through the mix of social practices that occur

Fig. 4.2   DJI Mavic Pro app interface

simultaneously in digital and in physical spaces" (de Souza e Silva, 2006: 265). The drone interface illuminates visual, locational, and digital information that may otherwise be invisible: satellite connections, wind conditions, local regulations, interfering signals, and so on. As such, aerial drone play also provides access to "networked place," meaning

> the everyday superimposition of real and virtual spaces, the development of a mobile sense of place, the emergence of popular virtual worlds, the rise of the network as a socio-spatial model, and the growing use of mapping and tracking technologies. (Varnelis & Friedberg, 2006: para. 2)

In this superimposition of real and virtual formations along with the near-instantaneous mapping and tracking functions, the aerial geomedium enhances "mobile senses of place." As such, consumer drones are "sensor media" in more than one way: They illuminate otherwise invisible networked sensor activities and engender personal mobile sensibilities toward the respective location. In the way the app layers the digital information on top of the aerial visuals, the drone interface also produces "augmented spaces" understood as physical environments "layered with informational augmentation of spaces and infrastructures" (Sheller, 2014: 278). Ultimately, the combination of the aerial livestream, digital sensor data, and virtual connections speaks to media scholars Jay David Bolter & Richard Grusin's (1999) framework of "remediated space": The drone combines the logics of transparency and multiplicity in this overlay of space and data.

In the simultaneous collection, arrangement, and mediation of networked information, aerial visuality, and multidirectional mobilities, camera drones afford *communication on the fly*. The busy communicative processes occur in different forms between space and drone system, drone system and user, as well as user and space. Here, the user's space can mean both offline and online environments and the respective infrastructures. Moreover, drone users not only have access to those hybrid, networked, and remediated spaces, *they also produce them*. Hobbyists create a visual record of their flight sessions when taking aerial photos and videos. In addition, drone apps like DJI's create an animated record of the flight path, drone maneuvers, camera operations, and warning messages (Fig. 4.3). This drone flight animation traces the mobile and visual practices on a two-dimensional map. The aerial play is thus carved onto digital space, allowing users to revisit where and how the drone traveled along with where images were taken in relation to their own geographical position and other conditions. In this sense, the flight records are geospatial diaries.

In addition, those automated flight records are reminiscent of creative practices that engender "emplaced visuality." "That is, a visuality that is part of place and makes place, and in this case traverses and connects the material-physical with the digital-intangible" (Hjorth & Pink, 2014: 46). The automatic post-hoc flight animation speaks to this concept of temporal, spatial, emotional, and geographic emplacement, which situates "movement at the center of our understanding of contemporary media practice" (Hjorth & Pink, 2014: 44; see also Hjorth, 2016). As mobile media, camera drones both substantiate and complicate this

Fig. 4.3 Animated DJI flight record

theory of movement. The technology is emplacing but also displacing the user in its operation at varying distances. As a result, the flying camera distributes mobile and communicative features of locative media, such as mobile phone photography and videography along with geo-tagging, across different temporalities, spatialities, and subjectivities.

Mediating Social Space

Beyond mediating physical and networked spaces, consumer drones also shape social spaces in distinct ways. The flying camera can create social environments in the physically co-present activities of drone flying and image-taking (embraced and encouraged by drone communities) in the subsequent sharing of aerial imagery offline and online and the virtually co-present practices of live-streaming onto social media platforms. However, consumer drones equal other mobile devices that "introduced new seams to the social fabric in the forms of disturbances, disruptions, and distractions for users and co-present others in shared space" (Campbell, 2013: 10–11). As can be taken from the polarizing discourse surrounding consumer drones as "unruly aerial objects" (McCosker, 2015: 3), their presence disrupts social spaces because they are noisy, look eerie, and raise issues about physical safety and locational privacy.

The broadcasting of drone-generated videos onto social media platforms such as Facebook or YouTube make for an interesting case of mobile communication. When users live-stream their visuals onto a selected platform, they can see the number of people watching along with any comments they may leave. Moreover, the videos can be juxtaposed with the audio the smartphone microphone picks up on the ground. Hence, users have the opportunity to not only see who is watching the live feed and what feedback they receive in the comments section, but they can also narrate the images and verbally respond to the social media comments. As mentioned in Chapter 3, Diego has developed a habit of narrating his flight sessions to his virtual audiences:

Now when I do my live-stream video [...], pretty much I just talk about what I am doing. So the last time I did live-streaming was on a sunrise.

So, I was like "Good morning guys, let's see what's going on over here by the water" etc. Almost like a blog you know? [...] And whenever I go live, I just talk with the microphone and I explain what I am doing. And the return is unbelievable. People love it. And it is something that is so new that people are like "Oh my God." But you know, I also have friends that are pilots, then it's all constructive comments. You're not gonna get the one that hates and is like "Oh no! You shouldn't be doing this" etc.

Occasionally, the audio from the ground will include Diego responding to his audience, emphasizing the dialogic affordances of this mobile medium. Moreover, this example speaks to "an essential idea behind locative social media" which is about enabling users to share their whereabouts with a network and thus "communicating something about [their] identity and the fabric of [their] everyday life" (Farman, 2011: 14). Camera drones operate as such mobile interfaces, which have "the fundamental attributes necessary for social engagement across mobile networks" (Farman, 2011: 14). As remote aerial media, socially-networked drones allow for distinct embodied productions of sociality distributed across hybrid space.

Diego's comment also points to the disruptive character of drones in the convergence of flight, camera, and communication. While this user is alluding to critical reactions to drone flying on social media, interviewees also point to negative encounters they have face-to-face. Next to the stigmatization of drones as "Peeping Tom"-spying tool, drone opponents point to the noisy nuisance drones present in public. Interestingly, this quality is what interviewees point out when rebuking accusations of privacy violations. In his rebuttal of drones as spying technology, Elliott, a professional drone pilot in his thirties, elaborates on how detectable the flying camera is not only visually but also acoustically:

When it comes to the privacy concern [...] spying and "Peeping Tom," that argument is absolute nonsense. Have you heard a drone? You know what a drone sounds like? [...] You cannot be inconspicuous with a drone. It's loud, it's noisy. And it is obvious to look at. No one is using a drone to be a "Peeping Tom."

According to Elliott, consumer drones make for an unlikely amateur spying tool because they are acoustically and visually detectable as well as temporally limited by battery life. While he dismisses the argument that drones make for suitable spying devices, he does confirm their otherwise disruptive noise and optics. Alignments with military drones such as the Predator or Reaper, which can similarly announce their threatening presence by their buzzing sounds (S. Graham, 2016), surface. However, Elliott's response implies that everyday socio-spatial structures are subject to different cultural codes than the extremely uneven power hierarchies in remote warfare. While the affiliations of personal drones with warfare and surveillance are undeniable, the recreational adoption of camera drones is more nuanced than what might be seen as an outright militarization of culture and society. Nevertheless, cases of drones used for spying have been reported (see for example Bilton, 2016), falling in line with other pernicious practices with visual technologies such as binoculars, telescopes, selfie sticks, and cameras more generally.

In light of the potential intrusiveness of the aerial gaze along with its noisy mobility, several users report adjusting their drone practices to not disturb others, as highlighted in Chapter 3. In my own auto-technographic engagement with the DJI Mavic, I can relate to this socio-spatial sensibility. Highly aware of how audible my practice is, I prefer locations that have only a few or no bystanders and inhabited buildings nearby. Moreover, I notice turning the drone camera away from people that have entered its visual frame when I don't have their explicit permission to record them.

Flying on a beach right after sunrise, I learned how disruptive the mere aerial presence of my drone might be. The waves drowned out the propellers' buzzing sound and my drone camera was facing toward the ocean. After I spent ten minutes spanning, traversing, and observing the wide-open space above the sea within the permitted parameters of the FAA, a police car parked behind me. The officer watched my activities from a distance without ever stepping outside of the car. After a few more minutes, Jay signaled that his battery was low, and I landed him. The police car left the lot. It remains unclear to me what triggered the police presence and what prevented a potential interaction. This incident made apparent, however, that the drone can augment not only my reach into aerial space but also my visibility on the ground. As I remotely explore drone-mediated spaces and create geospatial diaries (with often reduced awareness to my immediate surroundings), my own geographic emplacement is visually and acoustically enhanced to myself and others.

In the drone's mediation of physical, networked, and social spaces, Sheller's framework of "mobile mediality" as a "new form of flexible and mediated spatiality" applies (2014: 201). Referring to mobile art more generally, she notes that such creative practice

> involves phenomenological experiments with experiential happenings and performative interactional events that intensify and focus attention on the current spaces of mobile mediality in ways that potentially destabilize the everyday and deepen our perception of the conditions of the premediated real. (Sheller, 2014: 201)

In the interplay of aerial navigation, visual production, and digital communication, the drone medium furnishes such mobile mediality. Aerial drone play triggers experiential happenings and performative interactional events between user, technology, and space. As hobbyists confirm, the drone interface mediates and remediates experiences of their everyday horizontal and vertical environments. Hence, camera drone use parallels mobile art practices which, according to Sheller, extend "beyond relational aesthetics and beyond mobile gaming, effectively by re-spatializing and re-mediating our experience of embodied mobility and communication" (2014: 203). Personal drones are multi-mobile media that shape the way we relate to space, movement, ourselves, and each other.

Conclusion

The aerial camera presents an opportunity for expanding conceptions of mobile media along with how we can think of and with notions of communication on the move. In this chapter, I argued for the value of approaching consumer drones as mobile and locative media by exploring some of their unique spatial and social affordances. With attention to the multi-dimensional spaces drones operate in, I discussed how users access and manage geographic conditions; how they access and create digital formations; and how they shape and disrupt socio-spatial relations. The visual and informational data available via the drone interface brings attention to relevant hybrid, networked, augmented, and remediated spaces. Yet, personal drone ecologies also extend those concepts in the ambiguous arrangement of user and medium in the vertical and horizontal, the geographic and geometric, the remote and proximate. In addition, the aerial camera can create and disturb social environments. Drone-generated imagery can bring together physical and virtual bystanders alike. Nonetheless, drone presence is also disruptive. The potentially nosy camera and certainly noisy aircraft count as key factors for why the drone hobby faces criticism. Finally, aerial drone play is similar to other mobile art practices in how they involve mobile mediality and ultimately produce different attention to and awareness of personal emplacements.

Consequently, creative drone practices align with mobile communication practices in how they interface physical-material, digital-intangible, and socio-spatial dimensions. Drones are multi-mobile interfaces that afford performative cartography, emplaced visuality, and mobile mediality. However, camera drones also go beyond such communication on the move by extending human faculties and senses into the sky. As such, communication on the fly requires simultaneous attention to the vertical and horizontal, the immediate and hypermediate socio-spatial relations. On top of that, aerial drone play not only furnishes certain ways of making and sensing space but also making and sensing early degrees of mobile autonomy of communication technologies with respect to the increasing integration of intelligent flight modes (see Chapters 5 and 7). Consequently, understanding camera drones as mobile media along with the kinds of communication, movements, and environments they open up, allows for critically assessing such and other emerging, generative practices with mobile interfaces. Aerial media, such as consumer drones, and other socio-spatial technologies will continue to transform dimensions of visual culture, recreational mobility, and remote communication.

In this chapter, I have only begun to describe the mobile and medial character of personal drone use. In reference to her work on mobile mediality, Sheller (2014: 278) poses important questions that are equally relevant for the growing day-to-day uptake of consumer drones:

> What are the potentials of mobile mediality to afford new sites for creative interventions, public participation, and social interaction? On the other hand, what problems of privacy, surveillance, secrecy, and uneven accessibility are emerging out of the new patterns of mobile mediality?

Research into camera drones shares those questions over power, control, participation, interaction, privacy, surveillance, accessibility, and experience that occupy scholars in critical media studies, mobilities research, and mobile communication. This chapter presents an effort to open up the conversation on mobile media to socio-spatial technologies and practices beyond mobile media such as the smartphone. With this widening of the field, we can then address such pressing questions with critical attention to the full spectrum of mobile communication, *on the fly*. In the meantime, by approaching drones as mobile and locative media, we are a step closer to understanding the kinds of explorative, creative, and communicative practices underway in aerial drone play.

References

Andrejevic, M. (2015). Becoming drones: Smartphone probes and distributed sensing. In R. Wilken & G. Goggin (Eds.), *Locative media* (pp. 193–207). Routledge.

Bender, H. (2018). The new aerial age: Die wechselseitige Verfertigung gemeinsamer Raum- und Medienpraktiken am Beispiel von Drohnen-Communities. In N. Ghanbari, I. Otto, S. Schramm, & T. Thielmann (Eds.), *Kollaboration: Beiträge zur Medientheorie und Kulturgeschichte der Zusammenarbeit* (pp. 121–145). Wilhelm Fink.

Bilton, N. (2016, January 27). When your neighbor's drone pays an unwelcome visit. Retrieved October 17, 2018, from New York

Times website: http://www.nytimes.com/2016/01/28/style/neighbors-dro nes-invade-privacy.html.

Birtchnell, T., & Gibson, C. (2015). Less talk more drone: Social research with UAVs. *Journal of Geography in Higher Education, 39*, 182–189.

Bolter, J. D., & Grusin, R. A. (1999). *Remediation: Understanding new media.* MIT Press.

Campbell, S. W. (2013). Mobile media and communication: A new field, or just a new journal? *Mobile Media & Communication, 1*, 8–13.

de Lange, M. (2009). From always-on to always-there: Locative media as playful technologies. In A. de Souza e Silva & D. M. Sutko (Eds.), *Digital cityscapes: Merging digital and urban playspaces* (pp. 55–70). Peter Lang.

de Souza e Silva, A. (2006). From cyber to hybrid: Mobile technologies as interfaces of hybrid spaces. *Space and Culture, 9*, 261–278.

de Souza e Silva, A., & Frith, J. (2012). *Mobile interfaces in public spaces: Locational privacy, control, and urban sociability.* Routledge.

FAA. (2019, December 31). Proposed rule: Remote identification of unmanned aircraft systems. Retrieved June 4, 2020, from Regulations.gov website: https://beta.regulations.gov/document/FAA-2019-1100-0001.

Farman, J. (2011). *Mobile interface theory: Embodied space and locative media.* Routledge.

Farman, J. (Ed.). (2016). *Foundations of mobile media studies: Essential texts on the formation of a field.* Routledge.

Fish, A. (2020). Drones. In P. Vannini (Ed.), *The Routledge international handbook of ethnographic film and video* (pp. 247–255). Routledge.

Fish, A., & Garrett, B. L. (2016, December 18). Reframing drone methodologies. Retrieved September 1, 2018, from Centre for Mobilities Research website: https://www.lancaster.ac.uk/cemore/reframing-drone-met hodologies/.

Frith, J. (2015). *Smartphones as locative media.* Polity.

Goggin, G., & Hjorth, L. (Eds.). (2009). *Mobile technologies: From telecommu- nications to media.* Routledge.

Graham, A., Kutzli, H., Kulig, T. C., & Cullen, F. T. (2021). Invasion of the drones: A new frontier for victimization. *Deviant Behavior, 42*, 386–403.

Graham, S. (2016). *Vertical: The city from satellites to bunkers.* Verso.

Hildebrand, J. M. (2020). Drone-topia as method. *Mobilities, 15*, 25–38.

Hjorth, L. (2016). Mobile art: Rethinking intersections between art, user created content (UCC), and the quotidian. *Mobile Media & Communica- tion, 4*, 169–185.

Hjorth, L., & Pink, S. (2014). New visualities and the digital wayfarer: Reconceptualizing camera phone photography and locative media. *Mobile Media & Communication, 2*, 40–57.

Jablonowski, M. (2015). Drone it yourself! On the decentring of 'drone stories.' *Culture Machine, 16*. http://www.culturemachine.net/index.php/cm/article/view/589.

Jablonowski, M. (2017). Dronie citizenship? In A. Kuntsman (Ed.), *Selfie citizenship* (pp. 97–106). Palgrave Macmillan.

Jackman, A. (2019). Consumer drone evolutions: Trends, spaces, temporalities, threats. *Defense & Security Analysis, 35*, 362–383.

Jensen, K. B. (2013). What's mobile in mobile communication? *Mobile Media & Communication, 1*, 26–31.

Kaplan, C., & Miller, A. (2019). Drones as "atmospheric policing": From US border enforcement to the LAPD. *Public Culture, 31*, 419–445.

Katz, J. E. (2007). Mobile media and communication: Some important questions. *Communication Monographs, 74*, 389–394.

Klauser, F., & Pedrozo, S. (2015). Power and space in the drone age: A literature review and politico-geographical research agenda. *Geographica Helvetica, 70*, 285–293.

Ling, R., & Campbell, S. W. (Eds.). (2009). *The reconstruction of space and time: Mobile communication practices*. Transaction Publishers.

McCosker, A. (2015). Drone media: Unruly systems, radical empiricism and camera consciousness. *Culture Machine, 16*. https://www.culturemachine.net/index.php/cm/article/view/591.

McQuire, S. (2016). *Geomedia: Networked cities and the future of public space*. Polity.

Özkul, D. (2014). Mobile communication technologies and spatial perception: Mapping London. In R. Wilken & G. Goggin (Eds.), *Locative media* (pp. 39–51). Routledge.

Rothstein, A. (2015). *Drone*. Bloomsbury Academic.

Sheller, M. (2014). Mobile art: Out of your pocket. In G. Goggin & L. Hjorth (Eds.), *The Routledge companion to mobile media* (pp. 197–205). Routledge.

Varnelis, K., & Friedberg, A. (2006). Place: Networked place. In K. Varnelis (Ed.), *Networked publics*. Retrieved from http://networkedpublics.org/book/place.html.

Verhoeff, N. (2012). *Mobile screens: The visual regime of navigation.* Amsterdam University Press.

Wei, R. (2013). Mobile media: Coming of age with a big splash. *Mobile Media & Communication, 1,* 50–56.

5

Moving and Not Moving Up in the Air

Introduction

Picture the scene. We are in the grass slowly taking off from the ground. An open green field with several trees surround us. The sky is blue with puffy white clouds. We fly just above the grass tops. The movement is a little shaky. Now, we are rising up several feet off the ground passing between a sun chair and a small fountain. We pick up speed and fly into a curve toward a small lake ahead on the left. Our angle tilts toward the right, the lake is now to our right. Below we can see the shadow of… a large insect? It moves with us until we dip lower, flying just above the grass tops again. We tilt toward the left. Circling fast around a tree, we speed through another two trees. A set of white sun chairs appears in our path. A young man in an orange T-shirt sits on a bench behind them, leaning slightly forward. His head is turned away from us. In full speed, we crash into him.

We are a small quadcopter and the person in the orange T-shirt is operating it. In this 23-second video clip on YouTube, we experience the first-person point of view of freestyle drone flying—along with the remote pilot crashing into himself (doctorsnaketown, 2015). The clip is

© The Author(s), under exclusive license to Springer Nature
Singapore Pte Ltd. 2021
J. M. Hildebrand, *Aerial Play*, Geographies of Media,
https://doi.org/10.1007/978-981-16-2195-6_5

one of myriad drone-generated videos shared online. The example is also one of many featuring drone users crashing into themselves with their small aircrafts. Such cases raise several questions about aerial movement and its visual mediation by drone.

To further unpack what makes aerial drone play attractive and unique, this chapter focuses on the different kinds of mobilities and immobilities that the flying camera opens up. As the introductory clip suggests, the medium blurs the boundaries between drone movement and pilot stillness, being here and there. As such, a closer analysis of this mobile, motile, portable, and movable device in its multiple shapes and forms—from small DIY quadcopters to larger ready-to-fly consumer drones—not only helps assess the hobby's growing popularity, but has intellectual merit for mobilities research and critical media studies.

Who and what is moving in recreational drone ecologies? What kinds of movements and stillness happen? And, how do drone users experience these ways of moving and not moving on the ground and up in the air? In response to these guiding questions, I explore the mobile qualities of "first-person-view" (FPV) and freestyle quadcopters for racing next to those of off-the-shelf consumer drones for aerial photography and videography. As such, this chapter traces and discusses drone mobilities more generally, paving the way for future research into specific drone types and practices.

When referring to "mobilities," I am interested in multiple levels and forms of movement encompassing corporeal (the user's body), physical (the drone), and imaginative travel (the user's imagination), inspired by Urry's (2007) interdependent types of mobilities. This approach to movement includes forms of non-movement, stillness, and dwelling that are equally necessary for mobilities to take shape (Sheller & Urry, 2006). I complement those insights from critical mobilities research with key approaches from media ecology as the study of media as environments, and environments as media. Central to this intellectual tradition is the perspective of media as extensions of human faculties furthered by Marshall McLuhan, Sigmund Freud, Lewis Mumford, Edward T. Hall, and others (Strate, 2017). Approaching camera drones as an aerial extension of the human body—particularly our eyes and feet—into contested and ambiguously regulated public space (McCosker, 2015; Parks, 2005,

2016) can help us think about some of the promising and perilous ways of moving that such and other emerging mobile media bring about. In light of their "unruly trajectories, their multidirectional motility, and their accessibility to ordinary users" (McCosker, 2015: 4), the potentials of these uniquely mobile bodily extensions demand attention.

In the following, I briefly lay out the relevant theoretical starting point and drone-related literature before dividing the chapter into four main sections: (1) remediated mobilities, (2) corporeal mobilities, (3) imaginative mobilities, and (4) dis/embodied mobilities. Table 5.1 provides an overview and definition of the kinds of mobilities that build on Urry's (2007) typology of travel in combination with Bolter and Grusin's concept of "remediation" (1999).

In the first section, I shed light onto how the assemblage of the small aircraft, the wide-angle camera, remote control, and the smartphone *remediates* multiple modes from aviation, image-production, communication, and gaming. Those are skillsets drone users put to use in their mastering of drone flying and recording. The second section focuses on the minimal corporeal mobilities of the hand, fingers, and head necessary to operate the drone. In combination with those micro-movements, which leave the remote pilot comparatively still on the ground, the physical mobility of the drone as aerial technology animates new ways of moving and seeing. I discuss those imaginative mobilities in the third section and relate them to Verhoeff's (2012) concept of "panoramic desire." The ambiguous fourth component of dis/embodied mobilities comes into effect when drone users fully immerse themselves in the

Table 5.1 Types of drone mobilities, expanding on Urry (2007) and Bolter and Grusin (1999), relevant for this chapter

Remediated	Mobilities from previous practices that the user can draw from, e. g. aviation, image-production, communication, and gaming
Corporeal	Mobilities of the user's hands, fingers, and head as well as of the drone
Imaginative	Mobilities of the user's mind during drone flying, racing, and image-taking
Dis/embodied	Mobilities which merge the user's mind with the drone's body

drone's physical and their own imaginative mobilities. McLuhan's probes into media as extensions and amputations help assess the experience of disembodiment interviewees describe. Here, I also include theoretical considerations of how the spatially distributed cyborg of drone medium and remote pilot aligns with Vertesi's (2015) observations on "seeing like a rover" for remote missions on Mars.

The chapter concludes with thoughts on what such merging mobilities might mean for the future of human-technology movements and relationships: The flying system complicates boundaries between movement and stillness as well as the locatedness of subject and object. As such, contemporary camera drone technologies and multi-modal mobilities might well be a glimpse into the future; a future in which everyday media extensions and increasing cyborg configuration may be distributed across not only virtual but also vertical spaces.

Theory: Embodied Performances and Media Extensions

The figure of the drone inspires inquiries into its unique sensory capacities and multidirectional mobilities. Media scholar Mark Andrejevic (2015: 196), for example, recognizes "the promise of the drone as hyper-efficient information technology" in how "it extends and multiplies the reach of the senses" along with how "it automates the sense-making process" and how "it automates response." Similarly, media scholar Anthony McCosker discusses the "volatile and contested relationality hinging on the experience of 'wirelessness' more generally and shifting forms of visuality" (2015: 3). His work on the motility of drones, meaning the quadcopter's inherent capacity for movement, builds important groundwork for this chapter. The following pages add empirical depth to these arguments, drawing on concrete examples of how users experience this sensory and wireless extension into the air.

Similarly relevant again is Jensen's (2013) staging mobilities framework which consists of three major components for the staging and enabling of movement: First, "physical settings, material spaces, design" are key factors in mobile situations, which have been discussed in the context of drones in Chapter 3 and elsewhere (Bender, 2018; Hilde-brand, 2017; Jablonowski, 2015, 2017). "Social interactions" present a second component of mobilities. For drones, those social interactions for flying, image-taking, and image-sharing have been laid out by media scholar Hendrik Bender (2018), Jablonowski (2015, 2017), and myself in Chapter 4. Finally, "embodied performances" make up the third aspect of mobilities in situ according to Jensen, (2013). Those embodied perfor-mances are at the center of this chapter with critical attention to the staging of drone mobilities by users.

While research within the new mobilities paradigm (Sheller & Urry, 2006) views the act of physically, corporeally, communicatively, and imaginatively moving through environments as meaningful, media ecology attends to the environments, "their structure, content, and impact on people," (Postman, 1970: 161) that afford or constrain such multi-modal movements. Of special interest in this chapter on drone users' embodied performances is the concept of media as extensions of human faculties, specifically the drone as an extension of the human body and mind. McLuhan speaks to the idea and the consequences of media as means for extending ourselves into the world thus:

> Any invention or technology is an extension or self-amputation of our physical bodies, and such extension also demands new ratios or new equilibriums among the other organs and extensions of the body. (1964: 54)

Freud similarly addresses tools as means for perfecting organs and "removing the limits of their functioning" exemplified in such extensions as the "aircraft" or "photographic camera" (1961: 27–38). Mumford (1961) and Hall (1976) also draw from this metaphor of organ exten-sions, while philosopher Ernst Kapp (1877) speaks of organ projections in his historical analysis of tools.

Despite the empowerment of the human body and mind through these media, the technological prostheses and enhanced (im)mobilities can be problematic. Freud explains that "When [man] puts on all his auxiliary organs he is truly magnificent; but those organs have not grown on to him and they still give him much trouble at times" (1961: 38).

Addressing this "trouble," McLuhan highlights the processes of self-amputation that such extensions may initiate. What is amputated is our awareness of the relationship we have to the extending medium. To use Strate's (2017: 110) clarification, "as an extension, a technology mediates between ourselves and our world, extending us in one sense, while in another sense, as an amputation, coming between us and our world." How exactly do camera drones both extend us and our mobile ways but also come between us and our world?

Drone (Im)mobilities: Body, Drone, Space

Remediated Mobilities

To explore the movements and stillness camera drones afford as extensions of the human body, let's consider how different mobile and medial practices are configured. At the most basic level, consumer drones bring together aerial navigation, visual production, and networked communication. The technology thus reconnects the historically closely related concepts and practices of communication andtransportation (Adey, 2010; Carey, 1992; McLuhan, 1964). Complex modes of communication and signal movement occur simultaneously between user and remote control, remote control and smartphone, smartphone and drone app, drone app and small aircraft, small aircraft and satellites, small aircraft and user, and so forth, shaping hybrid drone ecologies (see Chapter 3). Multiple mobile modalities such as flying, piloting, racing, gaming, and image-taking further shape aerial drone play. As a result, those multi-modal elements become interrelated, mutually dependent, and transformative.

This intersection of different media and their respective mobilities (aircraft, camera, sensor, remote control, smartphone, satellite, etc.) is exemplified in the background of hobby users I interview and observe. In drone flying and image-taking, photographers meet pilots; technophiles meet travelers. Their respective interests and skills give them certain advantages in mastering the drone medium and mobile practice. Ethan, a drone hobbyist and racer in his thirties, points to his background in model and manned aviation as well as photography and film that helped him quickly adopt the technology:

> I fly remote-control helicopters and remote-control airplanes, and I also have my pilot's license. So, I love all things aviation. And then, I also have a background in photography. I went to film school and travelled the world as a photographer for a long time. So, I have this connection. And then, just recently I went on a trip with a friend and he had a drone with him and he said, "Dude, I cannot believe you're not into drones because you love flying and filmmaking and photography so much, this is like the ultimate combination of those elements." And that was kind of the trigger to get me back into it. [...] So yeah, I've learned a lot in those four months because I have a really good foundation in all the areas that matter.

While Mike, a drone hobbyist in his thirties, does not have a background in aviation, he mentions his gaming skills as advantageous to learning how to operate his first camera drone:

> The first time I picked it up, I was definitely struck by how easy it felt. The second thing that struck me is, you know, I am looking at the screen, moving this thing around, and this is a really familiar experience. I grew up playing video games since I was 5. And I was like "This is playing video games. This is very simple, and similar to, you know, playing HALO." So, I think all of those hours spent shooting things at HALO translated over nicely into flying drones.

According to this and other descriptions of drone users who point to the similarities of playing video games and flying drones, aerial drone play is a refashioning of gaming culture; one that has transpired into geographical space and became physically as opposed to merely virtually mobile. Thomas, a drone user in his fifties, speaks to this observation more directly:

> It's very similar to a video game, but it's real. You're seeing a real thing as it is in real life. If it's a construction site, what they're doing now, or

if it's nature or something, it's what's happening now. It's different than a video game because it's real, but it's really like a video game.

One characteristic of drone (im)mobilities then is the remediation (Bolter & Grusin, 1999) of video gaming practices, extended into aerial space. At the same time, video games along with model aviation "pre-mediate" aerial drone play; they provide "a form of medial pre-emption" (Grusin, 2010: 2). This means that video games and model aviation set the stage for the disembodied, imaginative mobilities users experience in drone flying and recording. Drone users benefit from such pre-existing media and mobility literacies.

Moreover, interviewees point to how challenging this coming together of movement, communication, and gaming can be. Ethan provides some details about the various media formats and mobile processes that define his drone racing practice.

So, there is this unique combination with these drones, where you have a culmination of a lot of different technologies. You've got the video-streaming, the goggles, you've got the remote control that controls the drone, and then inside the drone, you've got the electronics that are actually stabilizing it, and you've got the speed controllers which are controlling the motors, and each of those has evolved in a big big way in the last five years. So, all of the sudden, you know, you can do these things, but it does take a lot of practice. And that is what is, I think, the fun about this. It is easy to try and then it is very hard to master. So, it is kind of a good hobby in that way.

Mike, who is also a photographer and car racer, similarly addresses this unique interplay of different modes and motions as quite demanding when "having to balance all of this at once." He describes the experience of drone image-taking as

this crazy intersection of all the things that I like in the world. And then you are having to like balance all of this all at once. At the same time, I used to build and race cars. So, there was that element of it as a kind of vehicle. All these components that are interesting. So, you are effectively kind of racing when you are steering this thing, even when you are trying to do a steady shot, it's like a slow race. Playing a video game, setting up a shot, dialing in your exposure, setting your aperture, getting good composition, and assuring your histogram is balanced. *So it's literally like trying to make a peanut butter and jelly sandwich while skateboarding in the ocean.* You are like using every part of your brain. I think that is what's fun both then and now. You're using an intuitive, instinctual reaction. You're using this emotional quality of "Oh I need to move in and move the camera this way to get this kind of a shot like this," and you are using this kind of intellectual component where you are going "Ok, there is this thing here" while making sure you are not running sideways into a tree.

The complex interrelations and mutual dependencies of the mobile, visual, physical, communicative, and affective mobilities come into full light in Mike's illustrative comment. The drone user refers to how "every part of your brain" is involved and how he experiences "this emotional quality" and "this kind of intellectual component" when trying to maneuver the drone, operate the camera, and respond to the visual and computational data displayed on the interface. Adopting the full potential of drone capacities means handling multiple mobilities simultaneously while drawing on potentially pre-existing individual media literacies, such as gaming, piloting, racing, and image-taking.

Corporeal Mobilities

In aerial drone play, human corporeal mobilities and drone physical mobilities are uniquely configured. Distributing the grounded pilot and aerial camera across vertical and horizontal space, the drone medium blurs the boundaries of corporeal mobility and immobility. The user's comparative stillness on the ground contrasts the drone's exceptional maneuvers in the air. The remote pilot initiates and commands those macro-movements into three-dimensional space with micro-movements of the hands and head. In my own drone sessions with the DJI Mavic Pro Platinum drone, I notice just how immobile my body remains as I focus on controlling the device's motions. During chilly days, my hands and feet get cold because of the enduring corporeal stillness in my practice. As my drone ascends, hovers, flies, and descends to explore the vertical and collect exciting visuals, my body becomes and remains immobile; *grounded*.

Despite the limited corporeal requirements for drone flying, learning how to operate the system is demanding. Careful practice is required because—in contrast to gaming—the micro-gestures translate into impactful macro-movements across geographical space. Ethan compares learning how to fly freestyle drones to learning how to drive a car with manual transmission:

> When you first learn how to drive a car, it's not that fun. You have to think about how you have to break, use the clutch, the shift, you have to steer. That's kind of like to learn how to fly a drone. There's a lot going on. A lot you have to think about. But, once you get that kind of skill built in your brain, you can do it naturally. You just think about where you want to go and then go there at a hundred miles an hour. And go as high as you want or as low as you want. Upside down, right side up. It's exhilarating. It's really fun. It's like having your own rollercoaster that you can ride whenever you want and have it go wherever you want.

Hence, similar to driving a car, the process of flying a drone can become second nature. The car responds to the micro-commands initiated by the hand and foot operating the break, the clutch, the shift, and the steering wheel. To turn your drone experience into that of a rollercoaster, however, even less corporeal mobility is necessary.

When asked about the top three skills needed to be a "good pilot," Dimitris Rizikianos responds, "A good pilot has to know his equipment capabilities and its limits, respect the safety and the privacy of the people around him and during a flight, *pilot's senses and mind must be wired with his fingers*" (quoted in Jarret, 2015, own emphasis). Even closer to the practices of gaming and image-taking then, the hands inherit a special role for initiating and controlling the aerial movement of drones. This attention to the hand is reminiscent of anthropologist Tim Ingold's (2013) argument that the hand serves as an extension of the brain. Anthropologist Sarah Pink and her colleagues (2016) draw on this notion of the hands extending the brain and describe mobile devices as "technologies of the hand":

Thus when we cast mobile devices, their materiality, content, and sociality as technologies of the hand, we ask how they become part of this particular configuration where there is a certain intensity between the hand-mind-device relationship as people and phones move through everyday digital-material environments together. (Pink et al. 2016: 240)

This observation holds true for camera drones, which further intensify the "hand-mind-device relationship" in the drone-specific movements "through everyday digital-material environments." Frequently, the tactile smartphone screen serves as the remote control and touch interface for the drone app. Beyond the haptics of phone use for gaming or image-taking, the fingers remotely mobilize a physical object that directly responds to the corporeal micro-commands.

The immediate responsiveness of the aerial device extending the hand and ultimately mind is front and center in users' accounts of what they enjoy about drone flying and image-taking. Jasmyn Philipps, a "drone girl" interviewed by Dronestagram, recounts that "It was wonderful to feel the drone respond to my fingers on the joystick" (quoted in Dichtlerova, 2016). Moreover, the physical object follows the user's commands in ways that are so unlike human mobility. Diego is partic-ularly fond of his DJI Inspire prosumer drone because of the aircraft's responsive flight capacities:

> I love my Inspire. Because when you are flying out there, the drone is so responsive to you, your remote, *your moves*, it's fast, the way that it looks, the way the arms go up once the drone is flying.

"Your moves" are minimal yet powerful as they command significant physical mobilities beyond those of the human body up to several miles into the distance and (legally in the United States) 400 feet up.

In my own auto-technographic engagements with the Mavic drone, I've found its responsiveness not only noticeable in the flight maneuvers following my hand commands but also in the movements of the camera attached to the aircraft. To better understand why my own flight maneu-vers fail to produce the cinematic shots in drone videos shared online, I closely analyzed how I operate both the aircraft and the attached camera.

I realized that without proper training in the cinematographic craft, I instinctively use the drone camera the same way I would orient my gaze on the ground in a new environment. After going up, I panoramically scan the aerial surroundings before moving the drone into a direction of interest. The static 360-degrees-turn is insightful. Yet, the video misses the full aesthetic potential of the multidirectional drone mobilities. Sacrificing aesthetics for explorative play, I use the camera drone like I would use my body in search of orientation and visual cues. In those instances, I clearly prioritize a "seeing in the moment" over a "recording for the future." In other words, the photographic and cinematographic craft of aerial image-taking is subsumed under the desire for seeing (t)here and now. The physical mobility of the drone camera is a direct aerial extension of my personal gaze mediated by the manual steering.

At the same time, the user's gaze is challenged in the double attention to how the drone is moving in the air and what the drone is seeing via the visual live-feed. The FAA (2020) asks drone pilots to keep the flying device within visual line of sight at all times. However, the remote control and the app interface equally require the user to take note of the visualized telemetry including flight and camera settings and warning messages. Hence, while comparatively immobile on the ground and focused on the micro-commands of their hands and fingers, users find their head moving up and down between drone in the sky and remote-control screen in their hands. This shifting of visual attention from the view *onto* the drone and the view *by* the drone can burden safe flying practices. Mike notes,

> Honestly, if you are a single operator, trying to fly both line-of-sight and in the screen, in my opinion, is more dangerous. You really need to focus on one point or the other. And, if you try to do both, like trying to reconcile those two worlds, that's what's gotten me into a little bit of trouble at times. Trying to do both. You can't do either very well if you are trying to do that.

I can confirm the difficulty of distributing my gaze in this manner and have noticed myself focusing more on the screen than drone. Similar to the way in which automobile drivers may split their attention between the windshield, car instruments, and the phone screen, my focus on the drone in the sky and the screen in my hand requires different geospatial attunements to either the physical/geographical conditions in three-dimensional space or the visual/informational conditions projected onto the remote control. This continuous distribution of attention is cognitively difficult to maintain. When flying with company, which several of my interviewees do, a designated "spotter" can keep the drone in sight and look out for any aerial traffic and changing flight conditions. The upward head maneuvers for line-of-sight flying are thus outsourced to a second body. Meanwhile, users can focus *downward* (if not *inward*) on the drone mobilities mediated on the screen. Concentrating on the drone's view namely opens up powerful imaginative mobilities and affective sensations that fuel such aerial play.

Imaginative Mobilities

Along with such various corporeal mobilities, the drone practice affords and effects certain imaginative mobilities. Here, I employ Urry's notion of "imaginative travel" as movements with which

> people "travel" elsewhere through memories, texts, guidebooks and brochures, travel writing, photos, postcards, radio and film. Such travel can sometimes substitute for physical travel [...], but more often seems to generate the desire for travel and for being bodily in other places. (2007: 169)

In recreational drone use, imaginative mobilities encompass the sensation of movement and "being bodily in other places" via the transmitted imagery. The camera drone allows users to experience flight unlike the aerial navigation provided by helicopters and planes. Josh Haner, a photojournalist for the New York Times, remarks,

> Movement becomes really key with drone video, and that's very difficult to do with a helicopter at some altitudes. It's a unique experience to be able to navigate like a bird. (quoted in Estrin, 2017)

Bird-like aeromobilities are frequently referenced when interviewees describe the imaginative mobilities they experience with both camera and racing drones.

Another attraction of drone mobilities is the capability of hovering. Sam, a drone user in his forties, describes how drones allow users to tap into such mobilities of flight and hovering that are foreign to the human body:

> You can hover. You can hover in one spot and you can move to one spot then stop and then hover. I think that's an additional fascination with that type of movement. I think in its core, it's really about flight, and we like things that can fly for our fantasy because we can't do it ourselves.

Here, Sam alludes to the drone as mobile empowerment beyond human capacities. In his choice of words, he collapses his positionality and mobile capacities with those of the drone ("*you* can hover"). This choice of expression speaks to the effective merging of user and technology that is also discernable in the context of the car and other media. I will return to this aspect momentarily.

These new ways of physically moving the drone and imaginatively accompanying the aerial camera bring about new ways of seeing. Thomas, who is a drone user and paraglider, for example, tells me,

> I love to fly. [...] It's like a bird, it feels free. [...] There's nothing else like it. [...] It's freedom. [...] It's like a beautiful view that you wouldn't get from the ground. It's what life is all about, really, flying. It's so different from walking. [...] You can go wherever you want. It's like another world.

The imaginative aerial mobility allows for escaping the physical constraints of the human body and its corporeal mobilities ("You can go wherever you want") and thus accessing different views of both familiar and unfamiliar places. Maggie, a freestyle drone racer in her twenties, emphasizes how "you get to see even places that you're super familiar with, you get to see them in a way that you don't ever see them."

Users tell me how their views onto their surroundings change as a result, once they have gotten into recreational and commercial drone flying and image-taking. Ethan shares,

> I feel like it [drone flying] widened my perspective significantly. And whenever I am driving around, I am like thinking "oh that little gap would be so fun to fly through." You can loop around. Or, like I am used to seeing the mountains from the car and I would wonder what it is like on top of the hill, [...] and with the drone I can just go look. And that is really cool. And yeah, just sort of driving around or walking around *my brain has this sort of new way of looking at things* like a drone pilot for sure.

The imaginative mobilities afforded by the drone arise in Ethan's everyday travels. Having experienced the drone's unique vantage point, he wonders what other spaces may look like from this perspective. Hence, the imaginative mobilities can occur independent from the practice. Verhoeff's (2012) concept of "panoramic desire" applies in how it is "part of the regime of navigational visuality, which strives to escape the spatial constraints of embodied haptic visuality" (21). She compares the screen to the windshield "because both function as access points, portals or gateways to the moving image" (21). The drone interface presents such a portal for personal aerial mobilities which can turn into a gateway for other everyday navigational perceptions. With "panoramic desire," Verhoeff also argues for "the desire for perceptual, not physical, immersion" in the "visual arrangement or dispositif of spectator, visual field, and medium that organizes the gaze" (12). How then do such perceptual immersions and the experiential collapse of subject and object take place in aerial drone play?

Dis/Embodied Mobilities

Several of the previous interview excerpts point to a rhetorical and experiential merging of user and drone. Varying degrees of embodiment and out-of-body impressions take shape at the interplay of corporeal and imaginative drone mobilities. The remote users' micro-mobilities of the body and macro-mobilities of the mind lead to the sensation that *one's self is situated within the drone*. As the human body becomes still on the ground and the mind is mobilized in the air, users describe a *separation of body and mind*. The aerial device is thus both a disembodying and embodying medium. The technological extension of the human body can potentially "amputate"—in McLuhan's (1964) sense of numbing and replacing—the users' sensual relationship to their own corporeality. With varying and oscillating degrees of embodiment and disembodiment, the medium is "coming between us and our world" (Strate, 2017: 110). Several examples illustrate this point.

As previously noted, Sam frames the flying camera as a technological extension of the user, if not more. Instead of "You can make the drone hover," Sam says, "You can hover." Like other users I interviewed, he describes his practice in ways that merges the drone and user into one entity that hovers, moves, stops, and flies. My imaginative and the drone's physical mobilities become one as they meet in the transmission and display of the aerial visuals. Similar language which collapses technology and user appears in the context of other mobile modes such as the car. Sociologist Tim Dant (2004: 74) describes the "driver-car" as an "assembled social being" fusing thing and person. As a result, descriptions of car accidents often include "the person hit *me*" instead of "the person *hit my car*." Strate relates this phenomenon to the media extension model, claiming,

> Eventually [...] comes the point where we merge with the car, become the car, in effect are transformed into a cyborg as our body and sense of personal space merge with the car and expand to take on this exoskeleton, *where we put the car on* as McLuhan would have it. (2017: 109)

Drone users describe their aerial play similarly. Interviewees draw on metaphors of merging with the drone in the sky toward an aerial cyborg assemblage of organic and inorganic mobilities. Kristen, a drone hobbyist in her sixties, describes the mediated aerial views in this manner:

> I just enjoy the fact that with a quick jump, I'm in the air. [...] I always think of a quote by Leonardo da Vinci. [...] It says "Once you have tasted

flight, you will forever walk the Earth with your eyes turned skyward. For there you have been, and there you will allows long to return." I heard that, and it really resonated with me because it's true.

Like Sam, Kristen describes herself as "in the air" while on the ground. She refers to da Vinci's quote about flight as something she has tasted, a sensation and longing that rings true to her. The geomedium has changed her perspective without changing her position. As such, the drone is both embodying imaginative mobilities while disembodying corporeal mobilities.

Such processes of dis/embodiment are enhanced with greater immersion into the drone's visual field. First-person view goggles are powerful tools that achieve this amplification. Thomas explains to me that wearing the goggles during freestyle drone flying is "Intense. It's really scary and very interactive. You're in there, you're part of it. *I'm in my goggles*, it's like, *you're there*." With the goggles, Thomas and his flying camera merge more deeply, enhancing the aerial cyborg of user and drone. Here, my findings echo those of Jablonowski's research into first-person view drone flying when his interviewee describes the technology as "an extension of my body, it is something like my Iron Man suit, I can use it or… yes, partially wear it" (2015: 10). Thomas, too, states that he finds himself *in his goggles*. There seems to be more than a mere extension of human faculties: He becomes "part of it," his mind has moved "there." While the screen interface with its more limited perspective is less immersive, the goggles envelope the user's visual field with that of the drone. "You're really there and it will make your heart beat fast," says Thomas in reference to first-person view drone flying. The user's corporeal responses to the imaginative mobilities speak to the shifting boundaries of body, mind, technology, and space that the dis/embodying medium affords.

Studying mobile virtual reality and the kinds of movements possible within such a mediated environments, media scholars Michael Saker and Jordan Frith state that "digital motion is physically felt" (2018: 11). Similarly, visual motion is physically felt in immersive aerial drone play. Ethan tells me about when he first started to fly small quadcopters with a headset:

The first time it is kind of crazy because you kind of want to tip over trying to look around. So, you are trying to use your body to manipulate the drone, but that doesn't work if that makes sense. So, it's kind of disorienting.

Animated by the imaginative movements of the drone, the user's mostly immobile body wants to engage more in the cyborg mobilities, but cannot. Beyond the minimal hand and finger commands on the remote control, the human body is meant to be still, letting the mind and the aerial technology do the moving. To remedy the disorientation of first experiencing drone mobilities, the user mentally disengages from the bodily constraints. The result is a sensual numbing of the human body and imaginative shifting into the drone medium.

Such dis/embodied mobilities are particularly remarkable when users see *themselves* through the drone's lens. Emanuel, a hobbyist in his fifties, describes seeing himself through the drone as "an out-of-body experience," and Thomas, too, uses the words "Weird. It's like out of body. It's unreal." He continues,

> It's like you're in it, it's like you're floating around the sky. You're exploring, you're going to check out things. Then you come around and you check out yourself. Like how can I be checking out myself? It's weird.

Ethan is particularly evocative when he recounts the "weird" out-of-body moment of seeing himself. Here is how he makes sense of the experience:

> You start to get used to it [flying], and then you fly somewhere where you can see your body. And all of the sudden, you have like this moment that everybody talks about where you're like totally disembodied. *You're seeing yourself as someone else.* Because you're the drone for that time. And it's really cool. It's kind of a really, kind of a uniquely human experience of connecting to "Oh I'm actually not my body. I'm my brain. And my body just carries my brain around." So, right now *my drone is kind of carrying my brain around*. So, it's kind of a glimpse into the future I think.

Ethan positions his *I* inside the medium and outside of his biological body. For that moment, the drone has become his body and he understands himself as not only part of but immersed and integrated into the aerial cyborg complex. Having fully adopted the drone's visual mobilities, Ethan experiences his body as that of "someone else." The corporeal numbness seems "total" because "you are the drone."

What becomes visible in those accounts is not only the extension of human faculties into vertical space, but also the subsequent amputation of relevant senses as probed by McLuhan (1964). Thomas, Emanuel, and Ethan allude to a sensory numbness that occurs as a result of the drone medium coming between them and their world. In the case of camera drones, then, it is the comparatively immobile and physically restricted human body that appears removed from the experience after full sensory immersion. The amputation process shows in the sensation of seeing "yourself as someone else" in the drone's visual field.

Moreover, this transition from moving and seeing like a drone to shifting in and out of the drone confirms observations made by Vertesi (2015), who explores "seeing like a rover" in her ethnographic analysis of Mars missions. She discusses how the team members of the rover projects do

> not project themselves outwards, into the body of the rover as a human proxy. Rather, they themselves adopt the rover's bodily apparatus with its unique bodily sensitivities in order to understand and interact with Mars. (Vertesi 2015: 176)

Similar to how Vertesi's participants describe the "need to literally be that vehicle" and mention that "you're not you, you're the rover" (176), my participants share experiencing themselves as being with and becoming the drone. Just as the Mars rovers are more than proxies for the researchers, camera drones present more than technological extensions of human faculties into vertical space. Mentally leaving their earthly bodily conditions behind, drone and rover users step into the medium's body. Vertesi states, "embodiment is a two-way street" (176); this sentiment is captured in what I describe as ambiguous and oscillating dis/embodied mobilities.

Conclusion

In this chapter, I discussed the multiple mobilities and immobilities aerial drone play configures, even collapses. With attention to both freestyle drone flying and aerial image-taking, I brought attention to the remediated practices of gaming, piloting, and image-taking that hobbyists draw from. Those mobile modes equally premediate recreational drone flying and recording, allowing users to tap into such literacies to master the complex interplay of aerial navigation, visual production, and virtual communication of signals and sensors. The physical macro-mobilities of drones in vertical and horizontal space are initiated by the micro-mobilities of the user's body. The hands and, to a lesser extent, the head play a central role in controlling the powerful aerial extension.

As the body remains fairly still, the user's mind can travel with the drone. Flying like a bird and seeing the world from an aerial perspective are sensations that interviewees speak to from a—often unmediated—first-person point of view. The consumption of aerial views through the screen or the goggles transforms into an experience that rhetorically collapses pilot subject and drone object. Particularly with goggles that envelope the user's visual field, the merging of human on the ground and technology in the sky feels almost complete. The drone is where the *I* is located, leaving the immobile human body as a strange *not-I*. Those examples enrich McLuhan's probes into media as extensions and self-amputations. To describe the blurring boundaries of subject and object, movement and stillness at the intersection of body and mind, I introduced the concept of dis/embodied mobilities.

Consequently, the drone medium and its uniquely ambiguous mobilities complicate conceptions of everyday physical, corporeal, virtual, communicative, and imaginative movement. In the blending of the inorganic and organic, the physical/corporeal and visual/imaginative, the grounded and the aerial, the pilot-drone cyborg complex signals how multi-mobile and multi-spatial ways of emerging human-technology relations may "come between us and our world."

The merging of human mind and drone movement has promises and perils. For future avenues of research, we can ask: How might such a coming between us and our world be beneficial? The dis/embodying drone medium could, for example, serve as an empowerment for people with physical disabilities. The French project Handidrone from 2016 is one early campaign inviting people with mobile impairments to fly drones and explore professional developments into such directions ("Handidrone - Kindai," n. d.). Along with vocational opportunities, we should also explore therapeutic benefits and mobilities (Kaspar et al., 2019) embedded in the visual drone motion that can be experienced with minimal corporeal investment (see for example Dorando, 2020).

At the same time, the perils of imaginative over-extension and sensory self-amputation demand further attention. Questions about the risks of such immersive drone mobilities include concerns over the physical safety of drone users and bystanders. The drone medium certainly comes between us and our world if we accidently hurt the human body on the fly. At the very minimum, the goal is not to crash into ourselves.

References

Adey, P. (2010). *Mobility*. Routledge.

Andrejevic, M. (2015). Becoming dones: Smartphone probes and distributed sensing. In R. Wilken & G. Goggin (Eds.), *Locative media* (pp. 193–207). Routledge.

Bender, H. (2018). The new aerial age: Die wechselseitige Verfertigung gemeinsamer Raum- und Medienpraktiken am Beispiel von Drohnen-Communities. In N. Ghanbari, I. Otto, S. Schramm, & T. Thielmann (Eds.), *Kollaboration: Beiträge zur Medientheorie und Kulturgeschichte der Zusammenarbeit* (pp. 121–145). Wilhelm Fink.

Bolter, J. D., & Grusin, R. A. (1999). *Remediation: Understanding new media*. MIT Press.

Carey, J. W. (1992). *Communication as culture: Essays on media and society*. Routledge.

Dant, T. (2004). The driver-car. *Theory, Culture & Society, 21*, 61–79.

Dichtlerova, V. (2016, October 25). Dronestagram's drone girls: Chat with top pilot Jasmyn Phillips. Retrieved October 17, 2018, from Dronestagram Blog website: http://www.dronestagr.am/blog/drone-girls-chat-jasmyn-phillips/.

doctorsnaketown. (2015). AWESOME! Quadcopter pilot crashes into his own head *ORIGINAL*. Retrieved December 6, 2018, from YouTube: https://www.youtube.com/watch?v=36CTDiJjQ8I.

Dorando, J. (2020, July 22). Therapy drones: Could sUAS be the adaptive therapy tool of the future? Retrieved October 22, 2020, from Dronelife website: https://dronelife.com/2020/07/22/therapy-drones/.

Estrin, J. (2017, March 16). Democratizing the sky: Drones in visual journalism. Retrieved October 17, 2018, from New York Times – Lens Blog website: https://lens.blogs.nytimes.com/2017/03/16/democratizing-the-sky-drones-in-visual-journalism/.

FAA. (2020, February 18). Recreational flyers & modeler community-based organizations. Retrieved June 2, 2020, from Federal Aviation Administration website: https://www.faa.gov/uas/recreational_fliers/.

Freud, S. (1961). *Civilization and its discontents* (J. Strachey, Trans.). W. W. Norton.

Grusin, R. (2010). *Premediation: Affect and mediality after 9/11*. Palgrave Macmillan.

Hall, E. T. (1976). *Beyond culture*. Anchor Press.

Handidrone—Kindai. (n.d.). Retrieved October 30, 2018, from Kindai website: https://kindai.fr/campaigns/handidrone/.

Hildebrand, J. M. (2017). Situating hobby drone practices. *Digital Culture & Society, 3*, 207–218.

Ingold, T. (2013). *Making: Anthropology, archaeology, art and architecture*. Routledge.

Jablonowski, M. (2015). Drone it yourself! On the decentring of 'drone stories.' *Culture Machine, 16*. http://www.culturemachine.net/index.php/cm/article/view/589.

Jablonowski, M. (2017). Dronie citizenship? In A. Kuntsman (Ed.), *Selfie citizenship* (pp. 97–106). Palgrave Macmillan.

Jarret, G. (2015, September 30). #3 Top pilot interview—Dimitris Rizikianos. Retrieved October 17, 2018, from Dronestagram Blog website: http://www.dronestagr.am/blog/3-top-pilot-interview-dimitris-rizikianos/.

Jensen, O. B. (2013). *Staging mobilities*. Routledge.

Kapp, E. (1877). *Grundlinien einer Philosophie der Technik: Zur Entstehungsgeschichte der Cultur aus neuen Gesichtspunkten*. G. Westermann.

Kaspar, H., Walton-Roberts, M., & Bochaton, A. (2019). Therapeutic mobilities. *Mobilities, 14*, 1–19.

McCosker, A. (2015). Drone media: Unruly systems, radical empiricism and camera consciousness. *Culture Machine, 16.* https://www.culturemachine. net/index.php/cm/article/view/591.

McLuhan, M. (1964). *Understanding media: The extensions of man* (2nd ed.). Signet.

Mumford, L. (1961). *The city in history: Its origins, its transformations, and its prospects.* Harcourt, Brace & World.

Parks, L. (2005). *Cultures in orbit: Satellites and the televisual.* Duke University Press.

Parks, L. (2016). Drones, vertical mediation, and the targeted class. *Feminist Studies, 42,* 227–235.

Pink, S., Sinanan, J., Hjorth, L., & Horst, H. (2016). Tactile digital ethnography: Researching mobile media through the hand. *Mobile Media & Communication, 4,* 237–251.

Postman, N. (1970). The reformed English curriculum. In A. C. Eurich (Ed.), *High school 1980: The shape of the future in American secondary education.* (pp. 160–168). Pitman.

Saker, M., & Frith, J. (2018). From hybrid space to dislocated space: Mobile virtual reality and a third stage of mobile media theory. *New Media & Society, 21,* 214–228.

Sheller, M., & Urry, J. (2006). The new mobilities paradigm. *Environment and Planning A, 38,* 207–226.

Strate, L. (2017). *Media ecology: An approach to understanding the human condition.* Peter Lang.

Urry, J. (2007). *Mobilities.* Polity.

Verhoeff, N. (2012). *Mobile screens: The visual regime of navigation.* Amsterdam University Press.

Vertesi, J. (2015). *Seeing like a rover: How robots, teams, and images craft knowledge of Mars.* University of Chicago Press.

6

Seeing like a Consumer Drone

Introduction

It was a cold January afternoon in a local park, when I flew my camera drone for the very first time. My hands were freezing as I set up the foldable DJI Mavic Pro drone and its remote control. I had studied the instructions for weeks, watched dozens of YouTube tutorials, learned the local and national rules and regulations, and saw hundreds of drone-generated videos online. When the football-sized quadcopter finally zoomed into the sky, my sense of my neighborhood and the places I thereafter visited would be significantly changed. The Philadelphia skyline popped up in the background beautifully lit in soft blue and orange colors with the sun slowly setting. The children's playground on my far left became smaller and smaller turning into colorful dots and lines. The pathways on the other side of the park created curvy patterns on the ground. Higher, lower, left, right, forward, backward, the drone responded swiftly to my fingers' gentle commands. Meanwhile, the image-transmission onto my smartphone screen was smooth and focused. My head pointed down to the screen, but my mind was

© The Author(s), under exclusive license to Springer Nature
Singapore Pte Ltd. 2021
J. M. Hildebrand, *Aerial Play*, Geographies of Media,
https://doi.org/10.1007/978-981-16-2195-6_6

Fig. 6.1 Drone view of Philadelphia in the winter (taken with DJI Mavic Pro Platinum drone "Jay")

in the clouds, ready to see more of my world from my drone's view (Fig. 6.1).

Consumer drones give hobbyists around the world the opportunity to see their familiar and unfamiliar surrounding from such new perspectives. As the latest technological manifestation of the desire to fly and see like a bird, camera drones continue the tradition of other aerial modes of seeing such as balloons, airplanes, and satellites. Yet, the aerial gaze afforded by the drone medium also complicates those earlier ways of moving in and seeing vertical spaces. While researchers have started to address the growing uptake of camera drones visible not only in drone practices on the ground but also drone-generated imagery circulating on social media sites, the particularities of the recreational drone gaze warrant a closer look.

In this chapter, I address the potentials of drone flying and image-taking to create new kinds of socio-cultural environments, similar to how the advent of the airplane changed "air space" (Adey, 2010a). Drone enthusiasts such as Eric Dupin, founder of the social networking site Dronestagram, point to the powerful visual and mobile affordances of camera drones:

Drones are revolutionizing photography. These small and lightweight quadcopters can take pictures in places where no other devices are able to fly: monolithic buildings; moving vehicles, sports arenas; inaccessible landscapes. They allow you to see the world from dizzying new heights, providing the ultimate bird's-eye view. They also signal a new "layer" to traditional aerial photography, sitting somewhere in-between satellite, aircraft and street views. (Dupin, 2017: n. p.)

This new "layer" to traditional photography and videography demands critical attention in light of the powerful associations aerial views engender. Think of the earliest attempts of balloon photography by French cartoonist Nadar to Apollo 8's iconic Earth Rise image and contemporary military drone practices. Social scientist Saulo Cwerner and colleagues point out:

Both the aerial view and aerial access have promoted a globalization that includes remote areas alongside the major nodes in the global economy and provided new, three-dimensional features of contemporary social life. (2009: 4)

More specifically, they argue that those spatial and visual practices "have changed the dynamics of contemporary war, mapping, surveillance, art, journalism, urban planning and government, to name a few" (Boldrick, 2007; see also Cwerner et al., 2009: 4). Providing aerial views and access to three-dimensional space from the bottom of the ground to legally a few hundred feet into the sky, camera drones are significantly impacting those and other domains (Choi-Fitzpatrick et al., 2016). Moreover, the remotely controlled flying camera allows for the self-controlled, independent visual exploration of vertical fields hitherto much more exclusive to mostly professional aviation and data collection.

To lay the groundwork for a general typology of the personal drone gaze, this chapter asks, what do drone views convey that is distinct to other aerial modes? In what directions do those hobby drone images and practices encourage users to think and feel? Drones afford new ways of remotely seeing and moving. A closer look at the motivations, practices, and experiences of aerial drone play helps assess those medium particularities, their visual biases, and effects.

In the following, I briefly address the aerial gaze and its different theorizations with attention to the cosmic view (Kaplan, 2006), the imperial-aerial view (Adey, 2010a), and the possessive gaze (Urry, 2007), which is closer to map-reading than way-finding (Ingold, 2000). Similarly, I delineate the consumer drone view from the concept of the less agile and omnipotent military "drone stare" (Chamayou, 2015; see also Wall & Monahan, 2011). I draw on these approaches to the aerial gaze to compare and contrast the consumer drone gaze. After this theoretical groundwork, I consider interview narratives and my auto-technographic fieldwork in terms of *what* aerial drone play allows users and viewers to see. Here, attention is less on the specific motives chosen by millions of drone users around the world, but more generally on what *kinds* of perspectives such users seek out and why.

In the second section, I shift from *what* camera drones see to *how* the playful aerial gaze operates given its unique vertical and horizontal mobilities. I discuss the explorative hobby drone gaze as related to practices of way-finding (Ingold, 2000) and performative cartography (Verhoeff, 2012). This approach to consumer drones acknowledges but also nuances the authoritative visuality that is often associated with the aerial gaze. In the third and final section, I explain in what directions this recreational aero-visuality is encouraging users to think and feel. Ultimately, I propose the concept of "drone-mindedness" as a visual sensibility that drone users develop toward their geographical surrounding even when not engaging in their aerial play.

Theory: The Aerial Gaze

Exploring the fascination with recreational drone use, I follow in the footsteps of French artist and entrepreneur Gaspard-Felix Tournachon, the first person to take aerial photographs in 1858. Having modified his hot-air balloons, Nadar—as he was known to his public—captured stable images of the French village Petit-Bicêtre while 260 feet off the ground (Scott, 2015). The development of balloon flight marks what Kaplan (2017) calls "the balloon prospect": a new way of seeing the world by combining the cartographic gaze with the mobile and visual appropriation of space. As in many examples from the intertwined histories of transportation and communication (Adey, 2017; Carey, 1992; Hildebrand, 2018), the development of photography and later cinematography is closely linked with the development of balloon flight and motorized aviation (Cosgrove & Fox, 2010). The aerial way of seeing the world continues to be variously modified depending on the technology for such visual access. The dirigible, airplane, and helicopter offer distinct vertical perspectives as does the satellite and now military and civilian drone technology.

Researchers across disciplines, from geography to anthropology, sociology, and philosophy, have theorized the aerial gaze and its past and present manifestations (see, for example, Adey 2010a, 2010b; Adey et al., 2011; Graham, 2010, 2016; Kaplan, 2006; Lin, 2017). Reminiscent of geographer Hans W. Weigert's (1944) "global view" concept, Kaplan, for example, develops the framework of the cosmic view as "a unifying gaze of an omniscient viewer of the globe from a distance" (2006: 401). Access to such views means mastering space that had been hitherto unknown or unobserved, according to Kaplan. With aerial views comes aerial power (Kaplan, 2006). Similarly, Adey (2010a) discusses the imperial-aerial gaze as granting space for state control and together with geographers Mark Whitehead and Alison Williams (2011: 176) argues that the "aerial viewpoint appears to be inescapably entangled in the very genesis of modern systems of control, and the coeval development of the target." The newly-gained visibility of territory and established "systems of legibility" (2011: 176) are also what Urry recognizes when highlighting,

> air travel affords a god's eye view, a view of the earth from above, with places, towns and cities laid out as though they are a form of nature waiting for the "possessive gaze." (2009: 34)

Drawing on Ingold's (2000) approaches to map-reading and wayfinding, Urry (2009) argues that air travel generates "map-readers" rather than "way-finders." "While way-finders move around *within* a world, map-readers move across a surface as imagined from above" (2009: 34).

The same observation holds true for "the drone stare" that social scientists Tyler Wall and Torin Monahan (2011) theorize as a "type of surveillance that abstracts people from contexts, thereby reducing variation, difference and noise that may impede action or introduce moral ambiguity" (239). With his "vision machines," technology critic Paul Virilio (1994) joins the conversation about how aerial perspectives lead to aerial power via monitoring and control. More recent scholarly inquiries into aerial ways of seeing focus on modes of "remote sensing" as "a way of deriving information about the Earth's land and water surfaces using images acquired from an overhead perspective" (McCormack, 2018: 40). As such, "remote sensing" shows alignments with the analytical, cartographic character of the possessive, imperial gaze. Relatedly, Kaplan and Miller (2019) situate contemporary unmanned aircraft systems historically in the violent, colonial work of atmospheric policing. With similar attention to forms of atmospheric monitoring, Fish (2020) and geographer Neil Waghorn (2016) add how activists, too, use camera drones for corporate and governmental accountability from the air.

In light of these "politics of verticality" (Chamayou, 2015: 53) related to the aerial view and the remote drone stare more specifically, I wonder, how does everyday aerial drone play speak to those frameworks? Does the playful access to vertical spaces equal the verticalization of power, "above-the-ground authority," and volumetric sovereignty (Chamayou, 2015: 54) associated with other aerial modes? While the power of accessing and managing vertical spaces by drones is undeniable as shown in the context of military and police applications, the way hobbyists adopt consumer drones challenges us to consider aerial movement and mediation beyond exclusively political associations. Seeing like a hobby drone is clearly linked to, yet also different to seeing like a military and police drone. The swift and smooth quadcopter affords map-reading *and* wayfinding above and within everyday environments. In addition, the much more playful exploration of three-dimensional geographies, infrastructures, and architectures enhances visual attunement and environmental awareness beyond everyday socio-spatial sensibilities. In her analysis of the view from above, historian Jeanne Haffner (2013: xiv) asks,

What new conceptions of space will emerge in the late twenty-first century as a result of technologies being developed today, and their direct use not only by researchers but also by urban residents themselves?

This chapter explores such conceptions of space in the context of recreational drone flying and image-taking.

Drone Visualities: Auratic Vertical Play

What Consumer Drones See: Auratic Views

The kind of views I can access and collect with my Mavic Pro never get old. Having taken Jay out for a flight in front of my rowhouse several dozen times, I still experience feeling impressed, surprised, and el(ev)ated. New angles, colors, formations, and patterns await each time I get to vertically explore familiar and unfamiliar environments. How can one typify the manifold views available to users from a few to several hundred feet above the ground and at angles anywhere between straight down and straight ahead? It seems impossible to fairly classify the millions of moving images of urban backyards, sunrises over oceans, sunsets over rivers, first-person views of drone races through the woods or empty garages, or top-down perspectives onto ice patterns on the ground. Speaking to the biases and effects of those images rather than their specific content, I understand the recreational and artistic drone gaze as *auratic*. A brief review of Benjamin's concept of "aura" follows, before examples from the interviews and auto-technography illustrate what I mean with auratic drone visuality.

Walter Benjamin's "aura" framework helps describe the views and sensations my participants and I experience with the drone medium. In his seminal work *The Work of Art in the Age of Mechanical Reproduction*, the philosopher argues that classic forms of art, such as paintings and sculptures, evoke a sense of aura. Yet, changes in technologies of representation, brought about by photography and film for example, diminish this auratic experience according to Benjamin (1968: 217–251). Aura stands for a sense of the "here and now," an attitude of reverence by the viewer. The English translation of his famous definition of "aura" states:

> We define the aura [of natural objects] as the unique phenomenon of a distance, however close it may be. If, while resting on a summer afternoon, you follow with your eyes a mountain range on the horizon or a branch which casts its shadow over you, you experience [breathe] the aura of those mountains, of that branch. (W. Benjamin, 1968: 222–223)

The original text in German mentions a unique "*Erscheinung einer Ferne, so nah sie sein mag*" (W. Benjamin, 1963: 15), which is translated as "phenomenon of a distance, however close it may be." Yet, the original sentence may also be understood as a "vision/ emergence/ appearance /emanation" of a "remoteness/ faraway place/ foreign space" however "near/ familiar" it may be. From this angle, the aura seems to have visual and environmental qualities, casting itself around objects and emanating into space for it to be "breathed in" by a "Ruhenden," meaning someone who is resting or still. As such, the aura is a relational happening emerging from the impression of remoteness. Benjamin criticizes the efforts of bringing works of art spatially and "*menschlich*" (in human ways) "*näher*," meaning closer and more familiar, which ultimately destroys the auratic dimension because aura, its remoteness, is peeled off ("*Entschälung*") of the object.

It is the auratic as a relational happening emerging from the impression of remoteness, which users allude to when describing their drone practices. First, while the aerial view unquestionably aids in making the unfamiliar familiar by providing geographical orientation (see Mike's story about using his drone to carve out a running path on a vacation island from Chapter 4), drone hobbyists also speak of the sensation of making the *familiar unfamiliar* (in the way that Philadelphia is new to me every time Jay shows it to me). Whatever is near and familiar appears remote, far away, or foreign. Several quotes further illustrate this sentiment. Anne and Przemyslaw Chwalik, two camera drone pilots interviewed by Dronestagram, describe the phenomenon in this way:

> From the air, everything looks amazing! The images taken by a drone give an unexpected perspective to familiar situations and transform their appearance to become extraordinary. A tree near the road, a family house, some people working or playing, a ballet of an agricultural machine in

the field, or an old ship aground can suddenly reveal some beauty, when viewed from the sky. (quoted in Jarret, 2016)

Anne and Przemyslaw note how familiar situations "transform their appearance to become extraordinary." Everyday spaces and movements change into a vision that is special; it emanates uniqueness, an aura that can be breathed in. Whether this aura is what the consumer drone gaze lays onto those appearances or simply makes visible is a question of aura being either the bias of personal drones or their effect. Regardless of this puzzle, the surprising visual emergence, the emanation of remoteness, and the extraordinary within the ordinary are dominant themes relating to aura in conversations with drone users and my aerial play with Jay. While the mind anticipates certain views, angles, and insights, the consumer drone gaze opens up a hidden detail, a startling formation, and a stunning pattern. Mike, a drone pilot in his thirties, tells me about first experiencing the drone gaze on a trip with his friends:

> The very first time, I was hiking in southern Utah with my brother, and one of his buddies brought a Phantom. [...] And he put his drone up, and it went up, and then you saw us and you saw the canyon that we're in, and then it went up higher, and then there was just this flat landscape. But, he got up so high that this land that we were in, this Jurassic Park World, was basically at the bottom of a hairline in his screen. *It so completely just blew my mind.* I was just like "WOW." Like we're right there. And what that sees and what I see was like, "That looks like Mars. That looks nothing like where I am. But I am there, I am there. How is that possible?" *It just completely upended my concept of space and my relationship and my size with the world and nature and it was just so completely unnerving.* So that was kind of the first time where I went "I think I need to get one of these." [laughs]

Already deeply impressed by the "Jurassic Park"-like geography of the Utah canyon, Mike's sense of place is "upended" by the aerial vantage point of the consumer drone. As the flying camera looks back down onto him and his friends and the surrounding area starts to appear "like Mars," the hiker sees himself and his position within this environment from a new perspective. In how Mike compares the views to landscapes in fictional film and outer space, his descriptions speak to the auratic drone gaze mediating foreign- and remoteness in his "here and now" ("I am there. How is that possible?").

While Mike is both in an unfamiliar location and seeing it from a new perspective, other users share how the drone changed their impression of the familiar. Maksim Tarasov, a professional drone pilot, tells this story:

> When I showed to my grandparents a bird's-eye-view picture of their house they said: "We've been staying in this house for more than 45 years and didn't even have a clue how beautiful this place is." (quoted in Dichtlerova, 2017)

Because we usually see our familiar environment from a few feet off the ground, we can obtain "that unexpected view of something that we think is very familiar" explains Henry, a drone user in his sixties. An auratic emanation of remoteness sensed in the here and now opens up such aerial play. When I had the opportunity to show my own family our house in a small German village from the drone perspective, my parents and siblings were deeply impressed by what the drone visuals unveiled (Fig. 6.2).

Fig. 6.2 Drone view of Bavarian village at sunset (taken with DJI Mavic Pro Platinum drone "Jay")

We quickly engaged in a play of real-time geographical orientation and landmark discovery. The transcription of this interaction reads:
Drone camera points straight down at about 100 feet off the ground.

Susanne: Oh, look [*chuckles*].
Magdalena: Oh, our backyard.
Susanne: There is my window.
Julia: Exactly.
Susanne: There is the nut tree.
Magdalena: The leaves are so yellow from up there. The hot summer sun really took its toll on the poor tree.
Susanne: It did! And there is the terrace.
Julia: Look, that is our house. Now, I am taking a picture. And now, let's look up [*points camera toward the horizon; the visuals are now showing part of the village*].
Susanne: Wow! There is the church.
Julia: And here is the sunset.
Susanne: Very beautiful!
Julia: We can see all that directly from our house. There is the field, there is the next village.
Magdalena: Impressive!
Julia: Let's fly to the church! Look!
Magdalena: Wonderful! Wow! Amazing perspective!

The drone view encourages visual attention to spatial arrangements and relations ("there is my window") and seasonal characteristics (the yellow leaves) of the surrounding, fostering an enhanced geographical understanding and aesthetic appreciation of the place. Practices of map-reading are evident in this example when my bystanders allocate the screened visuals and thus orient themselves via familiar landmarks ("there is the church"). At the same time, those sense- and place-making efforts are accompanied by affective experiences of the familiar and unfamiliar emanating as extraordinary visions in the here and now through the auratic lens.

In elevating the human gaze above everyday perspectives, the camera drone familiarizes but also defamiliarizes gazers with their space. As a result, the unique visual emanation of a remoteness however close, familiar, or near it may be, resituates us spatially. As we "breathe in" or visually take in the aura, the recreational drone gaze changes our ways of relating to space. "Resting" the body firmly on the ground, the eyes embark on a mediated journey to visually explore anew the home, the neighborhood, the community, and the region. At the same time, the mobile gaze allows viewers to "follow" and trace auratic visions of nature such as mountains, fields, beaches, parks, and rivers, but also cities and villages, sunrises and sunsets. The tension between near and far that Benjamin alludes to is discernable when experiencing drone imagery. In extending out into vertical space, the flying camera creates new visual relations between the viewer and views, a relational experience that is auratic.

Here, I follow Bolter and his colleagues in their argument that "digital technology [...] allows the invocation of aura in new ways" (2006: 36). With attention to mixed-reality applications, they discuss how contemporary mobile platforms can indeed exude aura. According to them, mixed-reality applications seem to "take what is remote and unapproachable (and therefore auratic) and bring it near to the subject" (Bolter et al., 2006: 28) thus destroying aura according to Benjamin. However, the digitally mediated experience of a place can still be auratic. Bolter and his colleagues illuminate how in the bridging of the physical and the virtual, the viewer's situational awareness can be heightened. The same argument applies to the personal drone gaze: The viewer's awareness is not only heightened but is frequently accompanied by increased senses for the "here and now" and a reverence for the mediated views. The drone medium's bias and effect are auratic el(ev)ation.

As such, the drone gaze follows in the tradition of sublime aerial views initiated by early ballooning, raising "the most careless observer to a high degree, not only of pleasure, but of rapture and enthusiasm" (Kaplan, 2014; "Review of Airopaidia," 1787: 428). The "stimulating and beautiful views" and "scenes of 'grandeur and beauty,' 'rapture' and 'new perspectives' [...] breathlessly reported by successive aeronauts," noted by Kaplan (2014: 31) in her analysis of the balloon prospect, are reiterated in the narratives of contemporary drone users. The kind of aerial photography drones afford, hence, continues to establish what geographers Denis Cosgrove and William L. Fox see as a context for individual features on the ground, to place them in relationship to one another and to a broader topography, revealing patterns to the eye, or, we might say, to create geographies. Like maps, such patterns can be produced and viewed with an eye to scientific objectivity, accurately representing and documenting actual space, or they can be made and read artistically as creating and revealing formal compositions and patterns of light, colour and morphology. (2010: 9)

Hobby drone users typically fall into the latter category, artistically creating and revealing auratic vertical and horizontal geographies. Henry, for example, has grown particularly fond of abstract ice patterns, snow landscapes, and other geographical formations:

> What to me are just fascinating images of either straight downwards or some kind of an oblique angle that just show the ice without showing the shoreline or the horizon. So many different abstract patterns and forms that people don't know. Even when I show them to people, they don't really know what they are, and they always are confused by how high I am. Am I five feet up, or am I 400 feet up? It's very disorienting when you see ice that way. You don't see it when you're on the ground looking sideways or at the surface. It only shows up and surprises me when I fly up above it.

Such new, surprising perspectives anywhere between zero and several hundred feet up continue to be abundant due to constant geographical changes and transitions. Colin, a camera drone and helicopter pilot in his twenties, tells me how he notices different things every time he takes the drone for a flight:

> When you're up in the air and you see it all together at once, you will never ever ever see the same view. And that's so exciting, and I think that applies to anywhere. [...] It's the sky and the way drones are... or helicopters... there is literally an infinite number of places you can point your camera up in the air. So, even in a desert or forest or somewhere where there is no development, you can get a different view each time.

These examples of the drone gaze speak to an explorative, creative, and playful engagement with familiar and unfamiliar everyday vertical spaces.

Drone users describe their aerial practices as driven by curiosity for evocative patterns and formations and other unexpected geographical details. In an interview with Dronestagram, Maksim Tarasov explains:

> I continue searching. Nature creates incredible images hidden from the human eye. This secret world opens up to you when you are flying: an overgrown pond can appear as the cosmos; a fishing hole, a human eye; and in dying soil, there can be seen life. [...] Every new flight is wonderful and promises unexpected discoveries. (quoted in Karabuda Ecer & Dronestagram, 2017: 263)

As such, the auratic personal drone gaze seems to be less about an imperialist mastering and conquering of the world. Rather, it is about recreationally and artistically (re)discovering familiar and unfamiliar spaces by experiencing remoteness; it is about shifting our sense of scale in the explorative extending and collapsing of spatial relations; it is about "breathing" in the aura of our everyday worlds. Those drone views and the aura they evoke are different from those of violent, colonial work, and atmospheric policing. While military views center on control and information, the personal drone gaze allows for an affective letting go; letting yourself get immersed in the auratic visions the drone mediates. Moreover, next to the different visual feel for space, the drone gaze also encourages you to play with aura; to court it. While the gaze of the flying camera aesthetically succeeds the cosmic gazes obtained with balloons and other modes of aviation in the top-down practices of surveying and ordering, qualitative differences exist in how recreational users employ the remote sensor for always different, surprising, and evocative views that can upend familiar conceptions and perceptions of space.

How Consumer Drones See: Vertical Play

The unique aerial mobility of contemporary consumer drone models shapes this aerial gaze in specific ways. Camera maneuvers such as the "reveal," "crane up and down," "tilt up and down," "point of interest," "track in motion," or "fly out/dronie" and their combinations often distinguish those recreational and artistic moving images from those of other aerial modes. The drone-mediated experiences of flying, hovering, gliding, chasing, and whirling result in perspectives that reveal, survey, explore, tease, and so forth. This extreme mobilization of the gaze is visible across drone film festival and online archive categories such as "Landscape," "Architecture," "Dronie," "Narrative," or "Freestyle/First Person View." Hence, the consumer drone gaze presents an enhanced "mobile gaze" (Cresswell & Dixon, 2002) that can playfully configure vertical and horizontal levels.

Map-Reading and Way-Finding

First-person view (FPV) and freestyle flying with highly agile mini-quadcopters allow users to navigate those different spatial levels particularly swiftly. The quadcopter provides views onto Earth's surface as a large canvas similar to those of other aircraft (Adey, 2010a). However, the "airy" drone gaze also complicates the notion of a flat "canvas" by moving among top-down, bottom-up, and mezzanine levels. FPV pilots visually explore the present geographies in parkour-style going up and down, left and right, above, underneath, and through. The flying cameras thus open up not only auratic views but also entirely new sorts of visual mobilities in three-dimensional, volumetric space. The unique aerial maneuverability and subsequent visual impressions diverge from processes of visual equalization ascribed to the balloon prospect (Kaplan, 2014). According to balloonist Monck Mason's impression from 1838,

> the houses and the trees, the mountains and the very clouds by which they are capped, have long since been consigned to the one level; all the natural irregularities of its surface completely obliterated; and the character of the model entirely superseded by that of the plan. (quoted in Kaplan 2014: 37)

The vertical play afforded by FPV quadcopters and—to a lesser extent—consumer drones upholds both the character of the model and the plan, operating on multiple spatial levels.

In fact, "natural irregularities" within auratic views make for recurring attractions playfully explored in consumer drone flying. Infrastructures and architectures that are on the mezzanine level (Shapiro, 2016), i.e., light poles, cables, antennas, and the like, require special attention in drone flying to avoid falls and crashes (see Chapter 3). Nonetheless, during both drone flying and drone-video watching, I find myself particularly drawn to architecture and infrastructure that impressively reach into vertical space: skyscrapers, monuments, water towers, tall bridges, or large trees (see for example Fig. 6.3). Being able to fly closely under, over, and around, the drone medium courts the volumetric quality of such geographic features. Moreover, some of the most breathtaking drone shots give "unprecedented angles of some of the world's most emblematic monuments," such as the Statue of Liberty, Rio de Janeiro's Christ the Redeemer, and Gaudi's Sagrada Familia (Karabuda Ecer & Dronestagram, 2017: 13). As increasing regulation of drone flying and image-taking restricts access to such landmarks, the technology's visual bias toward verticality remains visible in more mundane shots (Figs. 6.4 and 6.5).

The recreational drone gaze, hence, differs from Urry's (2007) possessive aerial gaze because consumer drones mediate *both* "way-finding" and "map-reading" (Ingold, 2000). According to Urry, "while way-finders

Fig. 6.3 Philadelphia skyline seen from the "mezzanine" level (taken with DJI Mavic Pro Platinum drone "Jay")

Fig. 6.4 Philadelphia skyline at dusk (taken with DJI Mavic Pro Platinum drone "Jay")

Fig. 6.5 Bridge crossing the Philadelphia Schuylkill (taken with DJI Mavic Pro Platinum drone "Jay")

move around *within* a world, map-readers move across a surface as imagined from above" (2007: 34). The world can thus "be visited, appreciated and compared even from above but not really known from within" (34). The recreational drone gaze remains limited in the extent to which the world can be known from *within*. However, it allows for curious visual explorations of spaces and objects that lie closer to, in-between, and underneath, instead of just above. Early balloonists were able to "wander around" in "permeable place of encounters between the map and the landscape" (Kaplan, 2014: 34). Contemporary drone users can go even further when remotely but more readily wandering above, within, and beneath multi-dimensional geographies.

Techniques of Surveillance/Techniques of Vision and Visualization

Practices of both map-reading and way-finding are front and center in my visual fieldnotes. Despite over a hundred auto-technographic drone flights in urban and rural settings, over rivers and beaches, parks and forests, my drone gaze continues to convey first disorientation, then unsystematic multi-level drone and camera maneuvers in search of focal points, which leave me wishing for more cinematographic skills. As mentioned in Chapter 5, I have come to recognize the aerial camera movements as direct extensions of my head movements on the ground. The 360-degree panorama, which opens up many of my drone-logs, provides an initial impression of where the drone is located, and where interesting vistas lie. The panoramas make for compelling photographic, but less intriguing videographic themes. Yawing movements to the left and right further point to geographical curiosity being my driving force as opposed to systematic scenography. Carefully finding my way in volumetric space supersedes any tendencies for well-structured, abstracting, and all-encompassing aerial gazes. Compelling views may then invite me to engage with the auratic drone-mediated space, to court it, and to play with it. As such, my findings echo the argument of Klauser and Pedrozo that "deployment of drones for fun [...] is sporadic and punctual rather than well-ordered and sequential or systematic" (2015: 287–288).

They suggest "approaching drones as techniques of vision and visualization, rather than as techniques of surveillance" (Klauser & Pedrozo, 2015: 287–288). I agree that understanding hobby drone practices as techniques of vision and visualization more readily acknowledges both the kinds of orientational map-reading and explorative way-finding that shape aerial drone play.

In Chapters 4 and 5, I already pointed to Verhoeff's "performative cartography" (2012) which camera drones—particularly contemporary models with GPS connectivity—afford. Recognizing drone practices as performative cartography helps consider both the strategic ordering of location and experimental visual mobilities inherent to drone flying and image-taking. With camera drones as "techniques of vision and visualization," I want to emphasize the "performative" and playful character in those techniques. My active engagement with the plan and model of Earth's surface, the intentional and accidental vertical play above, between, and below is reminiscent of precinematic optical toys. Media scholar Wanda Strauven highlights how "the precinematic observer is playing, interacting with the toy, or – to put it differently – how the eye is depending on the hand" (2011: 154). As mentioned in Chapter 5, my hands maneuver my drone-extended eyes in the sky similar to how I move my head on the ground in unfamiliar terrain. The performative cartography afforded by drones then positions this technique of vision and visualization within the paradigm of "the player mode of the optical toy" as opposed to the "viewer mode of the optical theater" (Strauven, 2011: 155). This understanding leads me to other insights into *how* drones allow users to see: The vertical play of drone pilots equals the virtual play of gamers.

Virtual Play/Vertical Play

Analogies of drone flying and gaming lie at hand given the extremely similar setup for controlling the visual and virtual mobilities via controllers. In the previous chapter, I highlighted how drone users draw from their literacies in gaming to more quickly master the aerial practice.

However, the similarities continue when it comes to the visual representations of vertical play. In her analysis of early YouTube dronecam videos, media scholar Anna Munster is hesitant to describe drone use as "just another form of 'in the world' gaming" (2014: 152). Drawing on the work of digital media artist Simon Penny (2004), she argues that first-person shooter games, for example,

> function not at the level of representation but of enaction, where the body of the gamer is "naturalized" to a training regime of "seek and destroy movements" that work at the level of procedural navigation of the digital games' virtual space. (Munster, 2014: 152)

I agree that drone flying does not quite mediate a "training regime of seek and destroy movements." However, aerial drone play does function at both the level of representation and enaction and may well be understood as "in the world" gaming.

When I recently had the opportunity to play my very first first-person shooter game (Call of Duty), I was immediately struck by how much my gamer gaze reminded me of my drone gaze live-streamed onto the screen and recorded in my drone-logs. Unfamiliar with the virtual environments, my unsystematic and punctual gamer gaze was searching, exploring, and experimenting. The unfamiliar virtual space invited me to just wander around and look at the views, to explore the architectural setting, and to roam the space until the next attack comes. Both the virtual and aerial are what Virilio (1994: 62) calls "event spaces" and what McCosker (2015a: 9) describes as a "relative and relational place that enfolds heterogeneous human action, machine movement, perception, and location in one." The vertical and virtual event spaces show similarities even in the kinds of dialogues I exchange with my co-gamers and co-remote-pilots: "Where are you?" "I am to the left at 300 feet." "Ok, I'll stay at 200." "Did anybody catch that train passing by over there?" "I got it. So awesome." "Nice work." "Watch out for the birds." "Whoa, did you see that?" "That was close." With minor modifications, this conversation I had with two other drone users may occur in a multi-player gaming context. Here, drone flying and gaming further manifest themselves as related in the kind of visual mobility and play they afford. Given the military associations of first-person shooter games and drone use, the examples also illustrate dimensions of visual and mobile "play" inherent to war (Wright, 2008). Dan Burton (2017), CEO and co-founder of DroneBase, even speaks of drones as turning into a "real-world cursor in the sky" in the context of the augmented reality application AirCraft. This drone platform allows users to create virtual geometric formations with the drone in aerial space, which are then visible to other app users (Trent, 2017). AirCraft is an example of how vertical and virtual play is not only similar, but expected to merge into one multi-layered event space.

How Consumers Start to See: Remote Drone-Mindedness

In her research on the Mars rover missions, Vertesi notes how the NASA team learned "to see like a rover" (2015: 7). The same applies to drone users and how many mention seeing like a camera drone as a result of their hobby. Yet, those remote pilots reportedly don't just see like a drone when they engage with the aerial camera, they also start to see like a drone when *not using it*. In my auto-technographic transformation into a drone hobbyist, I have noticed myself developing a "drone-mindedness" in the way I look at familiar and unfamiliar surroundings. Consumer drones belong to optical toys that curate "new modes of circu-lation, communication, production, consumption, and rationalization," demanding and shaping "a new kind of observer-consumer" (Crary, 1990: 14). Similar to what Luvaas (2016, 2019) describes as "cultivating your own style radar" for becoming a street-style blogger, I developed a drone radar or, more closely, a "drone mind" that is attentive to vertical views. Ethan, a drone racer in his thirties, describes this experience thus:

> I feel like [drone flying] widened my perspective significantly. And when-ever I am driving around, I am like thinking, "oh that little gap would be so fun to fly through." You can loop around. Or, like I am used to seeing the mountains from the car, and I would wonder what it is like on top of the hill, but here you can't see that it is all forest, so I think, "I wonder where I am compared to this and that." And with the drone, I

can just go look. That is really cool. And yeah, just sort of driving around or walking around *my brain has this sort of new way of looking at things like a drone pilot for sure.*

With this "new way of looking at things," Ethan speaks to both the unique character of the aerial camera in terms of *what* it conveys and *how* it conveys volumetric spaces by, for example, flying through or looping around. He also mentions how his own positioning within larger geographical contexts becomes more apparent to him ("where I am compared to this and that"). As such, drone-mindedness includes a renewed attention to geographical features, to possibilities for vertical exploration, and to situational relations between oneself, others, and the environment.

This sensibility can seep into everyday routines prompting drone users to wonder about different ways of seeing and moving. As a result, Annie, a drone hobbyist and former jet pilot in her sixties, mentions that the hobby has made her

uniquely curious in a different way about my surroundings. I'm also more vigilant, too. I've always been vigilant, but I'm more vigilant now because I realize that the perspective of my world is not me walking straight ahead. It's also what's happening on all fronts. *I'm finding myself to be more visually cued.*

Drone users have a multitude of such "fronts" accessible to them, opening up additional imaginative mobilities and visual ecologies. Like Annie, I have noticed myself being much "more visually cued" to my surroundings. I wonder what patterns certain intersections and paths create when seen from up above, what I would learn if I flew my quadcopter underneath that bridge, or what hidden waterfall I might discover within the depths of the surrounding forest. A missed opportunity of recording a friend's wedding on a hilltop kept me fantasizing about what amazing aerial images I could have collected throughout the ceremony. Professional drone pilot Maksim summarizes his enhanced visual attention to space in this way:

Sometimes, I just stay still in such places, staring at them and thinking "what is there? What really is there?" It can be absolutely anything – a frozen lake or a forest or an endless field, it doesn't matter. Normally we got used to see everything in one plane, but from the skies, it looks totally different. And only when I fly high and look around, I'm able to find answers to these questions. Thus, for example, on the empty field, you can find mysterious signs. But while you are down on the ground, it's difficult to imagine their existence and, especially, to see them. When you realize all this, you start thinking how many hidden things there are around us. (quoted in Dichtlerova, 2017)

Hence, drone-mindedness means vertical attunement and situational curiosity. With consumer drones, the aerial access and resulting environmental awareness are available to people without the need to engage in general aviation. The flying camera presents itself as a powerful tool for vertical explorations, creative expression, geographical literacy, and imaginative mobilities beyond the more exclusive aerial gazes by air balloons, airplanes, helicopters, satellites, and military drones. The drone gaze mediates auratic visions of remoteness in the here and now. Not only am I extending myself out into vertical space, but the world seems to be extending itself to me, beckoning my drone eyes. Aura appears as an agential dimension of space affecting my relations and desires.

Of course, aerial imagination has a much longer history than that of manned and unmanned aviation. Cosgrove and Fox remind us that such spatial attunements are not exclusively "learned from flying or even from climbing to elevated viewpoints" (2010: 11). Practices of envisioning top-down views surface in, for example, the architectural arrangement of the Neolithic and Chalcolithic proto-city settlement Çatalhöyük (Cosgrove & Fox, 2010: 14). Cosgrove and Fox (2010) highlight how a loose geometrical plan of the village may have well been sketched by a contemporary geographer or captured by an aerial photographer. Similarly, the background of Leonardo da Vinci's famous La Gioconda or Mona Lisa from 1506 illustrates an aerial perspective onto a landscape with mountains and river valleys (Cosgrove & Fox, 2010: 17). Hence, imaginations and mediations of the world as viewed from above significantly precede the real-time perspectives from the air. Nonetheless, actively engaging with the auratic views in vertical play via optical toys has brought such aerial imaginations of my surroundings into my everyday in unprecedented ways. This affordance of consumer drones encourages me to think about what potential geographies and mobilities are in vertical proximity.

Finally, let me briefly mention to what extent "drone-mindedness" varies from McCosker's (2015a, 2015b) application of philosopher Gilles Deleuze's camera consciousness (1986) in the context of drone regulation and activism. Deleuze explains that camera consciousness is not "defined by the movements it is able to follow or make, but by the mental connections it is able to enter into" (1986: 23). Drawing on this concept, McCosker posits that "we think-perceive with and through the drone, with or without direct control over, or even access to, its first person perspectival vision" (2015b: 13). He describes the sensation and awareness engendered by drone camera use as "the system's media-affect" and a "new camera consciousness" (McCosker, 2015b: 9), each delineating what media ecologists would recognize as the medium's bias and effect. Concretely, McCosker argues that the figure of the drone prompts us to think about "the relation as seriously as the object" in technical assemblages (2015b: 4). He then centralizes "the experience of these perceptual systems, our troubled camera consciousness" and its impact "on the scene" (2015b: 7) in, for example, protest-counter-protest activities. My focus on drone-mindedness has alignments with camera consciousness but situates such mental connections in the playful merging of auratic drone visualities and imaginative user mobilities. I am both curious mapreader and casual way-finder with the optical toy affecting not only my recreational practices of visualization, but also vertical visions in passing. In contrast to an "anxious assemblage that fractures vision along with action" (McCosker, 2015b: 12), I understand drone-mindedness as *individual volumetric curiosity*, a quotidian spatial sensitivity enabled by the drone, free from "flat-earth" views (see also Jensen, 2020). Ultimately, my external self-extension into space and its potential for auratic emanation engender an internal attunement to everyday objects, subjects, relations, and environments.

Conclusion

Seeing like a camera drone means seeing vertical and horizontal spaces in ways that have been opened up by ballooning, motorized flight, and satellite imagining. As such, the consumer drone gaze aligns with traditional notions of the aerial gaze as top-down cartographic, ordering, monitoring, and managing perspective. However, drone play also complicates the aerial gaze in *how* and *why* the gaze is mobilized. Drone users allude to how the flying camera allows them to court auratic views, as the extraordinary vision/ appearance/ emanation of remoteness no matter how near or familiar it may be. The personal drone gaze allows users to transcend their immediate space, to sense different ways of relating and situating. This enhanced mobile gaze allows hobbyists to swiftly explore top-down, bottom-up, and mezzanine planes. Consequently, the imagery conveys imposing, centralized, and rational notions of the aerial gaze, but also the self-organizing, tactical, and tactile mechanisms of bottom-up locations of power (Shapiro, 2016). Both map-reading and way-finding above, underneath, and between local geographies belong to the recreational drone gaze. Yet, knowledge capture may remain secondary to aerial exploration and artistic creation. Reminiscent of optical toys and virtual gaming practices, camera drones open up vertical play, driven by performative orientation (map-reading) and multi-dimensional curiosity (way-finding). Hence, approaching camera drones as techniques of vision and visualization beyond surveillance accounts for the playful recreational practices that seek vertical self-empowerment without purposefully seeking aerial power over others.

That said, the mobile and visual affordances of flying cameras remain ambiguous and contradictory. The introduction to the photo-collection *Dronescapes: The New Aerial Photography from Dronestagram* states:

> The drone photography revolution is a game changer, with an ever growing and diverse range of users now having access to this technology and the new perspectives of the world that it offers. Unlike traditional aerial photography, drones do so much more than just going "higher" and "wider". They get closer to, and more immersed in, their subject;

they seek to trace, to follow. In this aim, however, they carry some major contradictions. Like the Internet, they offer unprecedented opportunities for discovery, access and liberation, but also a powerful means of surveillance and destruction. (Karabuda Ecer & Dronestagram, 2017: 11)

Besides discovery, access, and liberation, aerial drone play provides opportunities for enhanced visual attention, situational awareness, and geographical attunement, curated with what I call "drone-mindedness." While the potentials for harm regarding locational privacy and physical safety are undeniable, I remain curious about the extent to which recreational drone flying could open up avenues for not just technological literacy (Preble, 2015) but, moreover, environmental literacy to users beyond the geo and social sciences (Birtchnell & Gibson, 2015). In times when resource exploitation, excessive energy consumption, and global waste and pollution irreversibly damage our everyday vertical and horizontal spaces, to what extent might drone-mindedness help better understand, communicate, and act upon the changes to our Earth's surface? Being visually cued to our geographical surrounding and developing an understanding of our embeddedness within those contemporary human and nonhuman ecologies can be a step toward increasing attention to and action toward such realities.

As geographer Mike Crang remarks, "Images are not something that appears over or against reality, but parts of practices through and which people work to establish realities. […] Technologies of seeing form ways of grasping the world" (1997: 362). Hobby drones can serve as more than tools for individually and collectively creating visual archives of the environmental status quo. Research is needed to see how their uses can mobilize visions and actions toward maintaining and protecting the auratic views they open up. Ultimately, I agree with Jablonowski (2017: 12): The contradiction of drones as both powerful and playful "cannot be one-sidedly solved since both are constitutive parts of the cultural meaning of drones." Some of the rhetoric pointing to consumer drones as predominantly technologies of surveillance and dangerous weapons can be complemented with informed discourse on the aesthetic, creative, and educational value of their auratic visual potentials.

References

Adey, P. (2010a). *Aerial life: Spaces, mobilities, affects.* Wiley-Blackwell.

Adey, P. (2010b). Vertical security in the megacity legibility, mobility and aerial politics. *Theory, Culture & Society, 27,* 51–67.

Adey, P. (2017). *Mobility* (2nd ed.). Routledge.

Adey, P., Whitehead, M., & Williams, A. J. (2011). Introduction: Air-target distance, reach and the politics of verticality. *Theory, Culture & Society, 28,* 173–187.

Benjamin, W. (1963). *Das Kunstwerk im Zeitalter seiner technischen Reproduzierbarkeit.* Suhrkamp.

Benjamin, W. (1968). *Illuminations: Essays and reflections* (H. Arendt, Ed. and H. Zohn, Trans.). Schocken Books.

Birtchnell, T., & Gibson, C. (2015). Less talk more drone: Social research with UAVs. *Journal of Geography in Higher Education, 39,* 182–189.

Boldrick, S. (2007). Reviewing the aerial view. *Arq: Architectural Research Quarterly, 11,* 11–15.

Bolter, J. D., MacIntyre, B., Gandy, M., & Schweitzer, P. (2006). New media and the permanent crisis of aura. *Convergence, 12,* 21–39.

Burton, D. (2017, November 3). AirCraft: Turn your drone into a cursor in the sky. Retrieved December 6, 2018, from DroneBase website: https://blog.dronebase.com/2017/11/03/aircraft-turn-your-drone-into-a-cursor-in-the-sky.

Carey, J. W. (1992). *Communication as culture: Essays on media and society.* Routledge.

Chamayou, G. (2015). *A theory of the drone.* The New Press.

Choi-Fitzpatrick, A., Chavarria, D., Cychosz, E., Dingens, J. P., Duffey, M., Koebel, K., Siriphanh, S., Tulen, M. Y., Watanabe, H., Juskauskas, T., Holland, J., & Almquist, L. (2016). *Up in the air: A global estimate of non-violent drone use 2009–2015.* Retrieved from http://digital.sandiego.edu/gdl2016report/1.

Cosgrove, D., & Fox, W. L. (2010). *Photography and flight.* Reaktion Books.

Crang, M. (1997). Picturing practices: Research through the tourist gaze. *Progress in Human Geography, 21,* 359–373.

Crary, J. (1990). *Techniques of the observer: On vision and modernity in the nineteenth century.* MIT Press.

Cresswell, T., & Dixon, D. (2002). *Engaging film: Geographies of mobility and identity.* Rowman & Littlefield.

Cwerner, S., Kesselring, S., & Urry, J. (2009). *Aeromobilities.* Routledge.

Deleuze, G. (1986). *Cinema 1: The movement-image*. University of Minnesota Press.

Dichtlerova, V. (2017, February 2). Interview with Maksim Tarasov, Dronestagram's talented drone pilot. Retrieved October 31, 2018, from Dronestagram Blog website: http://www.dronestagr.am/blog/interview-maksim-tarasov/.

Dupin, E. (2017). Foreword. In *Dronescapes: The new aerial photography from Dronestagram*. Thames & Hudson.

Fish, A. (2020). Drones. In P. Vannini (Ed.), *The Routledge international handbook of ethnographic film and video* (pp. 247–255). Routledge.

Graham, S. (2010). *Cities under siege: The new military urbanism*. Verso.

Graham, S. (2016). *Vertical: The city from satellites to bunkers*. Verso.

Haffner, J. (2013). *The view from above: The science of social space*. MIT Press.

Hildebrand, J. M. (2018). Modal media: Connecting media ecology and mobilities research. *Media, Culture and Society, 40*, 348–364.

Ingold, T. (2000). *The perception of the environment: Essays on livelihood, dwelling and skill*. Routledge.

Jablonowski, M. (2017). Dronie citizenship? In A. Kuntsman (Ed.), *Selfie citizenship* (pp. 97–106). Palgrave Macmillan.

Jarret, G. (2016, January 29). #6—Top pilot interview—Ookpik. Retrieved July 7, 2020, from Dronestagram Blog website: http://www.dronestagr.am/blog/6-top-pilot-interview-ookpik/.

Jensen, O. B. (2020). Thinking with the drone: Visual lessons in aerial and volumetric thinking. *Visual Studies, 35*(5), 417–418.

Kaplan, C. (2006). Mobility and war: The cosmic view of US 'air power'. *Environment and Planning A, 38*, 395–407.

Kaplan, C. (2014). The balloon prospect: Aerostatic observation and the emergence of militarised aeromobility. In P. Adey, M. Whitehead, & A. Williams (Eds.), *From above: War, violence, and verticality* (pp. 19–40). Oxford University Press.

Kaplan, C. (2017). *Aerial aftermaths: Wartime from above*. Duke University Press.

Kaplan, C., & Miller, A. (2019). Drones as "atmospheric policing": From US border enforcement to the LAPD. *Public Culture, 31*, 419–445.

Karabuda Ecer, A., & Dronestagram. (2017). *Dronescapes: The new aerial photography from Dronestagram*. Thames & Hudson.

Klauser, F., & Pedrozo, S. (2015). Power and space in the Drone age: A literature review and politico-geographical research agenda. *Geographica Helvetica, 70*, 285–293.

Lin, W. (2017). Sky watching: Vertical surveillance in civil aviation. *Environment and Planning D: Society and Space, 35*, 399–417.

Luvaas, B. (2016). Urban fieldnotes: An auto-ethnography of street style blogging. In H. Jenss (Ed.), *Fashion studies: Research methods, sites and practices* (pp. 83–100). Bloomsbury Academic.

Luvaas, B. (2019). Unbecoming: The aftereffects of autoethnography. *Ethnography, 20*, 245–262.

McCormack, D. P. (2018). *Atmospheric things: On the allure of elemental envelopment.* Duke University Press.

McCosker, A. (2015a). Drone media: Unruly systems, radical empiricism and camera consciousness. *Culture Machine, 16*. Retrieved from https://www.culturemachine.net/index.php/cm/article/view/591.

McCosker, A. (2015b). Drone vision, zones of protest and the new cinema: Drone vision, zones of protest, and the new camera consciousness. *Media Fields Journal: Critical Explorations in Media and Space, 9*, 1–14.

Munster, A. (2014). Transmateriality: Toward an energetics of signal in contemporary mediatic assemblages. *Cultural Studies Review, 20*, 150–167.

Penny, S. (2004). Representation, enaction, and the ethics of simulation. Retrieved December 6, 2018, from Electronic Book Review website: http://electronicbookreview.com/essay/representation-enaction-and-the-ethics-of-simulation/.

Preble, B. C. (2015). A case for drones. *Technology and Engineering Teacher, 74*, 24–29.

Review of Airopaidia. (1787). In *The English Review, or, an abstract of English and foreign literature* (pp. 428–433). J. Murray.

Scott, A. O. (2015, December 10). The art of flying in the movies. Retrieved December 6, 2018, from New York Times website: https://www.nytimes.com/2015/12/13/magazine/the-art-of-flying-in-the-movies.html.

Shapiro, A. (2016). The Mezzanine. *Space and Culture, 19*, 292–307.

Strauven, W. (2011). The observer's dilemma: To touch or not to touch. In E. Huhtamo & J. Parikka (Eds.), *Media archaeology: Approaches, applications, and implications* (pp. 148–165). University of California Press.

Trent, S. (2017). Minecraft for your drone. Retrieved December 6, 2018, from YouTube: https://www.youtube.com/watch?v=ap3O5ZrBoGA.

Urry, J. (2007). *Mobilities.* Polity.

Urry, J. (2009). Aeromobilities and the global. In S. Cwerner, S. Kesselring, & J. Urry (Eds.), *Aeromobilities* (pp. 25–38). Routledge.

Verhoeff, N. (2012). *Mobile screens: The visual regime of navigation.* Amsterdam University Press.

Vertesi, J. (2015). *Seeing like a rover: How robots, teams, and images craft knowledge of Mars*. University of Chicago Press.

Virilio, P. (1994). *The vision machine* (J. Rose, Trans.). Indiana University Press.

Waghorn, N. J. (2016). Watching the watchmen: Resisting drones and the "protester panopticon". *Geographica Helvetica, 71*, 99–108.

Wall, T., & Monahan, T. (2011). Surveillance and violence from afar: The politics of drones and liminal security-scapes. *Theoretical Criminology, 15*, 239–254.

Weigert, H. W. (1944). Asia through Haushofer's glasses. In H. W. Weigert, V. Stefansson, & R. E. Harrison (Eds.), *Compass of the world: A symposium on political geography* (pp. 395–407). GG Harrap.

Wright, E. (2008). *Generation kill: Devil Dogs, Ice Man, Captain America, and the new face of American war*. G.P. Putnam's Sons.

7

Dancing with My Drone

Introduction

Meet Kelly Swanson, a young "drone mom." In a 45-second clip created by Betabrand from September 2016,[1] Kelly tells the story of how she got Clippy, her DJI Phantom drone, from the fictional "San Francisco Drone Rescue Society":

> So, I kind of knew that I wanted a drone, but I didn't know if I was going to have time in my schedule. Since getting her, it's been the best thing that has happened. I got Clippy about six months ago. We got her from the shelter. It took her a couple of weeks to get back in shape and just to get her charged right. She came house-trained, which was nice. She is really great with kids. We go to the park. She loves playing fetch. My husband said, "No drones in bed." But that lasted about a week. Now I see them cuddling all the time together. I can't speak highly enough of the San Francisco Drone Rescue Society. You think that you

---

[1] Betabrand is a San Francisco-based online clothing company. Its YouTube channel provides "an array of clothing-centric humor, as inspired by the journeys of our Model Citizens" (Betabrand, 2016).

© The Author(s), under exclusive license to Springer Nature Singapore Pte Ltd. 2021
J. M. Hildebrand, *Aerial Play*, Geographies of Media, https://doi.org/10.1007/978-981-16-2195-6_7

are making a difference in a drone's life, but really Clippy has changed my life. (Betabrand, 2016)

The short video shows Kelly in a chair softly stroking the DJI Phantom drone in her lap. Intersected are clips of her "walking" the flying drone through the streets of San Francisco on a leash, picking up "drone poo" (interestingly: a cell phone) behind the flying camera, and playing fetch in a park. As such, the parody of the camera drone and its users draws on discourses of animal rescue and pet ownership. The video has gone viral in online drone communities, liked and shared thousands of times. Apart from parodying drone ownership and care, the clip addresses two notions of user-drone interactions. First, the depictions of the drone on a leash and playing fetch with the owner allude to the interconnected mobilities between flying device and remote pilot, discussed in Chapter 5. Second, the narrative of the drone as life-changing companion speaks to the affective ties between human and medium. Such user-drone interactions and associations are in the center of this chapter.

Adopting the concept of *mobile companionship*, I look into the kind of human-machine relations that surface in aerial drone play. As touched upon in the previous chapters, the consumer drone holds a unique position as a mobile medium at the intersection of locative interfaces such as smartphones (Frith, 2015) and autonomous robotic systems (Suchman, 2006). McCosker points out,

> The drone's motility, its autonomous vertical and lateral movement differentiates it from the mobile camera as it generates distributed modes of vision across a number of bodies, devices, and platforms, not merely as spectacle, but as a new mode of relational experience. (2015: 2)

This "new mode of relational experience" is not limited to "distributed modes of vision" but includes affective ways of relating toward the technology itself. As sociologist and clinical psychologist Sherry Turkle argues in *The Inner History of Devices*, "Technology serves as a Rorschach over a lifetime, a projective screen for our changing and emotionally charged commitments" (2008: 13).[2] In this spirit, I ask, how do drones "affect our relationships and sensibilities" (Turkle, 2008: 3)? Concretely, I am interested in how subjective ways of relating unfold in recreational drone flying and image-taking.

While I continue to employ the frameworks of media ecology, mobilities research, and mobile communication, I also turn to science and technology studies (STS), feminist theory, and media psychology, particularly by Turkle (2005, 2007, 2008, 2012), anthropologist Lucy Suchman (1987, 2005, 2006), literary critic N. Katherine Hayles (2005), technology theorist Donna Haraway (1997), and feminist physicist Karen Barad (2003, 2007) to describe the relational dynamics at play. Shifting attention to affective, subjective, and relational phenomena in the context of hobby drones, this chapter seeks to expand consumer drone scholarship that focuses on the applied and aesthetic qualities of the flying camera. I consider drones as mobile companions that "[reach] out to us to form active partnerships" (Turkle, 2007: 308) and evocative objects "underscoring the inseparability of thought and feeling in our relationship to things" (Turkle, 2007: 5). This chapter also continues to centralize the embodied/disembodied engagements with drones in day-to-day uses, as satirized with Kelly and Clippy.

A closer look at the theoretical backdrop for this discussion follows, before I turn to specific cases of user-drone companionships. I first consider the affective ways in which users (including myself) *address* the technology. Second, I shed light onto the ways users *describe* the relational roles and dynamics between them and their drones. In the third section, I focus on the ways users *interact* and *intra-act* with their geomedia, paying special attention to the sophisticated autonomous flight functions. Those features allow users to take their hands off the remote control and engage the device in a kind of robotic partner dance, negotiating who/what leads and who/what follows. I conclude with reflections on how such emerging mobile companionships between humans and robotic technologies may shape our affective ways of relating to objects, space, and each other.

---

[2] "Rorschach" stands for a psychological test, which purports to examine personality characteristics and emotional functioning based on inkblot interpretations.

Theory: Human-Medium Relationships

Understanding media as extensions of human faculties and environments that are shaped by us and shape us back, media ecologists point to formative dynamics between humans and technologies. Mobilities research similarly provides rich analyses into human-machine hybrids and relations, such as the driver-car and associated automotive emotions (Dant, 2004; Sheller, 2004). In particular, I follow Spinney who studies affect broadly as "emotions, sensations, atmospheres, feelings [that] arise out of relational encounters between object, spaces and people" (2015: 235). Mobile communication research echoes those interests of media ecology and mobilities research with inquiries into locative media, for example, and the "ongoing relationship between social bodies, technology, and site-specificity" (Farman, 2011: 5). Besides those resources, I look to STS and feminist scholarship for frameworks to describe the relational and affective dynamics at play with personal drones as unique visual, mobile, and moderately robotic technology that has entered everyday spaces.

One key concept is Haraway's "figuration" (1997), which I employ to discuss how users address, describe, and interact/intra-act with the flying camera in a mobile companionship. In a footnote, Haraway explains,

> to 'figure' actions and entities nonanthropomorphically and nonreductively is a fundamental theoretical, moral and political problem. Practices of figuration and narration are much more than literary decoration. Kinds of membership and kinds of liveliness – kinship in short – are the issues for all of us. (1997: 284)

The notion of figuration can help highlight the biases and effects—as media ecologists would say—of nonhuman entities in "knowledge-making and worldbuilding encounters" (Haraway, 1997: 284). With this model, I look beyond a "narrow instrumentalism" (Suchman, 2011: 137) in aerial drone play and, like Suchman (2006, 2015), look into the distributed configurations between persons and machines. At the center of this chapter are the "inner life" (Turkle, 2008) and personal meanings in formation in such user-drone dynamics.

Similarly relevant is Barad's use of "entanglement" (2007). This framework recognizes entities as *effects of performative relations*, as arising "from the material-discursive practices through which boundaries and associated entities are made" (Law, 2004; Suchman, 2011: 121). Barad's (2003, 2007) companion term "intra-action" equally denotes the distributed agencies at play in subject-object entanglements. She explains that in contrast to interaction which describes separate entities, the term *intra-action* speaks to ontologically inseparable agential "relations without preexisting relata. [...] Relata-within-phenomena emerge through specific intra-actions" (Barad, 2003: 815). In other words, such feminist scholarship approaches "the robot not as an isolated unit but rather as part of an ecological whole that includes the humans with which it interacts" (Hayles, 2005: 136). This approach resonates with the constructivist approaches of media ecology and mobilities research, which address human-technology relationships as embedded in and emerging out of complex ecologies. Of special interest in this chapter are the "affective entanglements" (Myers, 2012) and user-drone figurations, which I make legible as mobile companionships. Here, I use "mobile" again in the comprehensive sense that includes corporeal, physical, virtual, communicative, and affective movements within and between humans, technologies, and spaces. This conception of mobility also includes notions of "liveliness as relational, involving entanglements of the organic and inorganic" (Stacey & Suchman, 2012: 23).

Central to those related frameworks is the sense that subjects and objects are in formation and in motion with each other. Latour clarifies this meaning of figuration and entanglement with this example:

> You are different with a gun in your hand; the gun is different with you holding it. You are another subject because you hold the gun; the gun is another object because it has entered into a relationship with you. The gun is no longer the gun-in-the-armory or the gun-in-the-drawer or the gun-in-the-pocket, but the gun-in-your-hand.... If we study the gun and the citizen [together] ... we realize that neither subject nor object ... is fixed. When the [two] are articulated ... they become "someone/something" else. (1999: 179–180)

What do personal drones and drone persons become as they converge, entangle, and configure? This question gains relevance as consumer drones are not only interactive toys that "exercise intellect" but "interactive robotic creatures" that "exercise the emotions" (Turkle, 2005: 228), as I will argue. Similar to the computational objects Turkle analyzes in *The Second Self*, personal drones are "relational artifacts" that exercise foremost vision, but also intellect and emotion, and invite "people to project animation, life, and personality onto them" (2005: 228) similar to drone mom Kelly. Turkle further explains that "Relational artifacts ask their users to see them not as tools but as companions, as subjects in their own right" (2005: 289). As I will show, recreational drone practices seem to achieve such relationships with drone enthusiasts celebrating their aerial cameras as "true companions" (Karabuda Ecer & Dronestagram, 2017: 17). In this context, I am also interested in what sociologist Deborah Lupton (1996: 98) calls the "psychotopography" of human-drone relationships, meaning "the way that humans think [of], feel [toward], and experience" their flying cameras as subjects.

Employing STS frameworks for the study of user-drone entanglements, my ethnographic work aligns with Fish's (2021) research on conservation drones. Explicating a "crash theory," he describes "the enfoldment of the technological, social, economic and ecological" when drones fly, and "the points of friction in the convergence of nature and culture" when they crash (Fish, 2021: 444). He concludes that "[c]onservation drones are apparatuses of multispecies and computational reworlding" (Fish, 2021, 445). With similar attention to intra-actions, entanglements, and processes of reworlding at the intersections of human, machine, and space, I apply such STS thinking in the context of recreational drone use.

By drawing on the lenses of figuration and affective entanglement, my goal is to further complicate exclusively aviation-centric and militaristic associations with the ambiguous hobby drone. While the consumer drone signifies a "military-inflected rationalization of everyday life" (Andrejevic, 2016: 21), additional, diverging dimensions exist in how users adopt and relate to the aerial medium. Beyond its promises and perils as "hyperefficient information technology" (Andrejevic, 2016: 22), aerial drone play points to compelling affective entanglements that expand notions of the "'droning' of interactivity" with triggered alarms, response protocols, and the "subtraction of the human element from the decision loop" (Andrejevic, 2016: 23–24). I follow Adey in making "the drone visible differently, and to begin to reorder, unsettle and reposition the drone within other relations, hierarchies, and aesthetic sensibilities" (2016: 326). Moving away from associations of drones as "archaic monsters of vision" (Dorrian, 2014), "winged fusion of human beasts and machine" (Crandall, 2014), and "a mythical creature not unlike a unicorn or a zombie" (Rothstein, 2015: xvi), I ground the flying camera within performative figurations and affective entanglements as mobile companion in everyday spaces.

Drone Relationalities: Mobile Companionship

The following discussion of user-drone entanglements and drone-user figurations is driven by three questions: How do hobby pilots address the aerial technology? How do they describe their relationship with the medium? And how do they interact with the flying sensor that marks those ways of being together as a companionship? Along with considerations of media as human extensions and human-machine hybrids from media ecology and mobilities research, the frameworks of affective entanglement and mobile figuration build the basis for this qualitative exploration into user-drone relations.

Addressing the Drone: Affective Relationships with a Relational Artifact

During a summer break, I had the opportunity to give my family a drone demonstration for the first time. As I fly Jay above our backyard and house in the quaint Bavarian village, my family members try to identify personal landmarks ("my window," "the stairs to our basement," "the church") in the live-stream video on my smartphone screen (see Chapter 6). I am caught by surprise when my mother suddenly asks: "So what is her name?" "*Her*?" I respond. How did she know it had a name and why did she assume that Jay was female? "Well, it's 'die Drohne,' isn't it?" my sister argues. The gendered article for the German translation paves the way for gender assumptions of a technology that only shows very limited humanoid features. Without me confirming the technological gender of Jay, my mother continues to refer to the quad-copter as female: "Don't lose her," she cautions me when I fly the device up to 200 feet. Similarly, as I carefully land the drone in our driveway, she applauds the machine: "Look how well she behaves. She is a good drone." According to my mother, the drone is thus not only female but also *well-behaved*.

This statement underlines Vertesi's observations during her research on the Mars rovers. She confirms that "the pronoun 'she' is associated with the notion of agency: the rover is, and always has been something that actually *does something*" (2015: 188). Similarly, Jay is referred to as an agent, one that *does something well*. My sister seems to be less sure of the technology's gender (and keeps switching between she, he, and it), but certain of its rightful agency when she tells me to let go of the command. "Let it return home by *itself*!" As I respect my sister's wish and the drone descends "by itself," she exclaims: "It's coming home. It says hello." Welcome back Jay, you good drone.

In the conversations with drone hobbyists and experts, similar anec-dotes about drone names, personalities, and associations come up. Helena, a hobbyist in her sixties, tells me this story about a near-fly-away which led her to name the device:

> I have one moment which I would call a "fly away" except it wasn't. It was a wind storm. [...] I've only had her for a month. So, I shot her into the air next to this beautiful lighthouse and this storm just blows in, and I mean *it blows in*. And it sweeps her off into the water away... and I'm like, "Oh my gosh," and I am running to go see her because she had flown away so fast. So, I am running and I find her and I am pulling her back. It shot up that battery in five minutes in that wind. But I got her down. So that was very... again, this is why I am afraid of wind. [laughs] She got her name after that. She is now Dorothy.

The incident leads Helena to make a special connection to her new drone, which she acknowledges in the choice of name. Like Dorothy, the fictional character who is swept away by a hurricane and taken to the world of the *Wizard of Oz*, so Dorothy the drone is caught by a wind gust, but rescued by Helena. Helena, Dorothy the drone, Dorothy the fictional character, and the near-fly-away get affectively entangled in this human-machine figuration. Helena inscribes a character into the materialized figuration that is the drone and charges the device with what Suchman describes as "associations stretching across diverse realms of meaning and practice" (2006: 227). The affective entanglement between Helena and Dorothy is further manifested when the drone hobbyist tells me that now she gets nervous when the drone is further away while still in line of sight: "It was a little scarier having her go two blocks away. I tend to keep [my drones] pretty close." Here, Helena's words not only echo my mother's concern about "losing her," but are more generally reminiscent of guardians speaking of their children and pets.

Such narratives point to Turkle's "Eliza effect," an impulse for treating objects "as though they were people" (2005: 287), or pets if I may add. She bases this "novel and evocative relationship between the living and the inanimate" (Turkle, 2005: 287) on reactive and interactive computers. This observation translates well to the user-drone relationships I learn about. Emanuel, a drone enthusiast in his fifties, describes his own affective entanglement with his drone thus: "It's my baby up there. [...] I would be hurt if something happened to it." As his "baby up there," the drone signifies an aerial extension of himself, something that is close and dear to him, and something that needs protection (potentially via insurance) and care. In the same vein, I have surprised myself affectionately greeting Jay as he descends toward me with "Hello, my little one." Turkle points out that next to treating things like people, we "project our feelings onto objects" (2005: 287). Philosopher Elizabeth Grosz (1994: 80) argues that in those moments of prolonged and intensified engagements with technology, "the object ceases to remain an object and becomes a medium, a vehicle for impressions and expressions." In its figurations with humans, a technology's medial character takes effect. Some of the medium's messages (McLuhan, 1964) within subject-object-ecologies become legible.

Despite the very limited humanoid features of contemporary drone models (imagine the camera lens as eye, the propellers as arms, the chassis as body), clear alignments exist between how eleven-year-old Fara recalls her play with humanoid MIT robot Cog, and how drone users refer to their aerial companions. Quoted in Turkle (2005), Fara explains "it's something that's part of you, you know, something you love, kind of like another person, like a baby." Hence, it does not take human-like features, movements, or reactions of machines to animate such and similar relational entanglements. Drone users, too, shift from what Turkle calls "projection onto an object to engagement with a subject" (2005: 293). Those engagements may be complicated by the fact that the drone is neither clearly male nor female, neither human baby nor pet. Nevertheless, there seem to be "good" and "bad" drone behaviors and personalities, such as "good" autonomous return-to-home maneuvers or "naughty drone" occurrences (according to Henry, a drone user in his sixties), when commands are not followed reliably. That many of those figurations evolve subconsciously, likely fed by previous affective entan-glements (such as Helena and the Dorothy character), surfaces when I eventually find myself navigating Jay in front of friends and fondly exclaiming: "He is such a good boy today!" My surprising figuration with Jay as an ultimately genderfluid pet (not to say, a flying baby shark) that accompanies me on weekends in the park and joins me on travels echoes the ways other pilots *describe* their user-drone relations.

Describing the Drone: My Friend, Co-writer, and Witness

"Let's go for a flight," I hear myself say to Jay in a drone-log, affirming the owner-pet relationship *we* have developed. I write "we" to recognize the flow of agency circulating between Jay and I during each session. Other drone users also point to such collaborative processes: Maksim, an award-winning aerial photographer, for example, describes the relationship to his drone thus: "The drone became more than just a device for me, it became my friend and 'co-writer' for my stories. Wherever I'm going it's always with me" (quoted in Dichtlerova, 2017). Maksim acknowledges the machine as a collaborator, contributor, even as a friend and steady companion. Diego, too, admits that he takes his Phantom "pretty much wherever I can take it." As photographers, Maksim and Diego may recognize how, according to mobility scholar Jonas Larsen, photography "does not reflect geographies so much as it produces them, *new* bodies and 'ways of being together' are constantly produced when camera action begins" (2006: 253). Moreover, Maksim and Diego's descriptions of a mobile companionship, even creative co-authorship, also speak to the "intimate relationship between the production of space and the bodies inhabiting those space" (Farman, 2011: 4) afforded by mobile interfaces. The personal drone is a unique mobile medium that opens up innovative ways for producing and inhabiting space, which motivate Maksim and Diego to seek drone companionship "wherever" they can.

Beyond the exploration of aerial space and the co-writing of visual stories, there seems to be another affective dimension at play. Several interviewees point out how relaxing, meditative, and stress releasing their drone flying and image-taking can feel. Diego, for example, tells me that "It is just so relaxing for me. Seeing [a sunrise or sunset] and seeing what I am doing [with the drone]" (Fig. 7.1).

Just as Diego uses drone flights to "release [his] stress," Terrence, a drone hobbyist in his forties, confirms, "It's like a good… release for me. Especially because I work maybe like 80 hours a week sometimes." He

Fig. 7.1 Florida beach sunrise (taken with DJI Mavic Pro Platinum drone "Jay")

tries to squeeze in at least an hour of flight on his days off. The reflective pause before choosing the word "release" and the reported effort to integrate at least some drone time indicate that the practice is more than a time-filler. The way Terrence describes his drone use is reminiscent of how one may speak of trying to exercise and make it to that yoga class once a week for personal well-being. To him, drone time means downtime. Similarly, I am drawn to the pet-metaphor parodied with Kelly and Clippy, considering how pets and tending to them can contribute to release and relaxation. Yet, how is the careful attention to physical-material, digital-intangible, and socio-spatial formations *on the fly* compatible with experiences of relaxation and release? McLuhan seems to provide an explanation for this phenomenon:

> As the age of information demands the simultaneous use of all our faculties, we discover that we are most at leisure when we are most involved, very much as with the artists in all ages. (1964: 301)

Aerial drone play appears to confirm this claim by affording users to be "most at leisure" while "most involved."

Experiencing drone flight as a release is not limited to consumer drones used for aerial photography and videography. Maggie, an FPV freestyle drone racer in her twenties, corroborates the description of drones as a means for release. While she admits that racing quads can be "a little bit nerve-wrecking," she tells me,

> When it's nice [outside], you try to get as much flying in as life permits. Just because it's a release. It's like when you go running, how you get that really calm feeling.

Notions of self-care resonate in those accounts, raising the question: Can drones be "nurturant technologies" (Turkle, 2005: 296)? Given the military background and common perception of drones as invasive surveillance devices, this angle seems somewhat provocative. However, in how users describe their drones and practices, the flying camera can reconfigure not only human vision but also thought and feeling. As Turkle notes, "*Objects are able to catalyze self-creation*" (2007: 9). Indeed, aerial drone play can catalyze forms of self-creation reminiscent of other forms of self-care such as exercise, meditation, or tending to a pet.

Moreover, the drone's aerial mobility and visual capacities add another, spatial dimension to this human-machine figuration. Annie, a drone hobbyist in her sixties, explains how her drone filled a gap in her life after she separated from her husband. According to her, the drone became "a witness":

> I wanted to be a witness to my own life. That's kind of like when I got married. [...] I got married because I wanted a witness to my life [...]. I just don't want to be by myself and with him being out of the picture for so long now, I just missed that and at least with the drone I've got a witness. I can have another witness to my life. I can videotape what I'm doing and take pictures. That kind of scratches the itch, if that makes sense.

The camera drone can be a witness to her life by recording her spatial whereabouts, contextualizing her travels, journeys, and visits in the widest sense. In the context of his mobile interface theory, Farman (2011: 17) explains:

> Spatial relationships have always determined the way we understand ourselves, our place in the larger context, and the cultural meanings infused into gestures, objects, and sign systems. Spatial proximity and how we locate ourselves in space affects every aspect of the cultural objects we create and interact with.

In Annie's case, the drone assists her in understanding herself and her place. As a witness to her life, the drone helps her keep a record of how she "locates [herself] in space." Here, drone technology aligns with GPS maps that enable "the user to recognize him/herself as 'located' – that is, to see him/herself as part of a dynamic geographical inter-face" (Parks, 2001: 213). However, while satellites as witnesses (Parks, 2005) remain comparatively invisible and inaccessible to non-specialists, consumer drones are relational objects that we can control and look toward as they look back at us. As artist Paul Klee fittingly notes: "Now objects perceive me" (quoted in Virilio, 1994: 59). This statement is highly applicable to camera drones as sophisticated "vision machines" (Virilio, 1994). Studying the reverse shots of the flying camera unto humans, also known as "dronies," Munster is right to point out how

> the 'first person' viewpoint [of dronecams] does not come from a person at all but offers us a hovering, probing perspective on the human instead, reminding us that this is indeed a drone, a 'personless' flying object. (2014: 152)

Nonetheless, Annie's description of the drone as a witness to her life gives an affective, relational, if not nurturant, quality to the "probing perspective" of the "personless" flying object. The relational practice of capturing dronies speaks to consumer drones as technologies of the self—the spatial self. Here, I follow Parks in her analysis of GPS not as "technology of military strategy but rather as a technology of the self" that can articulate personal positionality and mobility (2001: 211). More than in selfies, the geographical context is central in dronies, producing identity-forming figurations of how a body inhabits space. Descriptions of personal-drone and drone-person entanglements insinuate senses of co-authorship and companionship contributing to self-care and identification. The agential flow between consumer drones and their users sheds light onto additional affective dimensions in this human-machine relationship, which I discuss in how users *interact* and *intra-act* with their aerial device.

Inter/Intra-Acting with the Drone: Dancing with My Drone

Interacting with my drone can feel like dancing. Usually, I set the agenda by controlling the small quadcopter and its camera. Yet, Jay's Intelligent Flight Modes and reactive sensors allow me to occasionally hand over some control to the machine. With sophisticated functions such as Follow Me or Active Track, I let go of the remote control. Then the dancing begins. Jay tells me when to "GO," and my dancing body will show Jay's small mechanical body where to follow. Ideally, our bodies, paces, and rhythms are in sync and our signals are clear. Jay feels like an interactive medium with which not only I influence the mediated experience, but together we co-create embodied movement through space and "generate a visible register of that movement" not unlike Parks' (2001: 212) play with the GPS receiver. This experience goes further than what some would describe as "place choreographies" or "place ballets" (Seamon, 1980), meaning "creative, intricate and interactive 'dances'" (Moores, 2012: 54) of humans rhythmically moving through space and thus sensing and making place. Unlike other dances of bodies, things, and space (Thrift, 2009), the drone and human are uniquely configured, ideally synched up to attempt and create mutual rhythmic patterns, fostering a strong sense of not only place but also human-machine relations.

Just as Vertesi detects "members' shifting and dual sense of robotic agency [...] produced at the interface of the human and the machine" (2015: 190), the interviews with hobbyists and my auto-technographic partner dances with Jay point to shifting senses of agency between drone and user. This kind of "agential gerrymandering" (Vertesi, 2015: 189) applies to not only the playful Intelligent Flight functions that concern drone dancer and dancing drone, but also the sense-and-avoid functions in effect between the drone and its environment. In the context of the Mars rovers, Vertesi explains,

> Team members [...] engage in a kind of *agential gerrymandering*, linguistically drawing and redrawing the boundaries between human and machine. On the one hand, the machine is an expression of the team's actions and interactions; on the other hand, they have personalities and agency all their own. The team signals this tension by alternating between "we" and "she." (2015: 189)

In the same spirit, drone users like myself tend to switch between "she/he/it" and "I." The blurry boundaries between who and what flies appear in many of my drone-logs that start with statements such as: "I am connected to sixteen satellites, I am 36 feet high and 72 feet away from where I'm standing." The messy negotiations occurring in aerial drone play are not only semantic, as in this case, but also embodied. The recreational human-drone interactions encompass alternations between when to lead and when to follow, when to act and when to pause. I will address those questions in the following section about user-drone *interactions*. Here, the focus is on human-machine entanglements as the subject and object are *both oriented toward their environment*. I then turn to user-drone *intra-actions*, meaning entanglements of subject and object *oriented toward each other*.

User-Drone Interactions

Terrence tells me how impressed he is with contemporary drone models that feature steady and stable flight maneuvers, that automatically sense and avoid obstacles in their flight path, and will "return home" if prompted by the user or other circumstances like a low battery. The hobbyist points out to me:

> He's like a bird up there that does what you want it to do. The thing is, the autonomous features that these things come with just blow your mind. They'd be just steady, they'll follow you, they'll go where you want it to go [chuckles]. It's amazing.

The sensor-equipped "birds" ("he," "they," "it") come with Intelligent Flight agencies that can leave the human "pilot" completely passive during certain operations. I have this conversation with Thomas, a drone user in his fifties, who tells me how he uses the Focus Point feature on his camera drone:

> *Julia*: Okay, you're just letting it fly and… what do you do when it's flying?
> *Thomas*: You could choose a focus point like this tower. I do it with water towers down at the beach. You put a mark on it and then choose the height of the tower and then you program the course to go around it. The viewpoints will tell it where to go, but you also tell it where to aim the camera, so it's aiming at the water tower the whole time.
> *Julia*: While it is doing that, what are *you* doing?
> *Thomas*: Recording. Nothing, watching. I'm watching it, and it's recording the whole thing.

The drone operates on auto-pilot while Thomas is on stand-by until the maneuver is over. His qualifying of who and what is actually "recording" and what he is doing ("nothing," "watching it") alludes to the messy agential figurations that the capable aerial sensor affords. Handling the mobile medium can mean *handing over* agency and mobility altogether. The hobby *pilot* may be not only spatially *remote* but temporarily *removed* from the action.

Interestingly, it is this passivity and doing "nothing" that several of my interviewees recommend to me for safer aerial drone play. While the drone "doing what *you want* it to do" may offer an "amazing" flight experience, letting it do what she/he/it *wants to do* is suggested to me as more responsible pilot behavior. It seems as if agential responsibility is shared with the drone. For one, this point is conveyed in how the Mavic Pro drone will tangibly *notify* me of harm or danger. If one of the sensors notices an obstacle in the flight path, the remote control starts vibrating and beeping. The DJI drone thus palpably alerts me to find an alternative path. Another illustrative example for drone agential responsibilities comes from Bill, a hobbyist in his forties, who tells me that he sometimes has limited knowledge of flight restrictions:

> I don't think [my drone] will fly up if I'm in a restrictive place. I think the safeties are on on mine. It'd stop me from doing anything silly. [...] I assume mine won't [take off] if I'm too close to the Air Force base.

Bill relies on the drone medium to prevent take-off if flight restrictions apply. With the drone as seemingly responsible and *informed* (due to software updates) agent, Bill takes on the role of a co-pilot which the drone will keep from "doing anything silly." Yet, some uncertainty is conveyed in how the hobbyist "thinks" and "assumes" the safeties are automatically on, and the machine will respect local regulations on his behalf.

Since drone apps do not account for and act on all potential drone rules and restrictions, there are significant risks with drone users shifting such responsibilities to the medium. For better or worse, the example also illuminates the extent to which the aerial camera is not just seen as a mobile companion but dependable co-pilot and partner. Less focused on the medium's capacity to follow regulatory guidelines and more focused on its flight functions, Henry, a hobbyist in his sixties, explains that when he switched to a more recent drone model with GPS and sensing capabilities, he

> just felt like I could depend on it. I could trust the technology, and I didn't have to be scared I was going to crash the drone at any second. That transformation was pretty instantaneous from fear to trust.

Such trust in this human-drone mobile partnership is also conveyed in how Thomas affirms that "if it goes out of range, it comes right back. [...] There is no harm." According to those accounts, there is no need to be scared of crashing under normal conditions, and there is no need to worry about harm when minding typical drone ecologies. Similar to the kind of trust invested in computer technology more generally, the drone is described as a trustworthy companion that will come right back.

Moreover, Bill suggests to me that the drone's functions may be more dependable than my own actions and judgments. When I was still a drone novice with Jay as capable quadcopter, Bill assures me, "If you let go of the control, pretty much you're pretty safe. When you're in trouble, stop pushing, stop touching things and it takes a care of itself." Because of the Mavic's advanced flight functions, which will make it return home and avoid obstacles, I seem like the less dependable factor in this human-machine figuration. Simon, a hobbyist in his twenties, confirms that the object-avoidance system in his DJI drone has "saved me in the past." As such, the drone can make up for human error and can "save" the potent user-drone entanglements. Similarly, Georgine, a drone user in her sixties, suggests to me that I should "just let it stay put" in case I panic:

> With the joysticks, if you're not used to them, it's easy to panic and say, "Oh my gosh, I wanted to go this way and this way." Just keep it in place and think about it for a second. There's no need to panic unless you are low on battery or something like that. If you get lost with it or anything, just press the home button and it'll come right back. There's no need to start tweaking the joysticks around every which direction in a panic. You

just let it stay put, figure it out, figure out where it is, and then bring it in.

Because the GPS-connected medium is reliable, I can keep calm and drone on when ready.

Without actively choosing to do so, this is what happened in moments when *I lost Jay,* either by sight or by signal. While out on a flight on a large and flat rural area between four villages in Germany, my friend Sandra and I have this exchange:

Julia: I lost him. Oh there. No. Where is it flying to at the moment? I am still not seeing him again. Where is it flying to now? I don't see him. Look [pointing at the screen], it seems like we are really close to each other, but we are not.

Sandra: Is he exactly behind the trees now?

Julia: [looking at the screen]: And here is that village. And there is the other one [pointing at the wrong village]. I'll just have him fly toward there. So, we should see him now. Oh, there. Oh, he isn't flying to where I thought he was, this is the other village.

Sandra: Is he flying backwards?

Julia: [looking back at the screen]: What is that town? Is that [names wrong village]?

Sandra: [looking at the screen, too]: That is [names wrong village].

Julia: Oh dear. That is [names correct village]. Oh my goodness.

Sandra: That is [names correct village]? But, he is still over there [pointing at drone].

Julia: Do you see him? That feels too far for me.

Sandra: Now come down a little.

Julia: Cancel! Cancel! "Return home" just kicked in. Maybe I just let him return home?

Sandra: Yeah.

Julia: THERE he is [sigh of relief, both laugh]. Good.

Sandra: I still can't see him. Oh, up there [chuckles].

Julia: You think you have orientation, but no... it's the wrong village. Sometimes, I feel like I have no aerial orientation.

Sandra: But, it is crazy that the remote control didn't limit the flight.

This exchange has much to unpack. Besides the semantic tensions related to "he," "it," and "I" (see Sandra's question: "Can *you* come down a bit?"), the incident illuminates several agential negotiations in this disrupted human-drone entanglement. While virtually connected to the flying camera, I am visually disconnected from the device in the sky resulting in my aerial disorientation. Since I don't see Jay, I am uncertain about *what he is seeing* and what is shown on the screen. Because my surrounding looks similar with four quaint Bavarian villages in several directions, I misread the visual information and thus struggle to locate Jay above us. Interestingly, I ask "where *is it flying* at the moment?" when I am the one pressing the sticks on the remote control. Amidst this agential chaos, it seems as if Jay decides to take control over the situation himself when he returns home "by himself." Initially, this maneuver surprises me and I try to cancel it before I reconsider and indeed hand over to him. Sandra voices her surprise about the device not automatically returning home sooner, alluding again to a shifting of responsibilities to the technology and its design.

Noteworthy is also the comparatively limited amount of concern discernible in this exchange given that a football-sized, $1000-dollar quadcopter is aimlessly flying at 300 feet in the sky. Somewhat consumed by the risks and costs associated with a potential crash, fall, or loss, I experienced this event as mostly comical in the moment. While initially hesitant to let the drone take over, I felt a sense of trust toward the aerial device. Jay would be ok, I just had to visually locate him. In this affective entanglement, the human seems to be the weak link, a poor vision machine with a lack of "aerial orientation." Those examples show how

> robotic agency is constructed at the interface between the human and machine. As humans interact with a robot, they assign it varying types and degrees of embodied agency, limitations, and possibilities [...]. (Vertesi, 2015: 189)

Furthermore, those drone-user interactions illustrate how not only the robot but also the human is assigned varying types of embodied agency, limitations, and possibilities. This figuration is shaped by both what features designers integrate into the technology and how humans choose to respond and adapt to them. For safe and reliable aerial partner dancing, it seems as if the sophisticated drone should lead and the human should follow.

User-Drone Intra-Actions

The affective entanglements of users and drones are similarly complex when it comes to subject-object *intra-actions*. My focus now shifts from the human-drone figuration evolving in response to environmental factors, to the human-drone figuration evolving in response to each other. DJI's Follow Me and Active Track, for example, encourage embodied performances between drone and user beyond remote control operations. In the Active Track functions, the drone's movements adjust to the visual subjects' motions by flying and filming toward or away from them. It seems as if one has the machine on an invisible leash, similar to walking a pet like Kelly does with Clippy. The drone will spatially respond to the user's movement without any hands on the remote control. This mode affords more immediate intra-actions between the drone and myself as the small quadcopter engages with my body's movement in space.

In turn, the drone medium prompts me to perform in certain ways: I start running when the drone app commands me to "GO" for Follow Me maneuvers, I shape my hands in various squares to trigger a photograph, and I awkwardly pose flat on the ground for an interesting top-down shot. Munster argues that "we experience a sense of the nonhuman capacities of both the drone and the image" in moments when the drone is "cut adrift from human control" (2014: 153). I see those nonhuman agencies surface in instances of not only losing control, but also engaging with the device and actively handing over control. Contemporary drone models invite reciprocal movements, action, and reaction that can shape socio-material intimacies and amplify affective entanglements between human and machine. I borrow Suchman's concept of "collaborative world-making characteristic" (2011: 135) to describe the following agential negotiations of such intra-active notion, motions, and emotions.

Those examples bring about messy negotiations and further illustrate the agential entanglements of subject, objects, movements, and spaces.

In the first example, I try to have Jay track and record my friend Paul riding on his bicycle in a street that is closed-off to car traffic:

> Ok, we are doing Active Track [drone follows Paul on his bike]. Paul, watch out for… [enters a shadowy area and drone starts swerving]. Ok, please stop, Paul. I don't know what the drone is doing, but it is going kind of crazy. Can you get closer? It said that it had obstacles in the flight path. Ok, now you can go again, and you may need to go a lot slower because it is going crazy. I don't know if you saw that. Trace, yeah [talking to the drone app]. It lost you so…. Ok now it has you again. (Figure 7.2)

This excerpt exemplifies some of the semantic agential gerrymandering that Vertesi notes in the context of the rover missions. "We," "it," "you," and "I" are trying to make this human-machine movement happen. Agents in this complicated mobile entanglement are not only the drone and its app, Paul on the bicycle, and I, but also the shadows on the ground which ultimately confuse the drone's visual sensors and cause it to "go kind of crazy." Instead of me adjusting my usually reliable drone

Fig. 7.2 Jay follows the cyclist in a closed-off street in Active Track

companion, I ask the cyclist to get closer, go again, and be slower, so that the drone "has you" again, meaning visually detect his body and follow it in flight. The human factor again seems to be the one that needs adjusting to potentially accommodate the machine in this mobile figuration.

Adjusting bodily movements to the drone's biases and effects—in this case the technological limitations invoked by shadows on the ground—is a recurring theme. Sometimes, the object's needs remain obscure building up tensions and potential frictions in the intra-play of human and machine: "See, it is following me, but I don't know how to make it come with me. Come. Come with me. How can I make you track me, troublemaker?" reads one drone-log from an afternoon playing with Jay's Intelligent Flight functions. The video shows me running side to side, jumping up and down, and waving at Jay. I keep looking back down at the screen, trying to understand this thing. I look back up at Jay (into the camera) as if there lies the answer. This time, he won't dance with me. Maybe a technological limitation, lack of understanding him, or us giving "wrong" signals to each other. The drone can't *read* this human today. The image-transmission onto my smartphone screen and subsequent drone-log is lagging and shaky as if to visually underline how out of sync Jay and I are that day.

In the context of roboticists and their robots, social scientist Morana Alač (2009: 496) observes that users will shape their "own movements to accommodate the requirements of the machinic body." It doesn't always work. As user and drone intra-act, a process of encoding and decoding occurs. The human body sends cues to the flying camera, which reads those as visual messages, and the drone in return responds via physical movement and visual information on the screen. The drone system "connects" with me via the *sensitive* vessel and remote control. Amidst a plethora of communicative channels beyond our user-drone bubble (discussed in Chapters 2 and 3), it is no surprise that sometimes our movements don't *reach* and our sensors can't *read* each other. As such, the "collaborative world-making characteristic" in our affective entanglements is not always so collaborative. Yet, even here the (potentially underdeveloped) drone appears as an agent that is misunderstood or incorrectly configured.

Another drone-log of an early user-drone intra-action speaks to the complicated communication and ongoing agential negotiations between Jay and I. The longer transcription of a flight session one afternoon reads:

So, I finally figured out how to make it go Active Track. And, it is tracking me right now. And, the little screen has a green box around me as I walk here. The box is basically right here [signals where the box is around her body], and it tells me "GO" in capital letters. And then there is a little icon, a little man telling me to walk and to move [starts moving, nods and smiles to a bystander]. And, alright, I am going. So, the thing is, it is tracking me, but it is not coming with me. It's just staying behind. Oh, "Subject out of range." Now I have a little yellow box around me. Ok, walking toward you, is it gonna change? Is it gonna change? Yeah. Now I am back, it's telling me "Go, go, go". But, I still need to move the thing. Move the drone [drone flies toward and past me].

Oh, what happens now? It must have lost me. "Subject lost. Searching." Well, let's see if you can find me again. I am right here. Right here, right here [moves camera toward herself]. Do you recognize the subject? Do you recognize me? [looks directly at the camera]. Not really. Ok, maybe going back a little?

[Beep beep; battery low]. That was all the fun we have. [beep beep]. So, my colors are switching from green to yellow. [beep beep]. Still "Go" right around here [traces square around herself]. It's funny, I feel like I am part of a video game. Really. [beep beep]. But ok, let's get you down. I forgot what the… where I took off. [beep beep]. So, I am not sure if I want to do the autonomous return to home. So, I am just going to land it myself. [beep beep]. Turning you around. [beep beep]

Ok, and slowly coming down [beep beep]. Now it's telling me, it's too low. Oh. [beep beep] It's still trying to active-track me. Ok, I'll get you down, stopping Active Track. [beep beep]. Stopping Active Track. [different beeping now, "Returning home"] Oh no! No! [drone is ascending fast] Uh okay. Ugh. My goodness.

I just… I just… [beeping back to low battery noise]. I cancelled Active Track, and it automatically starts to return home, and it just kept on going up. [beep beep] I mean, it would have been okay. It was just 30 feet. It would have come down to the right place. [beep beep]. But, a person is standing not far from where I took off earlier [beep beep], so I really didn't want to risk it. So, I am just going to take care [beep beep] of this myself. That was kind of scary. [Landing]. On the ground!

The multiple levels of subject-object negotiations come to light again here. As I try to set up the embodied intra-actions between Jay and I via Active Track and try to read the drone's cues for me (green boxes, walking symbols, different kinds of beeping), I try to help the drone track, trace, and follow me by adjusting its and my positions in space. We are both teaching and learning from each other the steps for this partner dance. When Jay runs out of energy, the negotiations continue in how to get him on the ground again. He wants to go one way, I prefer another. As I vocalize my train of thought, Jay keeps interrupting with his beeping; it is an argument between two stakeholders. Again, the "collaborative world-making characteristic" between us is imbued with agential negotiations over who/what leads and who/what follows when, where, and how.

And then, that same afternoon—after switching batteries—I somehow ended up with significantly less means of negotiating. The app suddenly freezes as Jay smoothly dances with me in Active Track, following my movements at about 10 feet off the ground. Consequently, I am shut out from communicating with the aircraft by remote control. While the control turns into a useless brick, Jay keeps on hovering, flying, and playing in response to my bodily movements. With well over 60% of the battery left, I have about thirteen minutes or so to spend before Jay will "return home" by himself due to a low battery status. This is more dancing than I wanted in a public location with rain on the horizon. To my surprise, the SD card inside the quadcopter keeps recording me during the next ten minutes of trying to regain command over the robotic medium. With embarrassed side glances to bystanders nearby (can they tell I lost control?), I keep tapping and swiping the frozen interface.

I keep moving the sticks on the remote control, trying to bring the aircraft down, with no luck. Like a dog that is trying to decipher the human companion, Jay keeps looking at me, following me. When I give up on the app, I start walking Jay around randomly. I am careful not to have him accidently fly sideways into a light pole and hold my hand up at him when I feel he is getting a bit too close to me (Fig. 7.3). All the

Fig. 7.3 Drone tracks me while app is frozen (taken by DJI Mavic Pro Platinum drone "Jay")

while, I feel both helpless and empowered in how this flying thing will obediently follow me despite the comparative lack of control. I remember saying out loud, "This is as if I am in a reality TV show with a film crew following me." In the role of a perceived film crew, Jay has never felt so alive, so *animated*.

I am reminded of the "life force" tribal elders ascribe to the Mars rovers according to Vertesi:

> [Animacy] essentially is an extension of us. Other *things* don't have it. Cars don't have it, trains don't. It's not a possessive language, it denotes what something *does*, not what it *is*. (2015: 189)

That afternoon, Jay *does* what he would typically do in Active Track. Yet, without me *controlling* his settings, Jay mediates animacy. He appears as a lively extension of myself, ultimately mediating me back to myself in the visual record. Through the video, too, Jay's animacy is discernable in how his small aerial body follows me, but also in the subtle adjusting movements of the camera. His *eye* seems to be looking for me, trying to keep me in focus, remotely holding on to my body, and maintaining the invisible leash. In such moments of communicative disruption, spatial intervention, and agential negotiation, subject and object remain entangled in world-making figurations. In the affective assemblages of object, user, and space, the machine is an evocative, relational, and animated artifact. Throughout our collaborative world-making efforts, our inter-/intra-active successes and failures, our multi-spatial dancing with switching leads and follows, *we have become* mobile companions.

Conclusion

In her research on subject-objects relations, Suchman (2011: 135) asks, "But how then might we make sense of the mixture of objectifying and intimately intersubjective engagements between roboticists and their companion robots?" In this chapter, I turned to the frameworks of figuration and affective entanglements from STS, feminist research, and media psychology to describe the ways of relating between users and their drones. With attention to how hobbyists address, describe, and, finally, inter- and intra-act with the capable aerial camera, I discussed the personal drone as relational, evocative, and animated artifact that actively contributes to the mobile experiences of and in space. Associations of consumer drones as reliable co-pilots, creative co-writers, momentary witnesses, and "true" companions weave through accounts of such aerial play. Amidst semantic trials over she/he/it, parallels to other mobile companions such as pets and their character judgments manifest themselves with drones as "good" or "naughty." Hobby drones may be charged with personal meaning affecting and effecting subject-object-space figurations.

Moreover, I illuminated how drone use is akin to object play which Turkle describes as engaging "the heart as well as the mind" as "a source of inner vitality" (2007: 309). Drone users who describe their hobby as relaxing, a contribution to their well-being, and form of self-care allude to this quality. Finally, I considered several examples of user-drone inter- and intra-actions drawing on auto-technographic engagements with Jay and the metaphor of partner dancing. Along with ongoing agential negotiations of who/what leads and follows when, where, and how, our mobile companionship is shaped by tensions and frictions from spatial interventions and communicative disruptions. Our collaborative world-making dynamics are insufficiently described in terms of action and reaction. Rather, the relational dimensions of dancing with my drone comprise simultaneous reaching and reading, encoding and decoding, moving and pausing, controlling and releasing, understanding and mistaking, knowing and missing, succeeding and failing. Jay communicates with me via the app, the remote control, and the physical movements of his foldable, hard-shell body. Depending on the flight mode, I communicate with him with my gentle commands on the remote control and smartphone along with my moving body. Those channels can get disrupted, our signals unclear, our dancing out of sync. I adopted approaches to "more-than-human... geographies and philosophies" (Lorimer & Davies, 2010: 33) to interpret user-drone relationships as an example that complicates "the boundaries of where we stop, and the rest begins" (Suchman, 2011: 138). While not always in sync and not always together, Jay and I dance as an affective figuration.

Pointing to future research directions, I conclude with questions by Turkle about not

> what computers can do or what computers will be like in the future, but rather, what we will be like. What kinds of people are we becoming as we develop more and more intimate relationships with machines? (2005: 294)

How do the biases and effects of personal drones activated in our entanglements with them, shape the way we think, feel, and act? How will an increasing user-friendliness in optics and haptics, for instance, impact those figurations? This chapter opened up avenues for considering personal drones as relational, evocative, and animated companions beyond accusations of the aerial camera as dangerous aerial toy and invasive spying tool that contributes to the increasing militarization of culture and society. To understand what camera drones bring to the table in recreational human-nonhuman figurations, there is value in nonreductively acknowledging the complex material-discursive practices and shifting agencies in those subject-object ecologies. Evidently, there is more to consumer drones than their aerial and visual capacities. While Jay's and my affective entanglements do not match the parodical one of Clippy and drone mom Kelly, I started to see Jay as more than a flying camera. He/she/it is a dance partner, a mobile companion.

References

Adey, P. (2016). Making the drone strange: The politics, aesthetics and surrealism of levitation. *Geographica Helvetica, 71*, 319–329.

Alač, M. (2009). Moving android: On social robots and body-in-interaction. *Social Studies of Science, 39*, 491–528.

Andrejevic, M. (2016). Theorizing drones and droning theory. In A. Završnik (Ed.), *Drones and unmanned aerial systems: Legal and social implications for security and surveillance* (pp. 21–43). Springer International Publishing.

Barad, K. (2003). Posthumanist performativity: Toward an understanding of how matter comes to matter. *Signs: Journal of Women in Culture and Society, 28*, 801–831.

Barad, K. (2007). *Meeting the universe halfway: Quantum physics and the entanglement of matter and meaning.* Duke University Press.

Betabrand. (2016). San Francisco drone rescue. Retrieved December 8, 2018, from YouTube: https://www.youtube.com/watch?v=4mxnvOwaHSs.

Crandall, J. (2014). Ecologies of a wayward drone. In P. Adey, M. Whitehead, & A. Williams (Eds.), *From above: War, violence, and verticality* (pp. 263–287). Oxford University Press.

Dant, T. (2004). The driver-car. *Theory, Culture & Society, 21*, 61–79.

Dichtlerova, V. (2017, February 2). Interview with Maksim Tarasov, Dronestagram's talented drone pilot. Retrieved October 31, 2018, from Dronestagram Blog website: http://www.dronestagr.am/blog/interview-maksim-tarasov/.

Dorrian, M. (2014). Drone semiosis. *Cabinet Magazine*, 48–55.

Farman, J. (2011). *Mobile interface theory: Embodied space and locative media.* Routledge.

Fish, A. (2021). Crash theory: Entrapments of conservation drones and endangered megafauna. *Science, Technology, & Human Values,46*, 425–451.

Frith, J. (2015). *Smartphones as locative media.* Polity.

Grosz, E. (1994). *Volatile bodies: Toward a corporeal feminism.* Indiana University Press.

Haraway, D. J. (1997). *Modest_witness@second_millennium.femaleman_meets_oncomouse.* Routledge.

Hayles, N. K. (2005). Computing the human. *Theory, Culture & Society, 22,* 131–151.

Karabuda Ecer, A., & Dronestagram. (2017). *Dronescapes: The new aerial photography from Dronestagram.* Thames & Hudson.

Larsen, J. (2006). Geographies of tourist photography. In J. Falkhimer & A. Jansson (Eds.), *Geographies of communication: The spatial turn in media studies* (pp. 243–261). Nordicom.

Latour, B. (1999). *Pandora's hope: Essays on the reality of science studies.* Harvard University Press.

Law, J. (2004). *After method: Mess in social science research.* Routledge.

Lorimer, J., & Davies, G. (2010). Interdisciplinary conversations on interspecies encounters. *Environment and Planning D: Society and Space, 28,* 32–33.

Lupton, D. (1996). The embodied computer/user. In M. Featherstone & R. Burrows (Eds.), *Cyberspace/cyberbodies/cyberpunk: Cultures of technological embodiment* (pp. 97–112). Sage.

McCosker, A. (2015). Drone vision, zones of protest and the new cinema: Drone Vision, zones of protest, and the new camera consciousness. *Media Fields Journal: Critical Explorations in Media and Space, 9,* 1–14.

McLuhan, M. (1964). *Understanding media: The extensions of man* (2nd ed.). Signet.

Moores, S. (2012). *Media, place and mobility.* Palgrave Macmillan.

Munster, A. (2014). Transmateriality: Toward an energetics of signal in contemporary mediatic assemblages. *Cultural Studies Review, 20,* 150–167.

Myers, N. (2012). Dance your PhD: Embodied animations, body experiments, and the affective entanglements of life science research. *Body & Society, 18,* 151–189.

Parks, L. (2001). Cultural geographies in practice: Plotting the personal: Global positioning satellites and interactive media. *Ecumene, 8,* 209–222.

Parks, L. (2005). *Cultures in orbit: Satellites and the televisual.* Duke University Press.

Rothstein, A. (2015). *Drone.* Bloomsbury Academic.

Seamon, D. (1980). Body-subject, Time-space/routines and Place-ballets. In A. Buttimer & D. Seamon (Eds.), *The human experience of space and place* (pp. 148–165). Croom Helm.

Sheller, M. (2004). Automotive emotions: Feeling the car. *Theory, Culture & Society, 21,* 221–242.

Spinney, J. (2015). Close encounters? Mobile methods, (post)phenomenology and affect. *Cultural Geographies, 22,* 231–246.

Stacey, J., & Suchman, L. (2012). Animation and automation—The liveliness and labours of bodies and machines. *Body & Society, 18,* 1–46.

Suchman, L. (1987). *Plans and situated actions: The problem of human-machine communication.* Cambridge University Press.

Suchman, L. (2005). Affiliative objects. *Organization, 12,* 379–399.

Suchman, L. (2006). *Human-machine reconfigurations: Plans and situated actions* (2nd ed.). Cambridge University Press.

Suchman, L. (2011). Subject objects. *Feminist Theory, 12,* 119–145.

Suchman, L. (2015). Situational awareness: Deadly bioconvergence at the boundaries of bodies and machines. *MediaTropes, 5,* 1–24.

Thrift, N. (2009). Space: The fundamental stuff of geography. In N. Clifford, S. L. Holloway, S. P. Rice, & G. Valentine (Eds.), *Key concepts in geography* (2nd ed., pp. 85–96). Sage.

Turkle, S. (2005). *The second self: Computers and the human spirit.* MIT Press.

Turkle, S. (Ed.). (2007). *Evocative objects: Things we think with.* MIT Press.

Turkle, S. (Ed.). (2008). *The inner history of devices.* MIT Press.

Turkle, S. (2012). *Alone together: Why we expect more from technology and less from each other.* Basic Books.

Vertesi, J. (2015). *Seeing like a rover: How robots, teams, and images craft knowledge of Mars.* University of Chicago Press.

Virilio, P. (1994). *The vision machine* (J. Rose, Trans.). Indiana University Press.

8

Conclusion: Open Skies?

The goal of this book was to complicate, challenge, and complement discourses that approach consumer drones as unmanned aircraft systems, as technologies of surveillance and dangerous weapons, and as tools and devices for aerial navigation and data collection. Such assessments are accurate. Yet, they are incomplete. In exploring consumer drones as mobile media used in various forms of aerial play, I shed light onto the complexity of this technology along with the practices and associations it engenders. Focusing on camera drone ecologies, communication, movements, visualizations, and relationships, I made "the drone visible differently," reordered, unsettled, and repositioned the multi-mobile geomedium in what Adey calls "other relations, hierarchies, and aesthetic sensibilities" (2016: 326).

The flying camera uniquely configures principles of communication and transportation across hybrid geographies. As such, this topic provides fertile ground for continuously bridging media ecology, mobilities research, mobile communication research, human geography, and STS. To describe drones in terms of media and mobilities, extensions and environments, human-machine interactions, and affective entanglements, this book linked several theoretical frameworks and ultimately advanced comprehensive interdisciplinary perspectives. Such conceptual boundary-crossing based on fruitful alignments becomes increasingly relevant. More and more "emerging media," such as consumer drones and other advanced mobile, digital, robotic, intelligent, and autonomous platforms, challenge the way we think and talk about communication, movement, environments, and relationships. To understand these emerging dimensions and dynamics, their co-creation and co-dependencies, their conceptual and practical entanglements in comprehensives ways, we are served well to overcome disciplinary boundaries and draw on theories and methods from multiple intellectual traditions.

The book was driven by the goal to unveil the biases and effects of consumer drones as mobile media. Postman (1995: 192) helps clarify this principle one more time:

> Embedded in every technology there is a powerful idea, sometimes two or three powerful ideas. Like language itself, technology predisposes us to favor and value certain perspectives and accomplishments and subordinate others. Every technology has a philosophy, which is given expression in how the technology makes people use their minds, in what it makes us do with our bodies, in how it codifies the world, in which of our senses it amplifies, in which of our emotional and intellectual tendencies it disregards.

Each of the previous chapters speaks to some of the "powerful ideas" and technological "philosophy" discernable in recreational drone flying and image-taking. With an eye toward how the consumer drone "makes people use their minds, in what it makes us do with our bodies, in how it codifies the world," I discussed how personal drone use arranges dynamic spatial assemblages of human and nonhuman agencies; how the aerial geomedium affords communication *on the fly* and (dis)embodied (im)mobilities in auratic vertical play and user-drone companionships. My launching and landing point for this intellectual flight across drone spaces, movements, views, and relationships was the auto-technographic lens. This internal and external, el(ev)ating attention to the technological conscious and unconscious encouraged me to study not only the drone but also myself as I struggle, fight, dance, and fly with Jay.

More specifically, Chapters 2 and 3 set up personal drone use contexts and provided an inventory of common spatial, temporal, mobile, social, and affective elements in the aerial play. The juxtaposition of sky video and ground audio in what I called drone-logs encouraged me to zoom out, see the larger picture, and see myself within it as I engage with the medium and its powerful ideas. Auto-drone-technography can sharpen our perspectives onto media, mobility, communication, and culture as well as ourselves as we make sense of them.

Chapter 3 then shifted from the situating of the human to the situating of the thing. Here, in particular, I made a case for widening the definition of drones as "unmanned aircraft systems" to acknowledge constitutional factors of drone play beyond aviation. Manifold agencies within consumer drone ecologies and their ties to visual and digital culture in drone image-sharing and community-building come to light in this overview of the hobby. As a result, the unmanned aerial vehicle is more holistically approached as a geomedium that furnishes certain cybermobilities in hybrid space—affordances that will become more relevant when the drone, smartphone, and their processes of socially-networked communication merge further.

Building on this foundation of user and drone mobilities in situ, Chapter 4 introduced the concept of "communication on the fly." Consumer drones are mobile locative media that complicate how we think of "communication on the move" in their medium-specific configuration of aerial navigation, creative image-production, and virtual communication across physical, networked, and social formations. Those in turn shape user practices of place-making and place-sensing. Crossing physical, digital, and social spaces, consumer drones enable performative cartography, emplaced visuality, and mobile mediality similar to other mobile, locative media. Yet, as discussed, there is more. As the flying camera takes these affordances into the sky, they extend users' spatial awareness and capacities for making and sensing place beyond their body into vertical, volumetric space. We may be quick to dismiss these practices of communication on the fly as further evidence for the militarization of culture in hawkish intelligence-gathering activities. However, in the way hobbyists explore and explain their drone use, the performances appear as recreational self-enhancement and playful but also mindful environmental exploration.

Chapter 5 highlighted the distinct corporeal and imaginative (im)mobilities inherent to camera drone flying, causing a semantic and sensorial boundary collapse between movement and stillness, subject and object, here and there. Despite or because of the stillness of the body, the user's mind travels with the drone, leading to strange out-of-body encounters between the dronified mind and the corporeal self. Probes into media as extensions causing numbness and degrees of self-amputation fit those drone use narratives. To better describe the kinds of movement and stillness that effect the sensory boundary collapses, I introduced the concept of dis/embodied mobilities.

The critical analysis of drone-generated visuality in Chapter 6 showed how the aerial gaze of consumer drones can be a top-down ordering form of surveillance. However, we should also broaden this discussion by understanding drone visuality as auratic vertical play at the crossroads of curious aerial exploration, creative expression, and virtual gaming practices. Consumer drones are technologies of visualization for and beyond surveillance. Emphasized especially in Chapter 6 was the capacity of consumer drones to afford renewed visual attention, geographic awareness, and environmental attunement to everyday volumetric spaces. I used the term "drone-mindedness" to describe the curious imaginative mobilities hobbyists mention. The flying camera has the potential to provide geographical literacy in educational contexts, next to vocational and possibly mental benefits for people with disabilities, a point I will return to.

This last aspect also surfaced in Chapter 7 and the relationships drone users develop with the robotic medium. I turned to frameworks from STS, feminist theory, and media psychology to unpack playful user-drone interactions. Both ethnographic and auto-technographic engagements illuminated affective associations, agential negotiations, spatial interventions, and disruptive communication in recreational user-drone entanglements. Amidst semantic trials over what she/he/it and I do, personal drones emerge as relational, evocative, even animated artifacts. Jay and other drones can become mobile companions and nurturant technologies as trustworthy co-pilots, co-writers, friends, witnesses, and dance partners. In these encounters, we experience not only mobile companionships between human and machine, but also early degrees of mobile autonomy of communication technologies.

The goal of my critical engagement with consumer drones was to make visible the drone as a *medium*, make visible its *other messages*. In understanding the flying camera as a complex geomedium with multi-modal mobilities used in aerial play, its various messages become legible, helping us make better sense of this new technology in our everyday vertical and horizontal spaces.

Laws of Hobby Drone Media

To provide a final (h)overview, I formulate a set of explorative "laws" of recreational drone media based on the book's focus and findings (Table 8.1). Following McLuhan and McLuhan's (1988) tetradic "laws of media," I show to what extent my discussion responds to the four

Table 8.1 A tetrad of personal drone use inspired by McLuhan and McLuhan's "laws of media" (1988)

Enhance	**Reverse into**
• Auto-technography • Attention to hybrid space • Communication on the fly • Multi-modal, personal (im)mobilities • Techniques of visualization • Drone-mindedness • Mobile companionship	• Recreational drone bans or chaotic drone-filled skies? • Extreme techniques of surveillance + militarization of everyday spaces? • Nurturant technologies in place of interpersonal connections?
Personal Drones	
Retrieve	**Obsolesce**
• Virtual gaming practices • Personalized aeromobilities • Balloon prospect • Auratic impressions • Optical toys • Affective relationships (e.g. with pets)	• Clear distinctions between here + there, subject + object, mobile + immobile, immediate + hypermediate • Image-taking, surveillance, monitoring, etc. via manned aviation?

questions they recommend asking of every medium: What does the technology enhance? What does it obsolesce? What does it retrieve from the past? And, what does it reverse into when pushed to an extreme? This "tetrad" of media grammar is not meant to be sequential or universally applicable. Moreover, as the technology enters more and more domains, changes in design, and varies in adoptions, the consumer drone "laws" I present here are by no means complete. This tetrad primarily consolidates the book's key findings and probes into potential concerns when personal drone use is pushed to an extreme.

Enhancement

As discussed throughout this book, consumer drones enhance several ways of seeing, moving, and being. The aerial medium augments auto-ethnographic endeavors in its multidirectional make-happen and make-aware affordances. Personal drones encourage us to see the bigger picture and our place within it. The fruitful fusion and friction of self, system, and space can serve research endeavors in the form of auto-technography. In its function as a make-aware medium, the flying sensor also increases our awareness of hybrid geographies. Physical-material, digital-intangible, and socio-spatial conditions come to the fore in recreational drone ecologies and the novel affordance of communication on the fly. Here, flying, recording, sensing, networking, communicating, and disrupting merge in the mobile locative medium. These spatial crossovers also point to the multi-modal (im)mobilities of the machine and its user. Along with physical, corporeal, virtual, communicative, and imaginative movements, which are central in the new mobilities paradigm, aerial drone play enhances affective, remediated, and dis/embodied mobilities in the moving with and as drones.

When turning to the topic of drone visuality, I argued that the flying camera is a technology of surveillance, yet not exclusively. Consumer drones afford map-reading and way-finding in vertical play and thus enhance practices of vision and visualization. Those effects, in turn, impact user perceptions by increasing geographical curiosity and spatial sensibility. Last but not least, the motile medium and its sophisticated flight functions enhance forms of human-machine companionship.

Obsolescence

Along with these various enhancements, the mobile medium also seems to make several aspects obsolete. Those include clear distinctions between what is here and there in semantic descriptions, the subject and object in imaginative mobilities and agential negotiations, the mobile and immobile at the intersection of human body and mind, as well as the immediate and hypermediate in hybrid space. Moreover, aerial image-taking, surveillance, monitoring, and the like via manned aviation are likely to diminish and ultimately disappear when unmanned practices prove to be more cost-effective, accessible, efficient, and safer.

Retrieval

At the same time, drone play retrieves and remediates several ways of seeing, moving, and being on the ground and up in the air. Those include virtual gaming practices and personalized aeromobilities along with the sensations and aesthetics from early ballooning and other impressions of aura. As argued, consumer drones are reminiscent of optical toys. More-over, they retrieve efforts of visually archiving the surface of the planet. With millions of drone-generated still and moving images online and offline, the medium affords snapshots of Earth's landscapes, architectures, and infrastructures; its volumetric spaces and conditions at the begin-ning of the twenty-first century. In this context, consumer drone vision and views succeed older visual practices of recording and archiving the planet.[1] In addition, affective relationships, the kinds we may develop

---

[1] One example is the *Archives de la Planète* (1908–1931) initiated by French banker and philan-thropist Albert Kahn, which includes still and moving (including aerial) images from around the world (Amad, 2010; Hildebrand, 2017).

with pets or fictional characters for example, are retrieved in human-drone companionships. Those interactions may not only entertain but also nurture.

Reversal

Such retrievals stand in stark contrast to what the drone medium might become when pushed to an extreme via over-use or over-regulation. Drone users fear universal recreational drone bans while both enthusiasts and skeptics worry about drone-filled skies as more and more domains, from the military to commerce, find applications for the aerial technology. In such scenarios, concerns over extreme techniques of surveillance, excessive environmental disruptions, increasing threats to cybersecurity, as well as physical damage and harm among multiple other issues become more pressing. Similarly, as social robots enter spaces of care, service, and beyond to replace human-to-human and human-to-animal interactions (Turkle 2017), to what extent should we worry about the uptake of "social drones" and their effects? In light of this and other lingering questions, there are manifold avenues for future research.

Avenues for Future Research

This tetrad of recreational drone biases and effects, as discussed in this book, points to several future research directions about hobby drone media, mobility, communication, and culture. First, a key research agenda building on this work includes inquiries into how communication on the fly will advance or change as the aerial medium gains in technological sophistication. Future research could delve more deeply into the developing technological grammar of sensors, intelligent flight modes, and so forth, to further contextualize and specify some of the arguments made here. How will smaller, quieter, and smarter drones affect aerial play for users, bystanders, and virtual audiences? What practices of mobile mediality will emerge as a result of the personal

drone turning into a "cursor in the sky" (Burton, 2017) and digitally augmenting everyday spaces? This question about drone mobile
mediality addresses both "new sites for creative interventions, public
participation, and social interaction" (Sheller, 2014: 278) and problems of power, control, privacy, surveillance, justice, accessibility, and
equity. Consumer drones currently furnish certain ways of making and
sensing space as communication technologies that incorporate early
degrees of mobile autonomy. How might those ways change as mobile
drone autonomies increase? Moreover, how might other geomedia with
increasing capabilities of independent movement transform our practices, spaces, relationships, and ourselves? Turning to scholarship from
critical media studies, mobilities research, mobile communication, and
STS will continue to be conducive for understanding and responding to
such questions and concerns.

A second avenue for further research relates to the various consumer
drone mobilities and the forms of personal development and well-being
but also social disruption they entail. In Chapter 7, I highlighted the
benefits of recreational drone flying and image-taking, such as relaxation,
release, and escape. Additional empirical work is needed to more deeply
explore the hobby's merits. Similarly, as touched upon in Chapter 5, the
playful engagements with the dis/embodying technology seem to be of
therapeutical value (Dorando, 2020) and open up vocational opportunities ("Handidrone - Kindai," 2018) for users with certain disabilities.
As the potentials for drone leisure and work increase, so do the perils
of drone disruption and harm. Research across disciplines is looking
into drone disturbances and the counter-drone measures they provoke
(see, for example, Jackman, 2019). Users, regulators, and scientists would
benefit from more studies into unruly drone practices and resistances to
them specifically in the recreational realm.

In the context of creative drone visuality, questions remain about
how the new auratic perspectives of map-reading and way-finding in
volumetric space end up shaping our perceptions of the world. How
could recreational drone-mindedness and the literacies it entails be oper-
ationalized toward greater environmental awareness, communication,
protection, and conservation? Likewise, how can the vast visual online
archive of drone-generated views by hobbyists be of such service for

this and future generations? At the same time, concerns exist about drone manufacturers tapping into recreational drone visuals for political purposes. Fears over espionage by the Chinese government, for example, have already prompted the U. S. Armed Forces, the Pentagon, and the Department of the Interior to ground drone models manufactured by China, specifically the consumer drone market leader DJI (Hollister, 2020). The Chinese company denies any cybersecurity concerns, arguing that their drone platforms have been independently tested and validated by U. S. cybersecurity consultants and agencies (DJI Newsroom, 2020). Regardless of whether foreign actors are indeed accessing drone footage by recreational and commercial drone pilots, the possibility remains, and so the concerns over how public and private drone visuals are used and misused persist. Consumer drone imagery helps establish realities. What those realities mean and how they might be acted upon matters and warrants further critical research.

Last but not least, our understanding of recreational drone flying and image-taking will benefit from more studies into its users. Critical attention to how, for example, gender, age, race, ethnicity, disability, and class come into play in recreational drone adoptions will also help advance and refine media ecological frameworks such as media extending human faculties and consciousness. Such scholarly attention will also be relevant as we critically consider not just what the drone medium may become, but also what our environments and what we may become as a result of our playful entanglements with the flying sensor.

Right to Fly Remotely

As the FAA and agencies around the world continue to refine their drone rules and regulations, this work should be seen as a case for both protecting personal drone use as well as introducing, maintaining, and especially enforcing sensible recreational drone laws. Recognizing the growing efforts across commercial and non-commercial domains pushing for aerial access by drone, I conclude with the argument for an individual right to aerial space. I follow Garrett and Fish (2016) who problematize a "sneaky corporate takeover of the atmosphere," in the name of commercial drone delivery, for example, and the airspace being "diced-up to the highest bidder." They draw on the concept of "atmospheric commons" as "rights to the collective air" (Garrett & Fish, 2016) and point to geographer Jeremy W. Crampton's warning about the growing "enclosure of the commons" (2016: 140) via airspace privatization and other drone use restrictions. Understanding the sky as a regulated and governed, but nonetheless *shared* "atmospheric," "mobile" (Sheller, 2018), and "global commons" (Vogler, 1995, 2001) would allow for accommodating such personal drone aeromobilities in recognition of their social, cultural, recreational, artistic, and educational value. This may require airspace to be reconceptualized, consumer drone regulations to be more clearly defined and differentiated with attention to drone size, weight, payload, and noise level, and civilian drone flight education to be more strongly emplaced and enforced.

Current visions for unmanned traffic management in uncontrolled U. S. airspace leave little room for explorative, creative, and playful ways of drone flying and image-taking. The FAA's and NASA's focus is on "commercial services" "as the trade space changes and matures" to meet "business needs" and "consumer demand" (FAA & NextGen, 2020: 7–8). Plans for "UAS Volume Reservations" describe a future in which operators reserve a four-dimensional volume of airspace for approved types of "operations" (FAA & NextGen, 2020: 17). Despite language about "equity of access" for authorized users (FAA & NextGen, 2020: 32), it remains unclear whether drone hobbyists will be able to exercise a "right to fly" in those more creative and explorative ways that make recreational drone flying and image-taking meaningful. Points of entry into an educational hobby and often profession that combine technology, aviation, and science with communication, creativity, and the environment would be limited. As media, consumer drones are what McLuhan calls "means of extending and enlarging our organic sense lives into our environment" (2003: 155).

There is value in considering aerial drone play as such a means for extending our lives into vertical spaces, in particular when we draw maps of future manned and unmanned traffic in the sky.

My advocacy for personal drone use does not seek to downplay the significant risks and dangerous potentials of the practice when unregulated, irresponsible, unethical, and otherwise pushed too far. A growing body of important and timely drone scholarship is pointing to issues of locational privacy, physical safety, public nuisance, and the militarization of everyday culture, to just name a few examples. To complement this work, this book identified, illustrated, and discussed the more playful, creative, artistic, and restorative technological biases and effects of consumer drones to advance interdisciplinary theoretical frameworks, insightful methodological tools, as well as grounded (and aerial) research for understanding this mobile medium.

References

Adey, P. (2016). Making the drone strange: The politics, aesthetics and surrealism of levitation. *Geographica Helvetica, 71*, 319–329.

Amad, P. (2010). *Counter-archive: Film, the everyday, and Albert Kahn's Archives de la Planète.* Columbia University Press.

Burton, D. (2017, November 3). AirCraft: Turn your drone into a cursor in the sky. Retrieved December 6, 2018, from DroneBase website: https://blog.dronebase.com/2017/11/03/aircraft-turn-your-drone-into-a-cursor-in-the-sky.

Crampton, J. W. (2016). Assemblage of the vertical: Commercial drones and algorithmic life. *Geographica Helvetica, 71*, 137–146.

DJI Newsroom. (2020, January 29). DJI statement on U.S. Department of Interior Drone Order. Retrieved October 21, 2020, from DJI Official website: https://www.dji.com/newsroom/news/dji-statement-on-us-department-of-interior-drone-order.

Dorando, J. (2020, July 22). Therapy drones: Could sUAS be the adaptive therapy tool of the future? Retrieved October 22, 2020, from Dronelife website: https://dronelife.com/2020/07/22/therapy-drones/.

FAA, & NextGen. (2020, March 2). *Concept of operations v2.0: Unmanned aircraft system (UAS) traffic management (UTM).* Retrieved June 2, 2020, from Federal Aviation Administration website: https://www.faa.gov/uas/research_development/traffic_management/media/UTM_ConOps_v2.pdf.

Garrett, B. L., & Fish, A. (2016, December 12). Attack on the drones: The creeping privatisation of our urban airspace. Retrieved December 8, 2018, from The Guardian website: https://www.theguardian.com/cities/2016/dec/12/attack-drones-privatisation-urban-airspace.

Handidrone—Kindai. (2018, October 30). Retrieved October 30, 2018, from Kindai website: https://kindai.fr/campaigns/handidrone/.

Hildebrand, J. M. (2017). Visually distant and virtually close: Public and private spaces in the *Archives de la Planète* (1909–1931) and *Life in a Day* (2011). In T. Timan, B. C. Newell, & B.-J. Koops (Eds.), *Privacy in public spaces: Conceptual and regulatory challenges* (pp. 112–136). Edward Elgar.

Hollister, S. (2020, August 20). The US government grounded DJI—But here are the five drones it just approved. Retrieved October 21, 2020, from The Verge website: https://www.theverge.com/2020/8/20/21376917/drone-us-government-approved-dod-diu-uas-blue-china.

Jackman, A. (2019). Consumer drone evolutions: Trends, spaces, temporalities, threats. *Defense & Security Analysis, 35*, 362–383.

McLuhan, M. (2003). The book of probes. In D. Carson, E. McLuhan, W. Kuhns, & M. Cohen (Eds.). Gingko Press.

McLuhan, M., & McLuhan, E. (1988). *Laws of media: The new science.* University of Toronto Press.

Postman, N. (1995). *The end of education: Redefining the value of school.* Knopf.

Sheller, M. (2018). *Mobility justice: The politics of movement in an age of extremes.* Verso.

Sheller, M. (2014). Mobile art: Out of your pocket. In G. Goggin & L. Hjorth (Eds.), *The Routledge companion to mobile media* (pp. 197–205). Routledge.

Vogler, J. (1995). *The global commons: A regime analysis.* Wiley.

Vogler, J. (2001). Future directions: The atmosphere as a global commons. *Atmospheric Environment, 35*, 2427–2428.

Index

A
Active track 34, 35, 164, 171, 172,
    174–176
Actor-network theory 50
Adey, Peter 13, 17, 36, 41, 65, 66,
    102, 122, 124, 125, 135, 157,
    183
Affect 4, 21, 34, 36, 41, 50, 109,
    131, 144, 152, 154, 161, 178,
    185
Affordance 4, 13, 15, 16, 31, 46,
    49, 57, 66, 74, 77, 82, 88, 90,
    122, 144, 145, 185, 188
Agency 10, 14, 35, 36, 38, 47, 50,
    52, 57, 59, 61, 67, 158, 160,
    165, 167, 170, 171, 178, 184
Airmap 57
Airplane 20, 32, 40, 45, 57, 58, 64,
    76, 84, 101, 109, 122, 125,
    143

Airport 9, 56, 58
Airspace 2, 8, 9, 11, 46, 48, 57, 60,
    64, 83, 84, 193
Air Traffic Control 56, 57
Amputation 20, 100–102, 115–117,
    186
Andrejevic, Mark 74, 78, 100, 156
Animacy 176, 186
Animal 48, 57, 58, 152
App 9, 27, 28, 30, 37, 53, 54, 57,
    62, 63, 77, 80, 82, 83, 85,
    102, 107, 108, 141, 167, 171,
    172, 175, 178
Architecture 10, 14, 48, 64, 126,
    135, 136, 189
Assemblage 4, 17, 19, 46, 47, 49,
    56, 57, 63, 65–68, 99, 112,
    144, 177, 184
Atmosphere 13, 154, 193

© The Editor(s) (if applicable) and The Author(s), under exclusive
license to Springer Nature Singapore Pte Ltd. 2021
J. M. Hildebrand, *Aerial Play*, Geographies of Media,
https://doi.org/10.1007/978-981-16-2195-6

Attunement 31, 34, 109, 126, 143, 144, 146, 186
Audience 42, 48, 49, 62, 63, 66, 78, 87, 88, 190
Audio 18, 30, 32, 34, 36, 37, 41, 62, 65, 87, 88, 185
Augmented reality 74, 141
Augmented space 77, 84, 85, 91
Aura 18, 20, 127–129, 131, 132, 134, 138, 143, 184, 186, 189
Australia 60
Auto-ethnography 3, 28, 38, 40
Auto-technography 3, 4, 18, 28–30, 32–34, 36, 41, 89, 107, 127, 138, 184, 186, 188
Aviation 7, 8, 11, 21, 45–47, 49, 54, 68, 99, 103, 123, 125, 134, 143, 185, 189, 193
Awareness 20, 91, 102, 126, 132, 143, 144, 146, 185, 186, 188, 191. *See also* Location-awareness/Location-aware

B
B4UFLY 9, 54, 57
Balloon 20, 45, 76, 122–124, 132, 134, 135, 138, 143, 145, 189
Barad, Karen 153, 155
Battery 7, 54, 57, 84, 89, 158, 166, 168, 174, 175
Bender, Hendrick 74, 77, 80, 101
Benjamin, Medea 6
Benjamin, Walter 127, 128
Bicycle 29, 39, 48, 172
Birds 28, 39, 48, 58, 59, 140, 166
Bird's-eye view 33, 123, 130
Body 20, 29–31, 39, 40, 98, 101, 102, 105, 107–110, 112–117, 132, 140, 160, 161, 164, 171, 173, 174, 176, 178, 184–186, 189
Bolter, Jay David 84, 85, 99, 104, 132
Boundaries 20, 67, 77, 98, 100, 105, 113, 116, 155, 165, 178, 184
Brain 105, 106, 111, 114, 142
Bystander 19, 37, 38, 48, 49, 59–61, 63, 65, 66, 89, 91, 117, 131, 174, 175, 190

C
Camera 1, 5, 8, 27, 34, 35, 37, 39, 49, 54, 60, 62, 63, 77, 78, 84, 86, 88, 89, 99, 101, 102, 105, 107, 108, 110, 133, 134, 138, 141, 142, 144, 152, 156, 157, 159, 161–164, 166, 170, 173, 174, 176, 186
Camera consciousness 144
Campbell, Scott 75, 76, 78, 82, 87
Car 32, 48, 89, 104, 106, 108, 110–112, 141, 154, 176
Collapse 20, 80, 110–112, 116, 186
Comments 11, 63, 64, 68, 87, 88
Commons 21, 193
Communication 68, 99, 183, 191, 193
   digital 46, 90
   mobile 4, 5, 14, 67, 74–77, 82, 84, 87, 91, 92, 153–154, 183, 191
   networked 19, 32, 66, 76, 102, 185
   on the fly 19, 73, 75, 77, 85, 91, 184, 185, 188, 190
   virtual 41, 74, 116, 185

Companionship 21, 152–155, 157, 161, 164, 167, 168, 177–179, 184, 187, 189, 190
Co-pilot 59, 167, 177, 186
Cosmic view 124, 125
Crampton, Jeremy W. 193
Crash 29, 45, 55, 56, 58, 97, 98, 117, 136, 156, 168, 170
Cresswell, Tim 16, 135
Cybermobilities 65, 66, 69, 185
Cybersecurity 45, 190, 192
Cyborg 100, 112–116
Cyclist 28, 29, 173

D

Dance/Dancing 21, 153, 164, 165, 171, 173, 175, 177–179, 184, 187
Danger 12, 21, 53, 60, 108, 167, 194
Data 37, 38, 48, 79, 83–85, 91, 105, 123
Deleuze, Gilles 144
De Souza e Silva, Adriana 67, 75, 78, 85
Dirigible 125
Disabilities 117, 186, 191, 192
Disembodiment 100, 112–114, 153
Disruption 2, 3, 12, 20, 21, 37, 45, 87–89, 91, 177, 178, 186, 190, 191
DIY community 11
DIY culture 13
DJI 3, 6, 7, 21, 27, 53, 54, 57, 62, 80, 83, 85, 89, 105, 107, 121, 130, 151, 168, 171, 192
Domain 2, 7, 45, 123, 188, 190, 192

Drone-logs 18, 29–32, 34, 36–41, 138, 140, 165, 173, 185
Drone-mindedness 20, 124, 141–144, 146, 186, 191
Dronestagram 7, 62, 107, 122, 128, 134, 136, 145, 146, 156
Drone stare 124–126
Drone use
    activism 126, 144
    agriculture 2, 7, 12
    commercial 1, 5, 7–9, 55, 111, 192, 193
    conservation 2, 7, 12, 156, 191
    construction 2
    criminal 7, 12
    delivery 2, 3, 9, 11
    entertainment 7
    humanitarian 1, 12
    inspection 2, 11
    journalism 2, 7, 9
    military 1, 13, 81, 89, 125, 126, 143
    police 12, 126
    scientific 1, 7
    terrorist 12
Dronie 34, 134, 164

E

Education 7, 11, 21, 33, 54, 55, 67, 146, 186, 193
Effects 5, 11, 15, 16, 31, 38, 46, 51, 123, 127, 154, 173, 178, 184, 188, 190, 194
Embodiment 18, 20, 31, 36, 41, 50, 76, 88, 90, 101, 111–113, 115, 153, 165, 170, 171, 175
Emotions 18, 37–40, 154, 171
Emplaced visuality 75, 86, 91, 185

Emplacement 18, 28, 40, 42, 86, 90, 91
Empowerment 19, 81, 101, 110, 117. *See also* Power
Entanglement 4, 14, 18, 21, 47, 52, 75, 155–157, 159, 160, 164, 166, 168, 170–173, 177–179, 183, 192
Environment 14–17, 20, 21, 31, 40, 45, 50–52, 57, 61, 65, 67, 76, 82, 83, 98, 107, 108, 113, 126, 129, 142, 146, 154, 165, 183, 192, 193
Espionage 192
Ethics 33, 51, 194
Ethnography 18, 19, 29–31, 36, 38, 40, 62, 75, 186
Extension 14, 15, 20, 29, 31–33, 50, 75, 80, 81, 98–102, 106, 108, 112, 113, 115–117, 138, 144, 154, 157, 159, 176, 183, 186

F

Facebook 4, 7, 19, 30, 53, 55, 58, 62, 87
Farman, Jason 76, 88, 154, 161, 163
Federal Aviation Administration (FAA) 2, 4, 7–11, 28, 33, 47, 54, 56, 57, 59, 60, 67, 68, 89, 108, 192, 193
Feedback 63, 65, 66, 68, 69, 87
Feminist scholarship/Feminist theory 21, 153–155, 177, 186
Figuration 21, 154–157, 159, 160, 163, 164, 167, 170, 171, 177, 178
Fireworks 81–83

First-person viewing (FPV) 11, 20, 97, 98, 113, 135, 162
Fish, Adam 5, 33, 51, 77, 126, 156, 192, 193
Flight
    record 86
    restriction 9, 19, 57, 83, 84, 167
    time 1, 59, 61
Florida 80
Fly-away 158, 159
Follow Me 164, 171, 175, 176
Freud, Sigmund 98, 101
Frith, Jordan 75, 78, 113, 152

G

Gaming 20, 35, 90, 99, 102–107, 116, 139, 140, 145, 174, 186, 189
    shooter 35, 36, 103, 140, 141
Gaze
    aerial 13, 20, 36, 78, 89, 122, 124, 125, 134, 138, 143, 145, 186
    cartographic 124
    drone 14, 18, 29, 34, 37, 41, 122–124, 127, 129, 130, 132, 134–136, 138, 145
    gamer 140
    human 28, 37, 58, 108, 111, 131
    mobile 132, 135, 145
    possessive 124–126, 136
Gender 158, 160, 192
Geography/Geographies 4, 14, 19, 29, 56, 75, 83, 125, 126, 129, 133, 135, 138, 144, 145, 161, 178, 183, 188
Geomagnetic storm 55

Geomedia 65–68, 75, 77, 78, 185, 191
Global Positioning System (GPS) 9, 19, 28, 48, 54–56, 139, 163–165, 168
Global view 125
Goggles 104, 113, 116
Google Maps 56, 80, 82
Government 45, 55, 123, 192
Grasp 33
Ground control station 47, 49, 65
Grusin, Richard 84, 85, 99, 104

H

Hall, Edward T. 98, 101
Hand 14, 35, 99, 105–109, 114, 116, 121, 139, 153, 155, 171, 175
Handidrone 117
Haraway, Donna 153, 154
Harm 12, 29, 46, 146, 167, 168, 190, 191
Hawai'i 60
Hayles, N. Katherine 153, 155
Helicopter 20, 28, 29, 39, 45, 48, 54, 57, 58, 63, 76, 109, 125, 133, 143
Hildebrand, Julia M. 17, 47, 49, 77, 101, 125
Hjorth, Larissa 75, 76, 86
Home 10, 29, 48, 63, 84, 132, 158, 168–170, 174, 175
Hover 58, 105, 110, 112
Human-machine relationships 2, 5, 29, 46, 100, 116, 152, 155, 164, 165, 178, 183
Hybrid space 19, 67, 69, 76, 83, 84, 88, 91, 185, 189

I

Immediacy 40, 41, 66
Immersion 111, 113, 115
Immobility/Immobilities 16, 57, 66, 98, 105, 116, 186, 188
Infrastructure 2, 4, 9, 16, 17, 48, 52–57, 64, 65, 83, 85, 126, 136, 189
Ingold, Tim 106, 124, 125, 136
Innis, Harold A. 15
Instagram 7, 61
Intelligent flight mode 34, 91, 153, 164–166, 173, 190
Interaction 5, 15, 21, 29, 35, 36, 89, 92, 101, 131, 155, 165, 170, 190
Interface 19, 74–78, 80, 83–85, 88, 90, 91, 105, 107, 108, 113, 161, 163, 165, 170, 175
Internet 10, 14, 32, 48, 49, 64, 73, 146
Interplay 33, 38, 46, 50, 63, 65, 90, 104, 111, 116
Interviews 2, 4, 19, 21, 30, 53, 59, 75, 88, 111, 112, 127, 161, 165
Intra-action 155, 156, 166, 171, 174, 175, 177
Invisible 29, 31, 32, 41, 50, 85, 163, 171, 177
Island 79

J

Jablonowski, Maximilian 13, 34, 74, 77, 81, 101, 113, 146
Jackman, Anna 12, 46, 77, 191
Jensen, Klaus Bruhn 75

Jensen, Ole B. 16, 50, 52, 57, 69, 100, 101

K
Kaplan, Caren 12, 13, 77, 124–126, 132, 135, 138
Kapp, Ernst 101
Klauser, Francisco 5, 11–13, 16, 74, 138
Kp-Index 55

L
Latour, Bruno 50, 155
Laws of media 187. *See also* Tetrad
Line of sight 8, 9, 28, 54, 108, 109, 159
Literacy 20, 104, 105, 139, 143, 146, 186, 191
Live-stream 19, 30, 37, 61–63, 65, 76, 78, 82, 85, 87, 140, 157
Location-awareness/Location-aware 65, 66, 69, 78. *See also* Awareness
Locative media 67, 75, 77–79, 82, 87, 88, 90, 92, 154, 185, 188. *See also* Mobile media
Luvaas, Brent 38, 40, 41, 141

M
Map 7, 79, 80, 84, 86, 123, 133, 138, 163, 193
Map-reading 80, 124–126, 131, 135, 136, 138, 139, 144, 145, 188, 191
Material/Materialities 14, 15, 17, 18, 31, 36, 40, 42, 50–52, 56, 57, 69, 76, 100, 107

McCormack, Derek 126
McCosker, Anthony 16, 77, 78, 87, 98, 100, 140, 144, 152
McLuhan, Eric 21, 187
McLuhan, Marshall 14, 15, 21, 31, 32, 50, 98, 100, 102, 112, 115, 116, 159, 162, 187, 193
McQuire, Scott 65, 75
Media ecology 4, 14–18, 29, 31, 49–52, 67, 74–76, 98, 101, 144, 153–155, 157, 183, 192
Media life-form 67
Mediality 75, 90–92, 185, 190, 191
Media studies 4, 12, 65, 92, 98, 191
Medium 1, 2, 4, 5, 14–16, 31–33, 38, 41, 46, 50, 51, 90, 102, 111, 112, 115, 123, 132, 144, 159, 165, 187, 188, 192. *See also* Mobile media
Medium theory 15
Merriman, Peter 38
Metaphor 21, 28, 40, 101, 112, 162, 177
Method 4, 17, 18, 28–30, 33, 34, 38, 40–42, 184, 194
Mezzanine 48, 135, 136, 145
Microphone 30, 34, 37, 63, 87, 88
Militarization 46, 80, 89, 178, 185, 194
Military 6, 7, 15, 46, 124, 126, 134, 141, 162, 164, 190
Mind 29, 30, 40, 99, 101, 106, 107, 112–114, 116, 121, 129, 177, 184, 186, 189
Mobile art 90, 91
Mobile media 4, 12, 14, 16, 18, 19, 21, 74–77, 79, 86, 87, 90, 92, 99, 183, 184. *See also* Locative media

Mobilities in situ 19, 50, 52, 56, 69, 101, 185
Mobilities research 4, 12, 14, 16–18, 29, 36, 49, 50, 65, 67, 74–76, 92, 98, 153–155, 157, 183, 191
Mobility/Mobilities 2, 13, 85, 91, 98, 105, 155, 164, 167, 183, 188, 191
   affective 18, 29, 30, 38–41, 105
   communicative 16, 18, 29, 39, 41, 105
   corporeal 16, 18, 20, 29, 30, 39, 41, 98, 99, 105, 106, 109–111, 113, 186
   dis/embodied 20, 99, 104, 111, 114–116, 186, 188
   imaginative 16, 18, 20, 29, 39, 41, 98–100, 104, 109–114, 142–144, 186, 189
   physical 16, 18, 29, 39, 41, 78, 98, 99, 105, 107, 108, 112
   remediated 20, 99, 102, 188
   virtual 16, 18, 29, 39, 139
   visual 135, 139
Model aircraft/Model aviation 13, 45, 48, 57, 63, 76, 103, 104
Motility/Motile 16, 74, 75, 77, 78, 98–100, 152, 189
Mumford, Lewis 15, 98, 101
Munster, Anna 140, 164, 171

N
Nadar 123, 124
Narcissus-narcosis 32, 33
Narrative 3, 4, 15, 36, 80, 124, 132, 135, 152, 159, 186
NASA 141, 193

Nature 129, 132, 134, 156
Navigation 19, 32, 41, 66, 74, 79, 80, 90, 102, 109, 116, 140, 185
Networked place 84, 85, 91
New Mobilities Paradigm 16, 101, 188
Noise 30, 59, 88, 89, 91, 126, 193
Non-representational 30, 38
Nuisance 59, 88, 194
Numbness 32, 112, 114, 115, 186

O
Obstacle 58, 75, 166–168, 172
Optical toy 20, 139, 141, 144, 145, 189
Out-of-body 111, 114, 186
Özkul, Didem 75

P
Panic 168
Panorama 138
Panoramic desire 99, 111
Parkour 135
Parks, Lisa 4, 13, 17, 98, 138, 163, 164
Pedestrian 28, 59
Peeping Tom 59, 88. See also Spying
Performative cartography 75, 80, 82, 91, 124, 139, 185
Pet 152, 159, 160, 162, 163, 171, 177, 190
Philadelphia 27, 30, 56, 121, 122, 128, 136, 137
Photography 7, 11, 59, 60, 62, 85, 87, 98, 103, 123, 125, 127,

132, 138, 143, 145, 160–162, 189
Pink, Sarah 40, 75, 86, 106, 107
Play 2, 3, 35, 108, 134, 138–141, 145, 160, 177, 186, 194
Pokémon Go 77
Police 7, 58, 64, 89, 126
Policy 3
Positionality 28, 29, 40, 42, 68, 110, 164
Postman, Neil 14, 15, 50, 51, 101, 184
Power 13, 15, 34, 52, 64, 75, 89, 92, 125, 126, 145, 191. *See also* Empowerment; Superpower
Precaution 65
Premediation 20, 90, 104, 116
Privacy/Private 2, 10, 13, 45, 59, 77, 87, 88, 92, 106, 146, 191, 192, 194
Profile 19, 59, 63, 66
Public 3, 5, 7, 10, 45, 52, 59, 74–78, 88, 92, 98, 175, 191, 192, 194

Q

Quadcopter 3, 6, 20, 27, 30, 53, 54, 57, 97, 98, 100, 113, 123, 126, 135, 142, 158, 164, 168, 170, 171, 175
Questions 16, 33, 36, 52, 56, 61, 69, 73, 75, 92, 98, 117, 143, 157, 166, 178, 188, 190, 191

R

Racing 11, 98, 99, 102, 104, 105, 110, 127, 162

Real-time 9, 10, 30, 48, 62, 63, 65, 66, 68, 69, 78, 80, 82, 131, 143
Registration 8, 33
Regulation 9, 12, 30, 46, 60, 61, 64, 67, 85, 121, 136, 144, 167, 190, 192, 193. *See also* Rules
Relational artifact 4, 21, 156, 157, 186
Relaxation 162, 177, 191. *See also* Release
Release 32, 161, 162, 191. *See also* Relaxation
Remediated space 84, 85, 91
Remediation 90, 99, 104
Remote control 27–29, 35, 58, 62, 66, 80, 83, 99, 102, 104, 107–109, 114, 121, 139, 153, 164, 167–171, 173, 175, 178
Remote ID 10, 11
Remote sensing 126
Rights 60, 193
Risk 12, 21, 29, 40, 46, 58, 68, 117, 167, 170, 175, 194
River 1, 27, 28, 39, 53, 56, 58, 59, 127, 132, 138, 143
Robots 170, 173, 177, 190
Rogue 2, 46
Rothstein, Adam 3, 5, 6, 12, 15, 74, 157
Rover 17, 100, 115, 141, 158, 165, 172, 176
Rules 9, 27, 121, 167. *See also* Regulation

S

Safety 2, 7, 9, 10, 13, 45, 53, 61,
    77, 87, 106, 117, 146, 167,
    194
Satellite 20, 28, 32, 48, 53–55, 65,
    84, 85, 102, 122, 123, 125,
    143, 145, 163, 165
Science and technology studies (STS)
    4, 14, 17, 21, 67, 153, 177,
    183, 186, 191
Screen 30, 35–37, 39, 58, 62, 81,
    83, 103, 107–109, 111, 113,
    116, 121, 129, 140, 152, 157,
    169, 170, 173, 174
Security 2, 10, 13, 57
Self 13, 15, 32–34, 36–38, 80, 112,
    164, 186, 188
    spatial 33, 34, 164
Selfie 89, 164
Sense 32, 33, 36, 40, 67, 91, 100,
    106, 112, 115, 121, 132, 165,
    184, 193
Sense and avoid 75, 165, 166, 168
Sense of place 78, 79, 81, 85, 129,
    165, 185
Sensibility 89, 124, 142, 189
Sensor 7, 46, 47, 54, 74, 78, 83, 85,
    102, 116, 164, 166, 167, 172,
    173, 190
Sensuous turn 40
Sheller, Mimi 16, 17, 67, 75, 85, 90,
    92, 98, 101, 154, 191, 193
Signal 54, 65, 84, 85, 102, 169,
    173, 174, 178
Skypixel 7, 62
Sloterdijk, Peter 13, 34
Smartphone 27, 30, 34, 37, 54, 62,
    66, 73, 74, 76, 80, 81, 83,
    84, 87, 92, 99, 102, 107, 121,
    152, 157, 173, 178, 185
Social media 1, 7, 62, 63, 68, 74,
    78, 87, 88, 122
Social network 78, 122
Society 19, 51, 73, 80, 89, 178
Solar flares 48, 55
Speed 20, 53, 59, 84, 97
Spinney, Justin 36, 37, 154
Spying 1, 3, 46, 60, 88, 89, 178
Stillness 20, 66, 98, 100, 102, 105,
    116, 186
Strate, Lance 15, 50, 51, 98, 102,
    112
Strauven, Wanda 139
Suchman, Lucy 152–155, 159, 171,
    177, 178
Sun 48, 55, 121, 131
Sunrise 48, 54, 55, 87, 89, 127, 132,
    161
Sunset 1, 27, 28, 39, 48, 54, 55,
    59–61, 127, 130–132, 161
Superpower 81, 83. *See also* Power
Surveillance 2, 3, 7, 20, 46, 79, 89,
    92, 123, 126, 138, 139, 145,
    146, 162, 183, 186, 188–191

T

Technography 28, 31, 36
Technological unconscious 28, 31,
    40, 41
Telemetry 83, 108
Telephone 14, 67
Television 14, 32, 83
Temporal 19, 33, 50, 53–57, 65, 66,
    68, 69, 80, 86, 185
Tetrad 21, 187, 188, 190. *See also*
    Laws of media

Therapy 117, 191
Threat 2, 45, 77, 190
Thrift, Nigel 28, 30, 31, 40, 165
Traffic 1, 2, 11, 19, 28, 45, 48, 56, 57, 59, 64, 83, 109, 172
Transportation 102, 125, 183
Travel 16, 109, 111, 125, 160, 163, 186
Trust 168, 170, 186
Turkle, Sherry 152–154, 156, 159, 160, 162, 177, 178, 190

U

Unmanned aircraft system traffic management system (UTM) 10, 193
Unmanned aircraft system (UAS) 1, 2, 4, 5, 10, 11, 13, 19, 46, 47, 51, 68, 74, 183, 185, 193
Urry, John 16, 30, 39, 98, 99, 101, 109, 124, 125, 136

V

Verhoeff, Nanna 75, 80, 82, 99, 111, 124, 139
Vertesi, Janet 17, 100, 115, 141, 158, 165, 170, 172, 176
Vertical
   mediation 13
   play 20, 134, 135, 139, 140, 143, 145, 184, 186, 188
   space 21, 45, 76, 78, 83, 90, 100, 115, 122, 126, 132, 133, 136, 143, 193

Video 7, 18, 29, 30, 32, 34–38, 41, 62–66, 87, 98, 107, 109, 152, 157, 173, 176, 185
Videography 59, 85, 87, 98, 123, 138, 162
Virilio, Paul 126, 140, 163, 164
Vision machine 126, 164, 170
Visual
   archive 146, 189, 191
   culture 2, 17, 18, 49, 68, 91, 185
   production 19, 21, 32, 41, 46, 74, 90, 102, 116
   record 31, 37, 38, 85, 86, 176
Visualization 20, 73, 138, 139, 144, 145, 183, 186, 188
Volume/Volumetric 19, 48, 55, 57, 126, 135, 136, 138, 142, 185, 186, 189, 191

W

War 6, 89, 123, 141
Warning 56, 84, 86, 108, 193
Way-finding 124–126, 135, 136, 138, 139, 144, 145, 188, 191
Weapon 2, 12, 146, 183
Weather 19, 48, 53–55, 83
Wildlife 2, 7, 45
Wind 34, 48, 53, 83–85, 158, 159
Windshield 109, 111
Witness 36, 78, 81, 163, 164, 177, 186
World-making 171, 173, 175, 177, 178

Y

YouTube 7, 62, 87, 97, 121, 140